ALPHETON HALL

Diary of a Suffolk Countryman

by

James Mott

Published by Serpenpan Publishing
Printed by The Lavenham Press Limited

All rights reserved
No reproduction permitted without
prior permission

© James Mott 2011

ISBN 13: 978-0-9569600-0-9

Cover photograph: Alpheton Hall
Back cover photograph of Jim Mott courtesy of Rodger Welham

Edited by Ken and Judy Watkins

Serpenpan Publishing
The Nest, Old Bury Road, Alpheton, Suffolk CO10 9BT

The Lavenham Press Limited
Arbons House, Water Street, Lavenham, Suffolk CO10 9RN

ALPHETON HALL

Diary of a Suffolk Countryman

All costs of producing this edition have been donated, so that the money raised by your purchase can be given to:

St Nicholas Hospice Care

Our thanks to the following for their generous support:

John and Alice Pawsey, David Alston (Suffolk) Limited
Nic and Carol Willcocks, Alpheton Hall Barns
Suffolk County Council,
(Councillor Richard Kemp Locality Budget)
The Lavenham Press Limited

For
Cyril Douglas Mott
(Harry)
and William Frost

Acknowledgements

Our thanks go to the many people of Bridge Street, Alpheton and beyond, who lent a helping hand with the production of this memoir, in particular those who provided photographs.

Author's Note:
A chance meeting at Alpheton's 'Coffee Pot' between Judy and Daphne led to a discussion about certain matters in the book. Daphne happened to say, "Jim and myself would like to get it published with all proceeds going to St Nicholas Hospice Care," and Judy replied – "I think I can help you."

From then on, Judy and Ken organised everything, meeting the printers, raising the funds, coming to our house every week in exchange for a biscuit and cup of tea, and many, many hours of their time. Daphne and I would like to thank them for all their help, without which this book would never have been published.

PART ONE

Childhood – Days Of Freedom

*This is the story of my life.
If you are interested, read on; if you are not, don't read it;
the choice is yours.*

I was born on the seventh of October, 1925, the ninth child and youngest son of John and Lizzie Mott; eleven children in all, seven girls and four boys. Our home was Rose Cottage in Bridge Street, a hamlet on the main Bury St Edmunds to Sudbury road.

My mother rented three cottages from G Coulson of Clock House Farm, Shimpling – he was landlord of Rose Cottages. There were four cottages in all, we had three and another lady rented the fourth. They were thatched, one up, one down, with brick and slate lean-to's on either side.

Bridge Street was, as it is today, a hamlet standing in the valley of the river Chad, wetlands beside the Chad to the east, and a small wetlands meadow to the west known as Spring Meadow.

On one side of the main road was the parish of Alpheton and on the other was the parish of Long Melford. Rose Cottage was in the latter, situated next to the Rose and Crown, set back from the road with a long path up to the front door. Our three cottages had three staircases, but were joined downstairs by a passageway that ran along the back. A brick and slate lean-to at the side was our back'us, [backhouse], and our privy was in the garden.

My mother, known as Liz to all but us younger children, was a fiercely independent little lady. She ruled the household with an arm of iron and what she said was law. Up every morning at the crack of dawn to light the fires, get men off to work and children to school. Discipline was strict and obeyed by all.

These were her rules. Table manners: no elbows on the table, eat slowly and correctly. If you did not obey her warning, watch out if she walked behind your chair. Sit correctly at the dining table in your home or other people's homes.

'Please' and 'thank you' were to be said to everyone, in and out of the house, and if relations visit you, you do not speak until spoken to. Treat all your elders with respect, and stand correctly when being spoken to or speaking to people.

All of the above were accepted by the family without question.

The ages of the family stretch out by twenty-five years or more. I cannot remember some of my sisters living at home or going to school. There were four of us young ones. My brother Harry was christened Cyril Douglas. I was just Jimmy, and my little sisters were Beryl and Iris. We did not seem to be really hard up or impoverished in any way, perhaps having older sisters and brothers working made a great difference. We also had a quarter of an acre of garden and a quarter of an acre of allotments.

My father was known as Jack, and worked as second horseman for Mr Wallace of Ford Hall, Bridge Street, except for the years that he served as a soldier during the First World War. My two older brothers, Jasper (Jep) and Walter (Wally), both worked for Mr Ruffle at Bridge Street Mill.

My father was a hard-working, good-tempered man and the family was more or less self-supporting, or they had worked to make it that way. They grew their own vegetables, kept chickens for eggs, cockerels for eating and pigs and rabbits to turn into profit for clothes and shoes. Wood for fires was plentiful and there was a good supply of wild rabbits, pheasants, partridges and hares. Some of these were sold, the money going into the housekeeping petty cash tin. At Christmas time, we helped my mother plucking poultry for the orders she had taken from friends and neighbours.

All of the above was hard work which involved digging, sawing, plucking, skinning, planting, feeding and mixing pig food, and storing vegetables for the winter feed safe from rats and mice. The storage shed was a ring of gin traps and these were inspected twice daily and ferreted about once a month.

When my father sold some pigs, the money was kept aside for buying new stock, never spent next door at the Rose and Crown. On the odd occasion that my big brothers saw my father sitting glum with his newspaper on a Sunday, they would guess he was short of spending money. "Come on," Jep or Walter would say, slipping him a few coins, "the Rose will be open by now."

There were good times, too, and I remember my father once came home merry and he sat in the kitchen, bending forward, laughing and trying to remove his shoes without falling off his chair. My mother heard him saying, "Give me a hand, will you, boys?" "Don't you help him," she said sternly, so Harry and I waited until she wasn't looking before we ran to help.

One of my regular jobs as a small child, around four years old, was to take my grandfather Gott Mott's dinner up to him, and I felt this was a great responsibility. My mother packed it in a basket with a drink of beer, covered with a cloth, and off I went. I walked very carefully up to Gott Mott's cottage, which was on Aveley Lane, just before the allotments.

I would knock on the door and Gott Mott would open it, wearing shoes that were cut open for comfort. His cottage had a strong smell of pipe tobacco and mould, and I couldn't see his face properly as he had a big beard. I didn't really know who he was, to tell you the truth. I didn't think of him as a person like my mother or my brothers. I don't know what I thought, something like a woodland character from one of my story books, I expect.

When Gott Mott died, I remember standing with all the family along the main road as the bier was pushed past, showing our respect. Later, another family came to live in Gott Mott's cottage. The Frost family became very friendly with us, and my mother would walk with Mrs Frost down Dark Lane picking blackberries in the autumn. William and Lesley Frost were about the same age as my brother Harry and me, and years later their father, Bert Frost, and myself worked together at Alpheton Hall Farm.

This is the story of how I came to love the land I was born into, and the way of life that I learned, with all its good times and hard times, its beauties and its losses.

Defend Us From All Perils And Dangers

At five years old, I was given a new satchel, new shoes and socks, and off to school I went with other children from Bridge Street and, of course, my brother Harry who was two years older than me. I suppose I felt confident and well-protected with him around.

We all set off along the main road at eight o'clock one morning to walk the one and a half miles to Alpheton school. On arrival, everyone said the Lord's Prayer together. Then my name was put on the register, I was shown to my little desk and at this point my brother left me to go to his class in another room, assuring me he would see me at lunchtime. I was given a slate and chalk and immediately started lessons – A said ahh..., B was buh.... and so on.

By now, I was taking stock of the building. There was no ceiling and oil lamps hung from a chain attached to a beam. The room was huge, with an enormous black fireplace and a guard around. One couldn't see no fire. Whether it was hot or cold in the room, I did not know and at my tender years, I did not care.

At mid-day, the teacher said, "Chalks away. It's lunch-time," and my brother arrived as promised and I was relieved to see him. He took me to the cloakroom where my satchel hung on a peg. Then it was back to the classroom to eat our lunch, supervised by my teacher. Every day, before we started to eat, grace was said.

'Be present at our table, Lord.
Be here and everywhere a-told.
These creatures bless and grant that we
May feast in Paradise with thee.
Amen'

Harry had a bottle of cold drink in his bag and he gave me some. There were no hot drinks or nothing in those days.

When we had all finished, the teacher dismissed us. Harry took me back to the cloakroom and hung my satchel on the peg, gave me my hat and coat and I followed him outside. He took me to the toilets, which were in a small collection of buildings at the side of the playground. Then we played rounders with the other children, mostly from Bridge Street. The Alpheton children went home to lunch but after we had been playing a while, they began to drift back.

To my surprise, a bell started to ring. My brother told me it was time again for lessons. He put my hat and coat back on the peg, assuring me he would see me at half past three for going home. We had drawing lessons in the afternoon. Before dismissal, we all had to stand and say our end-of-day prayer.

> 'Lighten our darkness, we beseech thee, O Lord,
> And by thy great mercies defend us
> From all perils and dangers of this night. Amen'

These prayers we said every day, and I never forgot them. On the way home, it was getting dark. Men were off-loading sugarbeet on verges beside the road, and others had their horse carts in fields. Tramps sat around a fire at the top of Cold Hill and as we turned the bend, half-way down, we could see the smoke from the cottages at Bridge Street. It must have been a welcoming sight for someone of five years old and first day at school.

I think I walked to this school for about five years, until it was closed, around 1935. We were then bussed to Shimpling school, another church school with the same head teacher, a Miss Fisher. Lessons continued about the same as at Alpheton – maths, music, history, geography, sport, nature studies, English and politics. We still had prayers morning, midday and end of day.

The parson took scripture lessons once or twice a week and we also had to go to church on Ash Wednesday and Ascension Day and on these days we were given a half-day off school.

I must have been about ten years old when we started at Shimpling and can remember things more vividly from that time. We still took our dinner to school – there were no school dinners, no central heating, no hot water and no comfort. There was one, heavily guarded, open coal fire in the room.

Miss Fisher was Head Teacher and she taught me. She was probably the cruellest person I have ever met. She would get into terrible tempers, spit and shout and go red in the face, strike out with the flat of her open hand and knock children off their chairs and onto the floor.

This punishment was just for bad spelling, finger-marks on paper, talking in class, paper darting and suchlike. It's a wonder we weren't brain-damaged. Looking back, perhaps we all are.

More than once, I caught the full force of that right hand. It made me quite dizzy for a bit. You got no warning it was coming, no time to prepare for it. She would walk behind you, look over your head to your paperwork and if something didn't suit and the temper was up, which it nearly always was, the mighty right, open hand would fell you to the floor. She would shout and rave, spit all over one, and carry on like a mad person, and all just for an ink smudge.

Discipline was very strict. We were not supposed to be young. She didn't expect us to want to play or laugh. There was no room in her life for mistakes or accidents like ink smudges. If one was perfect, as she thought she was, we might all have got on well together.

No parents seemed to take her on about her cruelty to their children, but I think I lived my young life in very cruel times. There did not seem to be the love for people or for animals or for children as there is today. No-one was allowed to overstep the mark. Obedience was the answer if you did not want a clip round the ear-hole.

If I told my mother Miss Fisher had hit me around the head, all you would get for an answer would be 'You must have done something wrong'. She did not query whether it was justified or not, and did not appear to care, and so the beatings went on.

Most of the children hated her. Some were afraid to go to school and used to cry. Some used to bring flowers to school as a peace offering. I think the latter did help a bit, but we had two heroes – a Mrs Eady and her son Sam.

Mrs Eady had two children at school at that time and either one or the other must have got a back-hander from Miss Fisher. Sam stood up to challenge her and he must have had a lot of guts as this was only the second time I had seen anyone confront her – the other incident was years before, at Alpheton school.

A war of words broke out between Miss Fisher and Sam, but she stopped hitting when he raised his hands to her. She was furious, but seemed to know how far to go as this boy was about twelve or thirteen years old, and strong.

She could not let this rest, or be seen to have been beaten by the children, so she gave him five hundred lines to write – something like 'I must behave in school'. This must have been her one great mistake. This boy had a mother, and like her son, had a load of guts and spirit. It was not the done thing to challenge authority, but this lady did, and she was my hero.

The next morning, class said prayers and we all assembled for lessons, when the door opened and this lady, Mrs Eady, burst in. 'Miss' did not rise to greet her but sat firmly in her chair and she took all the abuse from this lady who told her a few truths about her cruelty to her pupils. She warned her never to touch her children again and her son Sam would not be writing five hundred lines for her or nobody else. She walked out with a slam of the door, and us children had at last seen our great dictator shot down in flames.

We were so excited, we all stood up and cheered as if we had been waiting for this day for years, for nobody had come to our rescue before and no-one seemed to care. We had played straight into her hands. She stood up and with one mighty screech – Sit Down! – she spat, and froth appeared at the side of her mouth and our mentor was back in control. Things carried on the same as before, with some improvements in her attitude.

In some ways she was quite clever for her time. She covered a lot of subjects. Music was her love and she played the piano beautifully. She taught us to sing professionally and entered us for the Clare Music Festival and the school won the Challenge Cup on three or four occasions.

Miss Fisher seemed good at maths, for her day. In politics lessons, we would hold mock elections. History was always interesting – tribes-people in Africa, pigmies in Sudan, talks on the Middle East and Far East – but of course, her knowledge of these countries must have been limited, as she read from books.

Nature studies were good. We would walk from school down Gents Lane in Shimpling, across beautiful old meadows covered with buttercups, daisies and ladies-hair where cattle grazed on the lush grass, then on to Alpheton Wood. I loved this walk, with the sun on our backs, the beautiful colours of the wild flowers under the great blue Suffolk sky, men hoeing in the fields, and the majestic call of the cock pheasants far away. It left an imprint on my mind which has stayed with me all my days. We would have to make notes of what we had seen and make drawings of flowers, grasses, cottages, trees and so on.

Later on in the week ahead, we would have to write compositions and draw pictures of what we had seen and observed. Perhaps this was one of my favourite subjects. I loved drawing and writing short stories.

There was a large playground at Shimpling and in those days, we had the use of a meadow with a football and cricket pitch. Sometimes matches were arranged with Cockfield school, and we would cycle there in the afternoon, accompanied by a teacher. I made friends with lots of Cockfield boys, who I worked with in later years and who are still my friends today.

I think cricket was my favourite sport but we always lost to Cockfield. They had one great advantage over us at Shimpling and that was their fast bowler, a boy named Jack Long. Not one of us could stand up to the accuracy and speed of his bowling. We were not trained to cope with a cricket ball travelling at perhaps sixty miles per hour, nor were we strong enough to stand up to it. He was a truly remarkable boy for his age and we all admired him.

Discipline at matches was strict. We had to behave ourselves at all times, shake hands with the whole visiting team, apologise for the mistakes or bad behaviour which sometimes does occur in sport. When the quarters of oranges were given out at half-time, visitors were served first. Failing to do this would result in being taken before the head teacher – Miss Fisher. Watch out! This was a very last resort as other teachers realised what she would do. We were generally taken to one side instead, and given a good talking to.

Winter

There were perhaps about six boys round about my age; we used to go to play at all sorts of games in winter. The winters were cruel; everything froze solid, sometimes for weeks on end, but we always managed to get water as the spring in Spring Meadow never froze. Water came in continuous from the bottom and flowed out at the top, along a ditch into a pond.

The rains would come in autumn – perhaps November, the river Chad was a raging torrent. The floodgates at the mill would be wide open to let the water through. Sometimes it would run over the catwalk and handrail. Spring Meadow would flood, as would part of the main road, and at Ford Hall, all the wetlands at the front and rear of the farmhouse would flood – acres of water, about two feet deep with rushes and long grass sticking out of the water.

We loved it. We would get an old galvanised tank from the farm and sail it on the flooded meadows behind Ford Hall. With poles pushing us along, it was great fun. Snipes would fly overhead, wondering what had happened to their homes as the flood dykes and the reeds had all disappeared under the water.

We may get one or two weeks sailing our tank, then would come the frosts, severe frosts. The floodwater and the Chad would be covered with ice, our tank a wetlands wreck aground in a sea of ice, but this brought another sport. Yes, you got it – sliding the Chad and the water meadows on acres and acres of ice. The miller and his friends had skates and glided along. How I longed for some skates! Not a hope. The blacksmith could not make them.

The days would be bright and bitterly cold, but we played on. What fun! Where could you get that today for nothing? The sun would go down in the western sky, the redness from it reflected onto the ice, a magic world to us children. It froze like hell, even the moisture froze on our noses, but we could still laugh and play.

At five o'clock, I'd go home to tea and a lovely fire blazing in the grate at Rose Cottage, where boiled eggs and buttered toast appeared at six o'clock. My working brothers and sisters would go to the ice with others from the hamlet, where the miller had put out hurricane lanterns for himself and friends. We were allowed to join in, some skating, some sliding. At seven o'clock, we had to be home to a wash, supper and off to bed – feather beds under three feet of thatch, warm and tired, we were soon asleep.

Up at the crack of dawn for hot tea and toast for breakfast. My older brothers had gone to work and us children would sit around the fire my mother had lit at five o'clock. It had all been black-leaded, ash removed and logs laid in the hearth for the day's burning. At half past eight, off I would go to meet my friends for another day's sliding and walking along the river banks to investigate the wildlife habitat.

Hundreds of birds would gather at the mill, where sweepings were thrown out to help them survive, for most nights the frost had been severe. Farm men would break the ice on ponds and rivers with pick-axes and heavy hammers. The ice could be over a foot thick. Water was taken in buckets to yarded cattle and pigs, and tipped into tanks. It was a regular job in frosty weather.

Everything was white, as far as the eye could see. Trees and hedgerows hung with hoar frost – even the rushes and long grass growing out of the ice – added a wonder to the scene. Horses would go past on ice-covered roads on their way to the blacksmith's to have frost nails put into their shoes, especially the yard horse who had to keep working in all weathers. They were needed to cart mangolds and swedes, and to cart muck from cowsheds and bring in fresh straw, as cattle had to be fed and watered and have dry beds. Most farmyards were stone and clay which turn to slurry in winter, so when it froze it formed into ice, and yard muck was placed on top of the ice to make it safer for man and beast.

Some days we would set off to walk the fields and hedgerows. Our wanderings would take us to farmyards such as Alpheton Hall, Ford Hall, Kiln Farm and Rowhedge Farm. The earth was frozen solid as a rock so we were able to walk across ploughed fields without getting mud on our boots and mostly we kept to the hedgerows. Occasionally, we would come across farm labourers cutting hedgerows. The big pieces, around four to eight inches thick, were trimmed and laid on the brew of the field, [the edge of the ditch that runs alongside the hedge]. These were picked up later for firewood. The smaller, thin trimmings were laid and tied into faggots. The rest – trash like bushes, very small pieces of wood and dry grass – were burnt.

We boys had a lovely time carting material to the bonfire, and it gave us a warm. The farm labourers smoked little pipes or rolled up cigarettes. They talked to us while they sharpened their cutting tools with carborundum stone rubs.

In our wanderings we came across pigeons feeding on kale, a last resort for them. Some lay dying and some were too weak to fly.

A lack of proper food for weeks in the severe cold meant frozen kale was their last hope of survival – a pathetic sight, but these birds were casualties of a harsh and cruel British winter. We would walk on, taking in all we saw in our young minds. Rabbits, and maybe hares, we would see eating bark off young wood as a supply of food, as nothing else was available.

The countryside was a stark scene: nothing grew, nothing moved. Everywhere frozen wastes, the winter wheat fields hundreds of acres laid black and bare.

One time, we arrived at Alpheton Hall farm. Coveys of partridges and pheasants were enjoying themselves around some straw stacks, searching the old chaff and kayvin [straw waste] heaps for food. We walked into the massive timber and thatched barn, where the stockman had heaps of chaff, mangolds, swedes, barley and bean meal for yarded cattle. Hundreds of linnets, finches, blackbirds, thrushes and sparrows were gathering here for the feast. The whole farm was a survival area for wild birds. They could all make themselves comfortable here, sleeping in the cattle yard buildings. The heat from the muck and the cattle kept them warm from the harsh conditions outside.

We boys helped the stockman, winding the handle on his mangold grinder and cake breaker for him. Then we pushed off into the churchyard adjacent to the barn, looked solemnly at each other, then continued on our way. We went up the steep lane from the church towards Alpheton, turning off onto the footpath that took us a triangular route back down to the main road and Bridge Street, where the Chad was well and truly frozen over.

The floodgates at the mill must have been closed for some time, as there was a good back-up of water, forming thick ice. We took to the river, walking and sliding right up to the floodgates, until we reached Spring Meadow. Then across the main Sudbury to Bury St Edmunds road, we called in to see the blacksmith. Mr Goldsmith was a huge man, with arms as big and strong as iron bars. He was a gentle giant to us kids and he appeared to love us all. We would watch him hit his white-hot metal on the anvil, with a steady rhythm – one, two, three backward, one, two, three forward, bang on the metal with his mighty hammer. Sparks would fly across the travis [traverse] and us kids would try to catch them. He would let us pump the bellows to blow the fire. We never stayed too long, because he thought we would get injured.

The weather patterns were such that sometimes it would thaw slightly, then freeze at night. Sometimes we would have quite heavy snow and prolonged showers. Deep drifts would form, whipped up by an East Anglian east wind, and it would be bitterly cold. This gave us the chance to play snowballs and build the greatest snowman in the world.

The few cars and vans that were around in those days would get stuck on Cold Hill, where the main road ran up from Bridge Street to Alpheton. This pleased us as we would run up from the village to give them a push up the hill. Sometimes we got a reward of one penny each or two pennies between us, but sometimes nothing at all. We might get someone up the hill and he'd just keep on driving. Then we'd fling snowballs at him, but he'd disappear with a wave of his hand. Some drivers ran off the road entirely, then we couldn't help and one of the farmers would bring up a horse to give them a pull.

It was during the winter months that the thrashing tackle would arrive on most of the farms – steam engines, drum and pitcher to thresh out the ricks standing in the stackyards. These were great hunting grounds for us boys, for the stacks were home to rats and mice, hundreds of them. As the farm men put the sheaves through the drum, the stack would get lower and lower. Small-mesh wire netting was placed around the stack so the rats couldn't escape. As the stack got lower, they would try to get away. It was our job and pleasure to hit and kill them with sticks, while the workmen would use their two-tined forks. The farm dog would have his share. We might get as high as a hundred and fifty rats. They were everywhere – in barns, pigsties, stacks – and man and dog could not keep their numbers down until poison was introduced.

Spring

As the weeks and months passed, winter gradually gave way to spring. The great east winds never fail to arrive in East Anglia at this time of year, drying out our heavy clay soils, ready for the sowing of spring crops. We say, 'An ounce of March dust is worth a king's ransom'. The severe frosts of winter had done their work, and the ducksfoot harrows would be out pulling down the ploughed land. The soil would smell fresh with a beautiful deep tilth, and dust – yes, March dust – would whip up from the tractor wheels or horse's feet.

The boys of the village would visit the farms, walk behind the old Smythe horse-drawn drill, drawn there by the newly spring-cleaned soil as if by magic – or was it the soil in our young veins, for each and every one of us had come from long lines, generations, of Suffolk farming families.

The Smythe drill, sowing the seed corn, was usually pulled by Suffolk horses and was a two-horse and two-man operation. The head horseman steered the drill with a labourer at the rear to watch that the Suffolk coulters did not block up, and he helped to fill the corn box at the end of the field when the horses took a rest. Two horses, and a set of light to medium harrows, worked behind the drill to cover the seed and level the soil.

Us kids would love it, even though the great east winds continued to blow their bitterly cold blasts. Snow flurries would race across the sky lasting a few seconds. Clouds of dust would sweep across the landscape. And then would come the sun and the horses and Smythe drill would appear again.

After the stillness of winter, every farm was now drilling, harrowing, carting, for this was mad March and everything else was mad as well – even the field roll, the lovely sound of its echoing jingle reaching across the fields for miles, and when the rolls were out, Suffolk fields were really dry. Even the blacksmith's hammer was working overtime to its 1-2-3-Bang! Even the usually tranquil mill waterwheel seemed to put on an extra effort.

Everything was coming back to life. The birds were finding food more plentiful, their feathers were putting on their marriage colours and the dawn chorus was increasing daily.

I would wander with other children from the old village where nothing changed and no-one moved in or out. We would visit all the farms in turn, to slide down the straw stacks, or pole vault the Chad. We used poles cut from the hedgerows or taken from the heaps of wood where men had been working. This was great fun, especially where the river was in a deep cut. Very often, one of us got a wet seat of the pants, but it didn't worry us much, a bit uncomfortable and cold for a bit, but the heat of one's body soon dried it out.

As the evening daylight extended, we were much more active after returning home from school. We would play football on Spring Meadow, or on the meadow behind my mother's cottage with its unusual name of Serpenpan and whether it was the correct name or not, I do not know. As the grass was shorter here, we would play cricket, rounders and similar games. The girls would go and pick bunches of violets from the banks at Cold Hill and Lavenham Lane, where they grew in abundance, and primroses which grew on Primrose Hill.

These were great, carefree days for me, and very adventurous. I loved every field in the valley, every footpath, cart track, lane, and of course the river, with its shallow, shining, silver waters and its wildlife. The winter flood left driftwood caught on overhanging trees, and on the flimsiest low branches moorhens built their nests. Stretching right out to the middle of the river, the nests rose and fell with the movement of the water. I looked out for freshwater mussels, tiddler fish, kingfishers, frogs, ducks, herons and otters. In the waters of the Chad and on its banks grew marsh marigolds, watercress, mint, wild roses, violets, primroses, rushes, bushes and grasses.

Tree trunks had been placed over the river at various points for crossing the shallow waters to the east side of the mill floodgates. The top surface of the wood had been adzed down to make a level surface and handrails nailed on. To the west of the floodgates were deep and dangerous waters, but the depth would decrease as one walked upstream and by the time one reached Aveley Bridge and Alpheton Hall water meadows, the water was back to normal.

In the deep water, we would fish for tiddlers. Our tackle was hazel sticks from the hedge, cotton thread and bent pins, complete with jam jar. Our catch was a stickleback, some little green and red fish, and the usual tiddlers. Frogs favoured the west side – perhaps they liked the deeper water.

All week long, horses and workmen toiled on the fields. Acres of winter wheat had been harrowed and rolled, leaving light and dark patterns on the fields. The countryside was now beginning to dress up with daffodils; buds were at bursting point, the grass was getting greener and people walked with a lighter step. Lambs did their dance in lush green meadows, hares fought their battles in great striped green wheat-fields, and rooks did their mass aerial displays over newly sown cornfields. Scarecrows with straw hair and battered hats appeared on the Suffolk scene, and more than one scarecrow exchanged his jacket with the tramps who walked the main road.

Time moved on towards Easter and the first holiday of the year. On Good Friday, men and horses were glad to have a break from their labours and the horses were glad to taste the new spring grass.

On gardens and allotments, the farm workers would be planting potatoes and other crops and at twelve o'clock sharp they would all be waiting for the key to turn in the door of the Rose and Crown. At the click of the lock they would march into the tap room and one by one order their favourite beer – something called mild and bitter – from the landlady, who would disappear down the cellar and return with their orders on a tray.

They all appeared to be very contented, for this was their pub. Hardly any strangers called in and they were, of course, very friendly to each other – they were more like brothers. They were all concerned for each other and their families. They would buy each other beer, if one had no money. They also helped out with rabbits, chickens and vegetables if one of them was ill. It really was a remarkable friendship.

They worked on farms with each other, they drank together, their awake lives were with each other, yet they showed no outward signs of friendship to each other's children or their wives. Nor did they ever – no, never – visit each other's homes or get into conversation with each other's wives except to wish the 'zeal of the day' as they called it, meaning 'good morning' or 'good afternoon', and never by their Christian names. They used the words ' Good morning, missus', and always touched their hats.

They were truly good workmen, ploughing, drilling, stacking and looking after stock. Everything had to be done correctly and with pride, but most of them were hard men who loved their beer and pipe tobacco and they also had their own special seat in the pub.

Easter
On Easter Sunday, the church bells of Long Melford and Lavenham would ring out across the countryside to let us know this was a special day. We would get an Easter egg, properly bought by my mother and older brothers and sisters. The four youngest of us and my older sisters would go to Alpheton church on Easter Sunday afternoon. We liked singing hymns but not the sermon, which seemed to go on and on. We got bored – bored – bored, so we were quite relieved when it was finished.

We enjoyed the walk to the church via Aveley Lane and Alpheton Hall private track. Then we would come home via the footpath from Alpheton to Bridge Street. My sisters would pick loads of dog violets from the field brews and place them in cleaned potted-meat jars as a centre-piece on the Easter Sunday tea table – a very great honour for a potted meat jar and you would be surprised if you knew how many potted meat jars would be awarded this great and noble honour.

On Easter Monday, my aunt and uncle from London, and an aunt and uncle from Bury St Edmunds would visit us at Rose Cottage. Two brothers had apparently married two sisters. They would arrive at Long Melford railway station, take a bus to Melford Green and walk from there to Bridge Street.

They were big, smart men, my uncles, dressed immaculately in fine grey suits with waistcoats and trilby hats, sporting silver watch chains with diamond gold medallions from their waistcoat pockets. Their ladies, wearing grand finery and hats to match, looked very elegant and posh, and it was obvious they did not belong to our village. Nevertheless, they were very friendly and perfect guests, shaking hands with all of us, including children.

On arrival, they were given coffee or tea and biscuits. The ladies stayed with my mother in the kitchen, while my mother cooked the dinner. Any changes to our tiny hamlet would have been discussed in great detail. A cluster of ancient Elizabethan houses stood along the old main road, at the bottom of Rose Cottage's long front path. They were of massive construction, with huge oak doors and were heavily beamed with a first-floor overhang. They had housed a number of Bridge Street families, including our own, when my mother had had a sweet shop there. Sadly, this was long before my time, as my mother said she had "too many kids to make it pay". Then the day came when these ancient houses were condemned by the council and its occupants were moved into newly built council houses nearby.

While my aunts were discussing this, the menfolk would go for a walk up the garden and to the allotment to look at the pigs, chickens, rabbits and ferrets. They would walk past Gott Mott's cottage – their father, my grandfather. After all, this was the village of their birth and of their schoolboy days, so it must have had a place in their hearts. Every time they visited, they called to see the village wheelwright, who was a great friend of one of my uncles in his schooldays, and no doubt they gave a glance towards their old Bridge Street school, closed long before. Returning from their walk, at midday it was time for the click of the key in the lock of the Rose and Crown and in they went.

On the dot of one o'clock, dinner was served around my mother's scrubbed pine kitchen table – beautiful Yorkshire puddings standing well above the top of the tins, roast beef, cauliflower or cabbage, roasted or mashed potato, carrots or parsnips and gravy. Out of this world! Then rhubarb pie and custard. All this from one little stove, one little oven, one little fire; all our saucepans and kettle black with smoke from the fire, for it had an open chimney and no fluepipe. This was my mother's dinner, served for twelve people. I look back in wonder. After lunch, with all the dinner crocks washed, my mother would go to her bedroom to wash and change and then appear as elegant as a queen in fine country clothes.

Then they would sit and talk, mostly about the past. At four o'clock, my mother made a pot of tea with very thin bread and butter for us all. These would be washed up and at half past four, the finest white cotton tablecloth one ever saw was spread over the table. Fine crockery, the best tea service, was brought out – a rose pattern to represent Rose Cottage. The table would look elegant with a small posy of wild flowers, peggles [cowslips] and primroses, for decoration. At five o'clock we would sit down to tea – cold meats, lettuce grown at the blacksmith's against a south wall, watercress from the Chad, boiled eggs, home-made salad cream and bread and butter were followed by home-made cakes and sponges. They would sit eating and talking until at a quarter past six, our guests gathered up their fine hats and coats, kissed and hugged my mother and thanked her for a great day and fine food.

My older brothers and sisters were given a handshake, and us kids had a kiss and a nip of the hand with one whole shilling pressed in. They departed up the main road towards Long Melford, with my father going some of the way with them. Then my mother and sisters would set themselves to wash the tea things, but not before the shillings were collected from us – as my mother always said, "to help buy you lot some clothes".

So, by the end of our Easter Monday, you would have thought they would have had enough, especially my mother who had been up since 5am. But no, at seven o'clock, motorcycles would roar into the yard with young men dressed in big mackintoshes, helmets and goggles. Three of them were my sisters' boyfriends. They would all come in with their bulky clothes and give my mother a very warm greeting. The other motorcyclists were my brother Jep's friends. They didn't stay long but roared off, and my brother with them on his BSA 250cc drip-feed motorbike, no doubt looking for girls all dressed up in their Easter finery.

Then, Easter over, the men went back to work and us children had a week's holiday. Ernie Bugg was my best friend, and his father was head horseman where my father worked, so we always had a welcome at Ford Hall. We would make catapults, cutting a wooden crotch from the hedgerow, and elastic bought from the local shop, with a piece of leather from an old shoe for the stone holder. We also bowled hoops, walked the towpath by the Chad, and looked for moorhen eggs which we would take to eat – very rich and tasty. We had an unwritten law between us that we would never strip a nest completely. We always left one egg in the nest and the moorhen would lay more eggs – take the lot and it would desert the nest. And we only took once from the same nest. We never took more than three eggs – four eggs in the nest, take three, leave one. All nests with more than four eggs were left, as these could be set on by the mother bird.

In those days, there was a footpath from the main road up the path to Rose Cottage, to a stile on the south side of the cottage. It continued in a straight line across Serpenpan Meadow, with the grass getting tall as this was a hay meadow in spring. Then over another stile into Three Acre Bit, which was an arable field, then over the top of another stile into Wash Meadow where a few cows would graze on the damp pasture, then still in a straight line to a five-bar gate. Over the top of that into the ten yard wide Dark Lane, which continued for about half a mile.

At the end of Dark Lane you came out into Lower Meadows, crossing wetland to the Chad, then turning right you followed the river for a mile and a half, past Hunter Bridge into Alder Carr Wood and along to Hare Drift adjacent to the Hare Inn at Long Melford.

This was my favourite walk over Serpenpan Meadow. Dark Lane was overgrown, not touched by man even for hundreds of years I would think. Its beauty was out of this world. On either side were tall, tall hedges of blackthorn, whitethorn, old crab apple trees and hundreds of blackberry bushes. Wild roses had climbed the tallest branches and cascaded down to the ground.

In June, I would gaze at the sides and roof of this lane, ablaze with wild rose and bramble blossom. Down the centre ran cart tracks, which gave it a fine country air. Wildlife was in abundance in this lovely lane, with fox, stoat, weasel, rabbits, pheasant, partridge and smaller birds in profusion.

Wild flowers grew in their season either side of the tracks – peggles and primroses, cornflowers, bluebells, foxgloves, pink wood or cuckoo orchids and many more in high summer. Hundreds of butterflies, of all colours and sizes, made this sacred place their home. Bees came here to drink their nectar, but some were greedy and crashed on their way back to the hive. It was a tunnel of broken sticks, ancient shrubs and bushes. Its light was by hundreds of sunbeams shining through many holes in its sides and roof – like chandeliers hanging from sky-hooks. In winter, it still had a stark and naked beauty of its own – old, broken, rusty farm machinery lay here and there, covered in bushes and dead grass. Nature was capable of taking these over in time. An old tumbrel, pushed to the side of the track, lying on its side, broken wheel high in the air, gave us kids a good ride on the merry-go-round.

A Walk In The Woods
April gave way and in marched May, the month of blossoms and good hay. Down to the woods! We would go along Dark Lane to Spelthorne Wood and Lineage Wood, the Queech and the Osier beds – this would take us a long way from home, out towards Sir William Hyde Parker's great Melford Hall estate, and other big landowners who didn't know our families. This was an adventure where there would be no familiar faces smiling down at us if we were caught, but exploring was a great temptation in such glorious countryside, and at that age we were just as much a part of it as the wildlife around us.

Spelthorne was a carpet of bluebells – a wonderful sight – but in the depths of the wood it was very quiet. Every stick that broke under our feet sounded to us like a twelve-bore gun going off. 'Trespassers Will Be Prosecuted' said the sign at every access to the woods, and we had to watch for keepers because this was pheasant nesting time and they were strict. So we would tread our way very carefully, listening for sounds of any human who would be stalking us. The cock pheasant would call out and it would echo through the forty acres or so of the wood. For a second, we would hold our breath, stop and listen, then go forward for we knew that if we were confronted by a keeper, we could easily outrun them as we had a good knowledge of the area. And we also knew where our poles were, for vaulting over the Chad.

Ernie and I move on slowly behind the others, not talking, but each taking in all around us – huge trees, with exposed roots and hollows beneath them where foxes or rabbits lived safe below for protection. We come across one tree with its huge trunk split open. We investigate with great interest and come to the conclusion it was caused by lightning. We had been told time and time again not to stand under trees while thunderstorms were in our area and if caught in a downpour, get wet and never take shelter under trees. We were young and learning first-hand about the countryside and the meanings of warnings from our elders.

We move on from the damaged tree with the cock pheasant and jays continuing to give our position away. We are travelling west to east, and getting out of our familiar area, but we head on towards a field we've spotted. The wood is beautiful with its canopy of green leaves and blossoms, but the going is getting tough. We are getting scratched and stung by thorns and nettles, so we turn south where the undergrowth seems less severe. We are looking for a woodland glade because walking through a thicket and holding one's direction is difficult, going round one obstacle then another. This time we make the right decision and come across a glade running west to east. West would take us back home, but we decide to go east towards Lavenham, because we had followed the hounds here once before.

The walking is easier now, and it is getting lighter meaning we are coming out of the wood. Ahead is a ditch, covered in brambles and nettles, so we stop and push them down with our feet and sticks, and stand surveying the area ahead. There is just a sloping grassy field, miles from nowhere. It seems it has never been cultivated as wild rose and cock bramble are growing everywhere. Hundreds of rabbits are sitting up straight to see who has invaded their private kingdom.

So by the rabbits we know no keepers, or anyone else, are around and we break our cover with confidence and march up the steep hilly meadow, sending the rabbits scurrying to their burrows. On reaching the top, we see the land falling sharply downhill before us. We are very exposed on top of this hill, and we quickly descend down to where a belt of saplings offer to provide us with cover.

But one thing is wrong. There is no wildlife alongside this belt of saplings – no rabbits, no pheasants, no nothing. We know there should be, for this is ideal rabbit habitat, but they are gone. As we did not scare them to their burrows, something else has. We lie under cover of wild rose bushes, discussing the matter and decide it could be a fox, a dog, a cat, or most likely – a human.

We watch and wait, not knowing what to do. Rabbits start to

appear, first one, then two, then lots more. Still we stay, watching. Everything seems quiet and peaceful but we know the countryside has eyes and ears, including our own.

Then, as we watch, a shot rings out and two rabbits fall squiggling to the ground, while hundreds more stampede to the burrows. A man emerges from the belt of trees, picks up the dead rabbits and puts them in his bag, then makes off along the meadow. We watch him go out of sight and decide it is safe to leave our cover. We make our way back to the banks of the Chad, flowing on its last leg to Long Melford.

We go down one bank and up the other, through nettles, reeds and a beautiful moss growing on fallen trees. Snipes swirl up into the sky on their twisting flight, as the land here is very wet and marshy. We struggle through reeds that are higher than us, trying to keep a straight line, and quickly find our objective – the railway track running between Long Melford and Lavenham. Hooray! At last we know exactly where we are, for this is border country. On the other side of the railway fence is L.N.E.R. property, and if the keeper appears, we can nip through the wire.

We wander on along the fence, north and east, through the bushes and lush spring grass. On our left, Lineage Wood is white with wood anemones. Such a wonderful sight, but now the east wind has a razor's edge.

On the railway track, four men on a rail trolley flash past, heading towards Long Melford. How these trolleys were propelled, I have never found out, but I think they had some sort of wooden connecting rod to one of the wheels, which was then propelled by hand until it got up speed, then it free-wheeled.

All the men wore caps and red and white wrappers around their necks, which were blowing quite strongly backwards in the slipstream, suggesting these trolleys were capable of quite a speed on a downward run. They all wave to us as they pass by and I remember thinking that if they had red and white trousers to match their wrappers, how like Rupert Bear they would be.

Walking beside the track on the farmland side, heading towards Lavenham, the profile changes from fill cut or embankment to deep cut. Here, we see a recess has been cut into the embankment, and a little hut stands, constructed of sleepers and a tin roof. This must have inspired us as we climbed over the wire fence and down the embankment to look inside. The construction of this shed was massive, like all things on the railway.

Inside we see all sorts of heavy tools, thick sleeper seats, an earth floor, a little fireplace still burning a heap of coal. It's very dark inside – there are no windows – and lo and behold, hanging from the wall are four or five haversacks, or grub bags, and a red and white wrapper. So this is where the Ruperts live.

"The men on the trolley," I say to Ernie. "They'll be coming back!"

We act as one to rush out of the cabin, up the embankment and over the wire, onto farmland and safe again – unless the keepers get us.

We haven't gone far when we hear the sound of a train running in the distance, coming from Long Melford. It is coming up a steep incline, the train is working hard as the chuff, chuff, chuffs are a few seconds apart. At first we see the smoke and steam, then the engine, coming very slow. We stop and look down to watch it go past.

The driver and fireman are hanging out of the engine on our side and they give us a blast of the whistle and a wave, and we all wave back. The crew are wearing red and white wrappers – more Ruperts. This time, their scarves don't blow in the wind, as the train is going so slow, hauling around twenty trucks laden with coal, timbered box vans and covered wagons.

We watch as the procession passes, then the guard at the rear raises his hand to us in greeting and we wave back. By now, we are almost at the railway bridge at Lavenham Lane and from the parapet, we watch our 'puffing billy' train make its way towards Lavenham until it is out of sight.

Now for the last leg of our journey home down Lavenham Lane to Bridge Street. What a lovely old lane it was at that time. Peggles growing in abundance on its verges and ditch banks, tall hedges in some places, grass banks at others. The road itself was just tar and chik stone. Only farm carts used it, and occasionally, thrashing tackle. We always, when in this area, looked in at the Gospel Oak. Not much to see, just another oak tree reputed to be haunted, so we never stayed here long.

We carry on past Keeper's Cottage and Duncan's Farm, round the lovely twisting bends. Now here we really have something to interest us! Council workers tarring the road, and one was our local length man [person responsible for the upkeep of a section of road], who knew us all and would always tell us tales of yesteryear.

Ahead we see the Tar Pot with a coal fire and a long chimney. The smell of steam smoke and tar is lovely. One never forgets it. They would empty a barrel of tar into the reservoir, get it heated up and pour hot tar onto the road with lipped buckets, feathering it out with squeegees. Workmen would spread a type of chik stone and gravel onto the hot tar.

Coming up behind, here was what we were most interested in – the steam-roller with a huge front roller and rear wheels, oil dripping from its cylinders and sizzling as it ran down the boiler, stones crunching under its mighty wheels. The brass boiler bands and copper chimney decoration shone like glass, its paintwork magnificent, everything seeming red hot. The whole machine was a show piece, and put the poor old Tar Pot to shame.

Yet somehow, to me, the old Tar Pot looked lovely in this beautiful Lavenham Lane. It had no finery, no brass, copper or paint. I don't think anybody loved it or cleaned it. It was just black with tar, with iron-type hurdle wheels, the longest chimney one ever saw, and there it stood billowing smoke up to the sky. Yes, I loved it. I didn't know it then, but I was to meet the old Tar Pot again one day.

Further on stood the horse-drawn steam-roller water cart, painted in blue and red – another cared-for implement. In a field gateway stood the steam-roller driver's van, painted green and red. Curtains hung from its little windows at the front and there was a stable door, complete with an access ladder. This was the home of the roller driver and his wife as they moved to different sites and contracts. Beside the van were two bicycles, a heap of coal and a linen line strung between van and hedge. The freedom of this living must have been great, but perhaps lonely for the lady of the van.

After taking in the busy scene, we walked on homeward, down the hill to the bottom of Lavenham Lane, where the road met the

Chad and took a sharp right turn to join the main road next to Mr Goldsmith's blacksmith's shop. There as always, stood this giant of a man with a huge smile, waving to us from the smithy door.

We split up and headed off to our midday dinner. My father and older brothers, Jep and Wally, were home and my mother, as always, had a wonderful meal on the table: suet pudding and rabbit gravy with rabbit, potatoes, cabbage and carrots. And for afters we had apple pie and custard. Drink was always tea. My mother stood up serving all dinner time and then had her dinner in peace when we had all gone back to work or play. While eating, the men would talk. The conversation would go on something like this:

"What does rolls pull down like?"

"Not very good."

"What's it, wet?"

"Yes, but it's for sugarbeet. He's anxious to get on. If the weather keeps up, it will haze behind me, then I suppose he'll put the rib-roll on, harrow up again with light harrows, then roll again."

"He'll need all that to get a good seed bed there. Ploughed up too late for sugarbeet. Get it up early and let the frosts do the work. 'Jack' works for nothing, but men and horses don't. He never seems to learn, that chap. It's not for me to tell him that."

"No."

It was farming talk and I took it all in along with my meat and drink, growing, I suppose, out of childhood and into the world of work.

Haymaking

Every day we took the bus to school at Shimpling and from the windows we could see the men working in the fields, sowing artificial manure by hand, horses and men harrowing the wheat fields, leaving wonderful stripes behind them. Sugarbeet would be coming through the soil, with men hoeing out hundreds of little plants by hand. We would see some labourers eating their breakfast – their 'nineses' – and they would wave their hoes in the air to us as we passed by.

Tramps would be inspecting their milestones as they tramped on forever and ever, mile after mile in their lonely journey to nowhere – a pathetic sight as they tramped on forlorn and alone. Dressed in rags, broken shoes on their feet, no bed, no home, no food, no money, no medical care, many were ex-servicemen from the First World War. Some were shell-shocked, some could never forget the slaughter and distress they had seen on the battlefields of France. They were mentally affected and some were physically ill. In the shelter at the top of Cold Hill, some were found dead and some very ill.

Listening to my elders, I heard they were taken off to the Union, or the Spike, as the workhouse was called. Many froze to death or starved as the severe British winter took its toll on these poor forgotten souls. Once they were heroes, now they were tramps. Christian Britain! But where was the Church of England? Politicians will force you to war and glorify it. They give medals for it. When it's all over, no-one wants you, especially if you are physically or mentally ill. They had money for guns and ships, but nothing for these lost souls. Justice they call it. A democracy. "Rule Britannia, Britannia rules the waves. Britain never, never, never shall be slaves," we sang at school. What a lie!

It was at this age, around twelve or fourteen, that I had my doubts about my country and its leaders. On the eleventh hour of the eleventh day of the eleventh month, they stand at the Cenotaph. Never were so many crocodile tears shed in one place. My dictionary describes a politician as 'cunning, artful, dealing with the distribution of wealth', but they did not distribute anything to the heroes who tramped the main road through Bridge Street – not even hope.

My mother, God bless her soul, would give them hot water when they came to her cottage door with their cocoa tins and wire handle. She would put a measure of tea-leaves on the hot water and milk and sugar, and a couple of buns or a piece of bread and cheese. Some were so cold, they would be shaking and trying to warm their hands on the hot tin. "Thank you, madam, thank you," they would say when they left. My mother would turn to us children as we watched with her near the door, and say, "Poor old bugger. We don't treat our animals like that."

My mother was very courageous. She would answer the door

in the dark to anyone. Nothing scared her. If there was someone having a baby, or somebody had died, we would see her putting her hat and coat on. She wouldn't tell you where she was going, and if we asked she'd just say, "Never you mind. You be in bed when I get home." And afterwards, she'd never tell you nothing, where she'd been or what had happened. It was always hid away from children in those days, but the district nurse lived in Long Melford, so there had to be one person who could be on hand in a village.

Time would move on to the season of haymaking – or haysel as it is called. From the school bus, I would see the hayfields of clover and grass being cut with the horse-drawn Sailor. This was a cumbersome looking machine with wooden sails, which rotated round, dipped to pull the grass to the cutting knife, then up to clear the operator at an angle of forty-five degrees. It was pulled by three horses abreast. In time it was replaced by a more modern machine, a grass mower with fingers and blade – far superior to the Sailor – and that was pulled by two horses and an operator.

There was a job for us in the hayfield, helping the gamekeeper with the beautiful smell of new-cut grass in the air. We would look for pheasants' nests and frighten the hen bird off the nest before it got its head cut off by the Sailor. We would collect the eggs and hand them over to the keeper as quickly as possible. He would put them under broody hens or bantams, which he would hire from cottages or farmers. As they hatched out, they were reared by hand and later released to the wild.

As the hay wilted and dried, in late May or June, the turner would be busy putting the drying hay into swaths. This machine would shake up the hay to let the sweet spring air into it, and the smell got better every day. Suddenly, as we came home on our school bus, our hayfield was being turned into haycocks.

We would race to our homes, anxious to get into the hayfield, but would be stopped in our tracks by our mother announcing, "You must wait a bit. The men are working late to cock the hay – the forecast isn't good."

We would wait until my mother had packed our father's tea. Tea consisted of the top from a cottage loaf, a lump of butter, cheese, onion and a milk can of very hot tea. She would hand this to my older brother Harry, who was still at school with me, and my second-youngest sister Beryl, and off to the field we would go, meeting our school friends on the way.

At five o'clock, the men would stop and sit under a haycock. I would watch as the men slid their hands into their trouser pocket and brought out their shut knives [penknives]. They would wipe the blade on their trouser leg, cut a chunk from their agricultural wafer [thick slice of bread], pop it into their mouth, then a lump of cheese and a piece of onion, all cut with their shut knives.

Then my father would hand out a packet wrapped in greaseproof paper that my mother had secretly hidden in his frail basket [woven straw bag]. In it would be a jam sandwich each and we were delighted. My father would give us a cup of tea between us, and the atmosphere was one of peace and contentment. In good weather, the warmth on our backs after a long winter, and the smell of hay and sweet warm air gave us kids a great sense of security.

We would play in and out of the haycocks, then make our way home and a kiss from each of us to our mother for our secret jam sandwich. I am sure it made her hard day seem lighter. Fed, bathed, and up the wooden hill we'd go, under the thatch of Rose Cottage and sleep.

The drying east winds would continue to blow, along with brilliant warm sunshine and wide blue skies with little white rag clouds floating below. This was real haymaking weather. We would see the farmer and workers taking samples from the haycocks from different parts of the field, checking areas of full sun, part shade and deep shade. The moisture content was crucial: too dry, no good; partial moisture, good; too much moisture – the stack would heat and catch fire. So it had to be just right.

They did it by feel, smell and experience – mostly the latter. I would stand and listen and this was how the conversation would go:

The farmer would ask his men, "What do you think, Sid?"

"It's a bit clammy everywhere but full sun. I think it'll be all right by tomorrow."

The farmer would turn to another, "What do you think, Jack?"

"Full sun, by tomorrow. If weather holds, all-shade and partial shade. I think we should shake haycocks down to let in more air, then we may be able to carry on from full sun area."

They'd all walk back towards the farm, no doubt talking over their opinions, but the final decision would be the farmer's.

From early morning, I would be full of the joys of spring, running to the dairy door at the mill to collect my mother's pint of milk before picking up my satchel to wait for the school bus. We would all be scanning the fields on our way to school, wondering if the men and wagons would start carting hay today.

On our way home from school, we would see other farms carting hay to the stackyards and knew they would be carting at home. We all went to the field with our father's tea and there would stand the great wooden hay wagons, painted blue and red with ladders front and rear. They were all pole wagons, meaning a pole was fitted from the front to the rear axle to strengthen the front axle supports. This method reduced the lock to half, for if one locked too sharp, or onto full lock, the wheel caught on the pole and would cause the wagon to overturn.

Haysel would last about three weeks from cut to stack, depending on the acreage and that depended on how many horses and cattle there would be to feed through the winter. It was, of course, a very valuable crop. The hayfield itself was either left for seed, especially if it was clover stuvver [clover crop], or ploughed up, known as barsted fallow. By now, the ground would have dried hard – too hard for horse or tractor plough – so most farmers hired in steam engines to cultivate the hayfield.

Then – in the mid-Thirties – a new machine appeared called a Gyro Tiller. This seemed a huge machine with rotating drums, with cultivator-type tines attached. It was tracked, with a huge wheel at the front, and an arrow attached to the wheel so the operator knew the direction of the wheel. I think they were of German manufacturer with huge diesel engines and I think some were made in England by John Fowler of Leeds.

The Gyro Tiller had two crew who lived in a hut and worked twenty-four hours a day in twelve-hour shifts. It was cheaper than steam and less labour-intensive, but reliability, I believe, was poor.

In contrast, the crew of the steam engines consisted of one cook, two drivers and a cultivator-steerer. They lived in a hut with great iron wheels and a ladder to reach the stable door at the front of the van. The operation was labour-intensive as farm men had to cart coal and water for the engine. It was a busy job when cultivation was taking place in distant fields and the source of water was the farm pond.

It was, of course, June, glorious June. Away from the fields, Spring Meadow was a wonderful sight – lush green grass, the yellow of the buttercups, the white of the daisies, the pink of the milkmaids and the calming effect of the water escaping from the floodgates.

Two Red Poll cows lie chewing the cud in this multi-coloured meadow. A village lady crosses the meadow with hoop and buckets from the village spring. No artist's brush ever touched this meadow, no-one ever wrote of its beauty. This was my home and its floral display was mine. The lady carrying the buckets was my mother. Visit it in early morning, when the first rays of sun penetrate the mist, turning it into a golden cloud, lighting the dewdrops on flowers and grass like golden icicles. The painting of this meadow hangs on no-one's wall, but it is framed in my mind forever.

Across Spring Meadow, follow the footpath to the first great bend in the river, where the water varied from one to six feet in depth. Half a mile back from the deeps of the floodgates, here was our waterhole. Village children bathed and swam through the long, hot summers of the Thirties in the pure, clean water. Shoeless, we spent hours playing and splashing, wearing just our underpants.

On hot summer evenings, our friends from Alpheton would come down the hill to join us for a swim at the waterhole. On Friday nights, our mothers would give us towels and a piece of Lifebuoy soap and we would all bath in the Chad. My older brothers and other young men from the village would also bathe or take a bath here, but the older men never seemed to bath at all, nor did they ever come near our waterhole. It was great fun for us boys and girls of Bridge Street and our friends from Alpheton, but of course, they were our school friends and great pals. There were lots of fish in the area so boys had to make sure to keep their pants on.

From the age of eight to thirteen, ten of us boys and girls were about the same age and usually went round together. Among the boys were Ernie Bugg, Herbert Newman, Digby Wallace, Lionel

'Barney' Andrews and brothers William Frost and Lesley 'Dusty' Frost. We never went to the towns or left our village except to go to school. I don't think we ever went to Sudbury or Bury St Edmunds. We had no need to, there was nothing there for us, we had all we required. We had the Chad to pole-vault, fish, bathe and bath in, moorhen eggs and watercress to eat, and jouncing boards across the river. These were meant for gamekeepers and labourers' ladies when out on their walks, but when we all loaded onto the board and jumped up and down together, they would spring up and down, hence the name we gave these wooden crossing points.

We also had thousands of acres to play and walk in, to hunt in, hundreds of secret places to explore, hundreds of animals to love, pat, scratch their bellies and ride on their backs. We had dogs to walk and take rabbiting, and we had horses, pigs, sheep, cows, goats and cats. We also hunted out bees' nests in old trees. Sometimes we managed to pinch some of their honeycomb to eat, but more often than not, the bees got angry and one or two of us, by being brave or foolish, would get stung. We would also stir up wasps' nests with long sticks, or try to smoke them out with paraffin rags.

One summer treat was boating on the Chad. For the rest of the year, Mr Ruffle's boat would be lying upside down in the grass on the riverbank near the floodgates of the mill. Then one warm day, we might unexpectedly be invited to have a ride in the boat. Mr Ruffle's son, Dick, sometimes did the rowing. On occasion, it was Mr Ruffle's housekeeper, Miss Underhill, who asked us. I remember one time, there might have been a few too many of us in the boat because when Miss Underhill stepped in, the water level rose alarmingly around us as she was a lot heavier than us children. We spent all that afternoon watching the water expecting the worst, and we were glad we could all swim. We weren't sure what would happen to Miss Underhill, though.

Of course, in those days, the water was a lot deeper. Now the floodgates have all gone but before that they used to have severe floods there at times. It's frightening, the Chad, when it's in full flood – or in those days it was. It used to hit trees and they would fly in the air. There was one occasion the water carried a pig off Spring Meadow and they thought they'd lost her. Next morning, they went looking and found the sow, none the worse, all the way down on the wetlands behind Ford Hall.

It was a different world when the water was still, and on a hot summer Sunday everyone seemed to come out and stroll by the river and walk across by the floodgates.

Harvest

Then would come the harvest. We would ride in the harvest wagons, slide down the straw stacks and visit the harvest fields, which were cut by binder and horses, later tractor-drawn. We would wait for hours, armed with sticks, for the rabbits to start to run out as the machine went round and round. The standing corn got smaller and further from the hedgerows and this meant the rabbits had a long run home when they were forced to make a run for it.

This was where our fun came in. We ran and chased these rabbits until we could run no more. Farmers shot hundreds of them, their guns could not be loaded quick enough – they had an area of field to themselves, which we were not allowed in for safety reasons. Dogs worked so hard some collapsed and had to be taken to the river to drink and be cooled off.

We made our way home in the evening, usually following the last loaded harvest wagon accompanied by the field gang of pitchers and loaders. The evenings were hushed and still, with just the creak of the harvest wagon as it rolled up the dusty track, its iron wheel-bands shining in the light of the setting sun.

The loaders and pitchers would be walking with a slight stoop, their two-tined forks on their shoulders, their straw frail baskets on their backs, the sleeves of their striped shirts rolled to the elbow, with their red and white wrappers and assortment of trilby hats, their skin tanned by the blazing sun and dust sweat marks down their faces, trudging the last mile home. The long day – from seven in the morning to eight at night – had taken its toll in these rolling wheat fields of Suffolk.

The crickets and grasshoppers were making their last calls of the day in the thick undergrowth beside the track. The wild flowers were surely closing their petals for the night, but were taking a refreshing rinse from the now falling dew. The butterflies were hiding under broad-leaved plants with folded wings to escape the heavy harvest dew. It was now the turn of the moths and bats as the last rays of the sun switched off its light in the far-off western sky.

The bats would start to flutter above our heads as we walked on, and moths did their ghostly flights in the warm night air. And now the harvest moon was shining over hundreds of acres of golden wheat fields, looking down from a perfect sky.

At last, our wagon, workmen and children rolled into the stackyard and a man stepped forward, released the trace horse [lead horse] and the filler horse [shaft horse], and with their heads bent, their harness loose, they made their way to the horse pond on their own. I watched as they drank gallons of water with the moon high in the sky and another moon in the pond reflection, the golden ripples flowing from the horses' lips as they drank, disappearing into the far-off bank of the pond. I stood in a silent and timeless place.

The horses went to their stable, where their harness was taken off. Sweat marks showed under their saddles and collars. The horses shook themselves vigorously, as if with relief at last from this heavy load. They were given oats and chaff for their tea. Their coats were groomed and they were later turned out on lush green meadows.

The workmen and children made their way to the village, the cottage oil-lamps flickering in the window. All the men turned into the pub for a well-earned pint or two of mild and bitter. The kids went home to mum, a bath, drink, food and up the wooden hill to dream of tomorrow.

Next day, after my father, and my brothers Jep and Wally had gone to work, my mother would get us younger ones out of bed at six-thirty, telling us it was a lovely morning and the sun was high in the sky. In her opinion, no-one who felt well should be in bed on a wonderful morning like this – anyway it was harvest time, and no time to laze around.

She would usher us downstairs to the bowl in the back'us, already filled with warm water and standing on a high oak bench with hedgerow legs. She would rub the flannel over our tired-looking eyes and sometimes we would protest about the pressure applied to the flannel. She would answer, "No kid of mine goes out of this house with grubs in their eyes."

After the wash, we were lined up for a quick hair inspection and she would brush and comb it with vigour. With us still lined up, she would stand a few paces back and inspect us, standing in our pants. Then we would get dressed, boys in shirts and short trousers and my sisters in dresses, after each shirt and dress had been inspected for cleanness. If dirty, to the wash basket, and a clean one was taken and given to us out of a drawer.

Breakfast was a choice of buttered toast, toast and poached egg, marmalade and tea. After this we were free to go where we liked. I would meet the boys from the village and go to Ford Hall where my father worked, hoping for a lift out to the harvest fields again.

The men would be working in the stackyard. Yesterday's half-built corn stack had its stack cloth removed and laid out to dry, and wheat sheaves were being unloaded from last night's wagon. The field gang loaders and pitchers had a wagon up on the wooden jack, greasing the wheel axles from a bucket, to make it run easier for the horses.

This job done and as if by clockwork, they would climb aboard the wagon with their frail baskets, two-tined forks and straw or trilby hats. Us kids climbed up the back wheel, which was higher than the front and easier for our short legs. We were always made to sit down in the wagons. The floor was covered in chaff and every living insect was here. The chaff heaved from these thousands of creepy-crawlies, but they didn't sting or harm us in any way.

The men were dressed, as usual in their collarless shirts, red and blue striped with grey background, buttoned to the neck. Their trousers – some cord, some pepper-and-salt – were mostly with stable-door flaps instead of flies. They had wide braces and belts which were dog-collar leathers or string, tied just below the knee. On their feet they wore hobnail boots with grey army socks, and most would also have foot rags tied like a bandage round their feet, why, I do not know. One man sat sideways driving, the wagon rolling and bumping along the dirt track. The men were all smoking their pipes and talking of the wonderful morning.

Coming up behind us, the wind was twisting the dust into small spirals, travelling slowly closer.

"Hello," said one of the men, "here comes Roger, the sign of good harvest weather."

Within a second, it caught our wagon and the chaff, insects and headgear went spiralling into the air. The wagon stopped, everyone covered in chaff and insects. We all got to our feet, brushing ourselves down.

"Get down and collect those hats, boy." I did it immediately, and one man turned to another. "You said it was a wonderful morning," and the other gentleman agreed.

As we jogged down the track, it became hot.

"Going to be a scorcher today. It'll fetch the gravy out of us."

"Sure will, my old partner," came the reply.

It was a beautiful track we were travelling on, right beside the Chad. We sat high in the wagon looking out over the wetland meadows covered in wild flowers, seedy stalks and rushes along the dyke banks. It was a lovely and lazy place. As we jogged along, the men seemed to look out into space, then we reached the end of the lane and the wagon drove into the wheat field. The men got to their feet and the first one down was handed the frail baskets and he searched for a tree or stub to hang the baskets off the ground and in the shade.

Then they began loading the wagon with wheat sheaves, the smell of the heavy dew lifting off the stooks evaporating into the fresh morning air, giving one's lungs a boost for the day.

One boy stayed behind to help the field gang, riding the filler horse from stook to stook, sitting straddle-legged between the saddle and the collar, feet resting on the wagon-shafts if his legs were long enough. The flies tormented the horse continually. It would lift up each leg in turn and slam it down on the ground to shake off its tormentors, and so it was not the most comfortable seat in the world for a boy.

Us other boys and girls would walk along by the osier beds and up the steep slope of Hangen Hills in our young days. These fields were never farmed, left to the wild and the wind. Here and there were wild roses, huge rabbit burrows and along its hedgerows there were great trees with huge girth and very rough bark, with some sort of poor-looking grass growing here and there. Poppies seemed to like the impoverished soil. This was a favourite place of ours, perhaps because of its wildness, its hilly terrain, or because it seemed forsaken. But above all, it was a great place to be on a very hot morning.

We continued our walk beside the Queech, which ended in a strip off Sunny Summer Meadow, with its seedy grass and great blue scotch thistles. We turned right, up to the bank of the Chad, to lovely clean water running over washed gravel.

The temptation was great, and off went our shoes and socks. The girls tucked their dresses into their knickers and into this cool rippling water we went. Carrying our shoes and socks, we walked upstream, pulling freshwater mussels from under stones. We watched thousands of tiddler fish take left or right turns to avoid us. Then we made a line across the river from bank to bank, and the tiddlers had only one option – to go through our legs. We liked this. We would bend down to try and grab them but it was very difficult to hold a tiddler fish.

Harnser birds [herons] would rise into the sky ahead of us on a slow, cumbersome flight, no doubt scared off by our shrieks and laughter. When we reached the spot where the heron had taken off, we would find empty freshwater mussel shells, so perhaps herons do manage to open the shells and eat them.

At last, we would climb out of the river and sit on our jouncing boards that spanned the river and we would watch the fish go past, never-ending masses on their way to the river Stour. Kingfishers would fly past – over and sometimes under – our jouncing board, travelling at great speed. Just a streak of blue was all we saw.

Wonders never ceased in our world. We were never bored, never lost for something to do, and we lived and played as a family of happy village children. The only difference between us was we lived and slept in different houses. There was a great bond of friendship between us. We seemed to have lived and played as brothers and sisters. Even on wet days, we would play marbles, and noughts and crosses in barns and disused buildings. No-one organised our play or walks, but we had all that a child wished for:

security, food, warmth, freedom, a river, a field, a meadow, buildings, ice, floods, carts, wagons, horses to ride on. And above all – good discipline and secure parents. We had everything except money and we did not really need that. In our play world, it was all free.

So our long, hot and brilliant summers continued. Mobile hen-huts were pulled onto the golden stubble fields for the chickens to shack the last heads of corn left behind by the reapers. Water became scarce at this time of year up the hill in Alpheton and three-wheeled horse-drawn water carts from the farms would arrive at the Chad, near the blacksmith's, to fill up with water for cattle and so on when the ponds and little streams had dried up.

Lots of Suffolk villages became short of water. Drinking water was taken daily from the spring at Spring Meadow for the people of Shimpling. A man named Ted Bruce carted it in his old Model T Ford, with a tank secured in the back.

Cattle on the high ground, on meadows out of the valley, were moved down to the lush pastures beside the Chad, as drinking water in their ponds had dried up. It was a lovely place for cattle as blackthorn bushes and hazels grew on both sides of the river, giving glorious shade and cool feet away from the many flies that always follow the herds. In fact, it was the perfect place if you were man or beast.

In my mind's eye, I see the standing corn, the fields of stooks, the stubble fields, all stretching out in different shades of gold; the faded paint of the blue and red harvest wagons, the heat shimmering on the harvest breeze and little whirlwinds making their way lazily to the unknown cottage ladies in their flowery pinafores and hats, with baskets on their arm. They are strolling down Dark Lane on their way to the woods, gathering hedgerow fruits as they amble along enjoying their summer walk, listening to the skylark singing up high above the field and the lovely soothing voice of the lonely turtle-dove in a hedge nearby.

And in the fields, great golden corn stacks rose majestically up into the sky as if by magic – built by men of nature who perhaps could not even write their name – but artists did paint them, and they hang in halls of fame. They stood as great golden temporary monuments to signify the end of the farming year and the bounty thereof.

Autumn – We Go To Long Melford

As our long and lovely summer holidays came to an end, mists would rise over the stubble fields and heavy moisture would appear on the grass and the fields. What a magic sight, like delicate lace softly touched by autumn dew. In late September and early October, sugarbeet clamps would appear on the verges of the main road. We could see the men knocking and topping the sugarbeet in the fields in all weathers, old hessian bags wrapped round their legs to keep out some of the cold and the clay.

Sometimes on a Saturday morning I would ride on the road wagons going to Long Melford railway station with sacks of corn to be loaded onto trucks standing in the sidings. My father Jack, the second horseman at Ford Hall, and Ernie Bugg's father, the head horseman, would be in charge of the wagons. There would be two shaft horses to each wagon and one trace horse to help pull the heavy loads up hills.

The road wagons, painted green and orange, had a seat at the front. The horses would have braided tails and manes and the best harness, with all brasses cleaned. These wagons were kept in tip-top condition, for these were the show-offs of the farm. A cast-iron plate was screwed onto the side with the name of the farmer and the name of the farm.

Proudly we set off from Ford Hall, stones crushing under the weight of the mighty iron-bound wooden wheels. Sid Bugg led the way, my father following behind, each man sitting high up on their wooden seats with real leather reins in their hands. I sat on my father's wagon, and my friend Ernie sat on his father's.

Reaching the top of Ford Hall drive, near the Rose and Crown, we turn left towards Long Melford. Our two mothers wave to us as we pass through the village. Within a short distance, we have reached Primrose Hill, taking us up and out of the valley. Both wagons stop, the trace horse is attached and the iron brake, or slud, is attached behind one back wheel as a safety device. It would lessen the weight in case the wagon stopped, going up the hill.

Ernie and I are told to walk up the hill, following the lead wagon until it stops right at the top. Then Ernie's father unhooks the trace horse, gives Ernie the lead and tells us to lead it back to the second wagon waiting at the bottom of Primrose Hill. Then my father couples up the trace horse with the brake slud in position, and proceeds up the hill. On reaching the top, the trace horse is tied behind the lead wagon until we reach Highcross Hill. Then the procedure is repeated, one wagon at a time.

At the top of Highcross Hill, with both wagons stopped, the brake sluds are brought from the rear wheel to the front before preparing to descend the other side of Highcross Hill. Both wagons again stop and one rear wheel on each wagon is run completely into brake slud, and both horseman signal to each other that they are ready to go and we all have to walk down the hill.

Both wagons now have only three wheels turning. One wheel is stopped, just riding along on the brake slud. Two white marks appear on the tar and stone surface of the road as the iron slud slides over the surface. The horses are laid hard back in their britchons and every link in their hold-back chains is at breaking point to hold the weight of these mighty wagons back.

The horses seem to know that they must get their act right, as they work together to hold the load. They are being pushed forward by the sheer force of weight on this downhill run. The iron shoes on their feet are slipping on the hard surface as they struggle to hold it back. The muscles in their legs, back, belly and neck are forced up to full capacity. Sweat marks appear as they make the descent.

I glance at the head horseman. His face is taut. Beads of sweat stand on his forehead and I notice he has clipped the verge with the wheels of the wagon all the way down the hill, maybe as another brake. He walks upright, leather reins in his hands, saying something to his horses in a language I do not understand.

Safely reaching the bottom of the hill, the lead wagon stops. We three, the head horseman and two boys, watch as my father completes his descent of the hill, also clipping the verge on the way down. There was skill in steering two horses and their great load by clipping not too far into the verge. The wheels could have sunk into the soft soil, but by their practical knowledge, the horsemen just chafed the wheels against it in an effort to make their horses' struggle a bit easier.

I understand why a great distance was put between the wagons, for safety in case of an accident to one of them. At the bottom of the hill, the brake sluds are removed from the wheels and hung on a chain on the side of the wagons, provided by the makers for this purpose. With the horsemen back on their high seats, Ernie and I sit on top of the corn stacks, and off we go on the last leg of our journey to the station.

Reaching the outskirts of Long Melford, both wagons pull into the forecourt of the Hare Inn. It did not take these two chaps long to get a thirst. The landlord, a huge-bellied man, appears at the door with two pints on a tray. The horsemen sank these within seconds, and the landlord toddles off to refill and returns again. They are emptied in record time. They pay up, thanking the landlord for his tray service and return to the wagons. Both men fill and light their pipes and on a chosen word, the horses tighten up in the shafts and we move off, the sound of flints crushing under the wheels of these heavy loads.

The going was easy through Melford, with one or two people raising their hands to the horsemen and both men raise their hats in acknowledgement. On reaching the station, the porter points to their box van and Ernie's father pulls his horses into a half-circle, in line with the van, reversing up to the door. Then our two fathers load the sacks of grain onto the train, using a sack barrow, and collect a receipt. We make our way back through Long Melford, stopping at the Hare Inn again on the way. The horses have an easier pull back home to the farm, where they get a generous helping of oats and chaff, and my father and Ernie's disappear into the Rose and Crown.

This was not the only time I would go to Long Melford. From the age of seven onwards, Harry and myself would walk the four miles there and four miles back, about once a month, to have our hair cut at Percy Drury's in Hall Street. Sometimes we had a shopping list.

"Get me an ounce of loose shag tobacco and a box of matches, will you Sonny?" said our father, handing Harry some money.

"You could get me half a dozen candles while you're there," said my mother.

After we'd had our hair cut, we walked on to Belfry Beales' shop, also in Hall Street. We opened the shop door and there was a tall, thin man standing behind the counter, arms stretched out, resting on it.

"Yes, sir?"

"Could I have an ounce of loose shag tobacco, please?" asked Harry.

"Yes, sir."

There were no shelves in the shop and the man stooped down behind the counter and came up with a tin of tobacco. He pulled some out of the tin, put in on the scale and rolled the tobacco up in newspaper.

"Anything else, sir?"

"A box of matches, please."

Down he went, out of sight, then stood up again, spreading both arms out across the counter. Looking me straight in the face, he asked, "You did say a box of matches – do you want those that strike both ends, or those that strike one end?"

That fooled me, so I said, "Just one end, please."

"Well, you tell your father when you get home that those that strike both ends will run out a lot cheaper. Anything else, sir?"

"Yes, half a dozen candles, please."

Down he went behind the counter, and up he pops again.

"Do you want those that light in the dark, or the daylight ones?"

We scratched our heads at that one. Harry said, "Well, we always use ours at home in the dark, so we'd better take those."

"Yes, sir." He wrapped those in newspaper as well. "Now you tell your mother the daylight ones are very good because they last a lot longer, and tell your dad that those matches that light both ends are very good as well."

"Thank you," we said.

"When you come to have your hair cut again, do come in and see me."

"Yes, we will."

Outside, Harry said, "Funny old man. Got matches that burn both ends and candles you light in the day."

We passed on the messages to our mother and father when we got home. That pleased the family, although it didn't take much to bring a smile to my father's face. "Well," he said. "There is some very clever people out there, trying to catch you out, so you two want to wake up – and fast, too."

Bonfire Night

At the beginning of October, we started preparing for Guy Fawkes night – a great event in our lives. Every one of us, boys and girls, carted wood off fallen trees, hedge cuttings, anything that would burn. This occupied our minds and souls as the November daylight was short. We had to work hard for five to six weeks as we had no industrial waste – no wooden pallets, no nothing. We had to cart everything on our trolleys, which were pram wheels and an axle with a Tate & Lyle sugar box with handles nailed either side.

We had one great friend – Mr Wallace, the farmer of Ford Hall. Every year he gave us a load of straw, delivered to the site on his meadow, next to his drive. Also, one gallon of TVO paraffin to start the fire. We were all very grateful for his generosity, as no-one gave anything away in those far-off days.

On the night of the Fifth of November, with a cloud-laden sky, we would step out of Rose Cottage – my brother Harry, my two sisters, Iris and Beryl and myself. In our hands, we each carried a paper bag, its contents a packet of sparklers, a box of 'special' matches, one 'catherine wheel', one 'flower fountain', one banger – and we were thrilled with all this.

My mother asked my brothers Jep and Wally to accompany us, fearing for our safety, I suppose. We met our friends outside the Rose and Crown and proceeded down to the fire we had worked so hard to build. As promised, Mr Wallace had sent his men to round up the fire and place a tumbrel-load of straw on top. The TVO stood ready to start the fire.

The young men of the village took charge of the fire, paraffin was poured on and the match struck. There was always a terrific bang as the paraffin ignited. The flames lit up the night sky and all the surrounding area, with the smoke taking a horizontal line in the damp and heavy November air.

The young men, with their two-tined forks, looked after the fire. Us kids were busy letting off our fireworks, helped by our brothers. The air was thick with the smell of smoke and gunpowder. Old men and ladies would be watching from the main road, no doubt remembering their younger days when they had carted wood and let their fireworks off on the same meadow.

As the flames died away and the lovely red embers turned into charcoal, from charcoal into ash, and the remains of firework cases lay shattered on the grass, we made our way home to Rose Cottage. The excitement of the event and the cold night air had dampened our enthusiasm for fireworks and everything else. All we needed was our beds.

Our mum would insist we must be washed, and all our protests were in vain. A bowl of hot water, soap and towel appeared on the kitchen table, we were undressed and washed all over. We were so tired we were crying and protesting at what we thought was unnecessary, but my mother – Liz – had her way, adding, "There is no pleasure without pain."

In our pyjamas and nightdresses, mother said, "There you are. That looks much better. Your faces shine like little pigs' bottoms. You couldn't go to bed with half of Wallace's meadow on your knees and hands." Then she gave us all a kiss and said "Goodnight, my old beauties," and so to our lovely feather beds in the timber-beamed bedrooms of Rose Cottage.

Christmas

Towards Christmas, the heavy rains of autumn gave way to severe frost. Ice and hoar frost hung on every tree, bush and shrub, so the scene was nearly always set for a white Christmas.

At school we rehearsed plays and carols. On the evening of the day before we broke up for our holidays, we would arrange a concert in the school and all the people of Alpheton and Bridge Street were invited. The school was usually full to capacity, for this was quite an event in those days, as most families had no entertainment at all. Lots of families had no radios or gramophones or anything. It gave everyone a chance to enjoy our Christmas play and join in with our carol singing, accompanied by Miss Fisher on the piano.

It also gave a chance to see some of the work we had done during the year, and to admire the decorated school. All the Christmas lanterns and chains were made by the children. Sprigs of holly appeared here and there, given by farmers. Oil lamps hung on oh-so-long chains from the apex of the roof, for there were no ceilings in these Victorian schools.

At the end of the concert, the parson and the wealthier farmers would give a speech thanking parents who had helped, and thanking the teachers, Miss Fisher and Miss Bixby for making Christmas a time to remember.

The head teacher, Miss Fisher, would reply, thanking Reverend so-and-so, Mr so-and-so and all the other names who thought they were important people. At last it got to 'ladies and gentlemen' – these were, of course, our parents, the so-called poor of the parish, but without them there would have been no children, no labourers to work the farms. So you see, we are all important in this world.

When the concert ended with the singing of 'God Save the King', and hand clapping and handshakes, our elder sisters would round us up. With other children from Bridge Street and all the other parents and elder brothers and sisters, we would walk the long dark miles down Cold Hill to Bridge Street. I don't think we ever met a car or anyone or anything. It was cold, frosty, and very still, dark except for the thousands of stars in the sky.

"A great night for Father Christmas to travel," said someone. I looked around me at the desolate fields, with the moon's soft light reaching down to gently touch Earth's frozen face. It looked desolate and forsaken. Skeleton-like objects stood out dark and forlorn, desperate and deserted. But of course, it was just sleeping, and it would wake from its slumbering.

In my child's mind, I thought of Father Christmas and I believed he was really out there somewhere. Was he, like me, scared in this desolate place? Had he got a home like mine to go to, with a fire to keep him warm, like me? A lovely bed to go to when tired, like me? A lovely mum to make the fires and beds, and wait on us, like mine? No, he can't have. He's too old. But I suppose he could have a lovely wife like my dad has.

My sister said, "Come on, lift your foot over the step."

My dream was over, and there I stood in my mum's kitchen, with flames roaring up the chimney. My mother gathered all of us round the fire, fussing over us, and I got as close to the fire and my mother as I could and I wondered if Father Christmas was circling those desolate fields, waiting for Christmas?

For a long while after, when I was tucked up in my bed at night, my mind always went back to those lonely fields, and for some reason, this scene has stayed with me all my life. Even now, I still stand and look out across this dark, still and mysterious landscape as if drawn to it.

Once, when the adults let little things slip, my brother Harry asked my father, "Do Father Christmas really come down the chimney, Dad?"

"He would get his arss burnt if he did," came the response, which brought shrieks of laughter from us kids, and my elder brothers and sisters.

My mother was quick to reply, "The fire is always out before Father Christmas comes."

My five older sisters May, Florence, Nora, Constance and Margie were mostly cooks or cook-housekeepers for the wealthy in the Sudbury area and had a half-day off on Thursdays, which was market day in Sudbury, and they would cycle home on Thursday evenings. They would always bring us presents, such as a cream bun, sweets, or an orange each. But near to Christmas, parcels would be secretly given to my mother and we would ask, "What is that?" and would be told not to ask questions.

Of course, these were the little things for our stocking. When our mother was out of the house, feeding the chickens and so on, one of us would watch out of the window for her to return, and shout a warning. The other three of us would look in cupboards, drawers and secret places in search of the mystery packages, but to no avail – we never found them.

The next morning, when my mother went to feed the chickens, we would all be waiting to resume our search. I remember her turning as she was leaving the house, and raising a finger she said, "It's no good you looking in those drawers and cupboards. There is nothing for you there and besides, I have to keep tidying up after you and I have enough work without that." That, to us, was a nice, kind warning to lay off searching.

The excitement would increase as we approached the day of the Christmas Party, when we'd see Father Christmas come running down the road, ringing a bell. Now we know it was Mr Ruffle, the miller, all dressed up, bringing each of us a little present. He put on a party in the Bridge Street Mission Hall every year where we all had jam and cream sandwiches. We loved to go and sing our hearts out in the little tin Mission Hall, especially at Christmas.

As the great day dawned near, my mother's cockerels were kept in their sheds and in the evenings the hurricane lanterns were lit and hung in the outhouse. My older brothers would visit the poultry shed and there would be a hell of a noise as they proceeded to catch them – feathers, dust and wings were everywhere. They would catch about eight per night, break their necks and bring them down to the outhouse.

All us kids, or anyone who could pull a feather or two, were rounded up to help with the plucking. We sat on stools, upturned buckets, old boxes, with a cockerel each between our legs, plucking away. There were feathers everywhere – up our noses, in our hair – and in the dim light of the lantern, it looked like a snowstorm. The down of the cockerel would stick to the moisture on our noses and tickle, and everyone was scratching and rubbing themselves, but somehow, the white flesh of the cockerel would appear. One by one, the first plucked cockerels were taken to the house to be dressed by my mother and hung up by the feet to drain the blood to their heads, to keep the flesh nice and white.

We brushed each other down with a stiff brush, took off our vests, shirts and pullovers, and these were shaken vigorously by our older brothers, who also wiped us down with towels as chicken lice would creep all over us – very uncomfortable.

"Never mind," said my mother, "they only live on a human for two hours." But two hours is a long time to be tormented by poultry lice.

The procedure would continue for about three evenings. By this time, us kids were red all over with scratching and rubbing. The feathers would be bagged up, the seats returned to their rightful places, and the house was getting back to normal. All the poultry lay on a table in the back'us, each with a label, weight and name of the order.

The best, and loveliest time of all was when the copper fire was lit and one by one we sat in a tin bath on the earth floor in the outside wash house. This outbuilding, where mother washed the bedlinen, was known as the bake-house or 'bake-us' because of the huge bread oven.

It was heaven, even if it was mid-winter, and the north wind blew around the door and under. Afterwards, with all clean clothes and a lovely clean bed, I felt like a prince. My mother had, by this time, changed all our bedding with sheets washed by hand and all out on the line to get a fresh blow, but the drying was finished off in the house because of the damp December air.

The cottage was decorated by my sisters. Home-made paper chains were stuck together by Beryl and Iris, and bells were bought by my older sisters. It was difficult to hang the paper chains, and they had to do a precarious line around the rooms because of the oil lamps and open fires. We had no Christmas tree because there was no room, but the front room would also be decorated.

Christmas was the only day of the year we were allowed to sit or play in this room. It was a place we were brought up to respect. I suppose it was my mother's show room. Everything was kept immaculate. The furniture and brass was always polished – why, I do not know, as no-one hardly ever saw inside it, only the family. There were stuffed birds in glass cases, a beautiful walnut Victorian piano, horsehair armchairs, overmantle, loads of Victorian vases, some dripping with china roses, lustres, trinket boxes, brass fender and brass companion set. All tables in the room were covered with cloths, some dark green, some dark blue, and, of course, a mantle-cloth in gold and dark blue, hung with a dazzling display of coloured tassels. So, looking back now, the whole room was a glorious setting for a real old-fashioned cottage Christmas.

On Christmas Eve, my mother would be busy cooking ham

and pork and neighbours would come up to the cottage to collect their Christmas cockerels. My mother would chat to them and everyone was offered a glass of port or sherry, and a heap of mince pies stood on the white, scrubbed pine table. The baker, grocer, butcher and postman and anyone else who came to the door was offered a Christmas cheer. Some were quite tipsy as they had already called at several houses before they reached ours, and most cottagers were generous with their drink at Christmas, and home-made wine was potent stuff in those far-off days. Our kitchen took on a lovely smell of cooked ham and pork, with a slight aroma of sherry and port but, alas, us children were not allowed any alcohol.

In the evening of Christmas Eve, we would sit round the blazing fire in our kitchen and play games. Everything seemed in place for the great day: brussels sprouts had been picked and stood in the back'us in a bucket; the Christmas pud was given the once-over by my mother; the cooked meats stood on the table in the back'us; and the family cockerel lay trussed up on a big blue and white plate. A huge log pile had been placed near the door for whoever stoked the fires; the single-burner oil lamp stood on the kitchen table with its dull-burning yellow flame; the flames round the roaring fire flickered and danced on the walls. It was warm and cosy and I am sure we all felt secure in our humble cottage home.

On this holy and quiet night, my mother opened the great oak door of the back'us and we all stood around her, staring in amazement into the night sky where a thousand stars twinkled. Not one word was spoken, we all stood silent looking up at the heavens hoping upon hope that we might, just might, see the Star of Bethlehem.

My mother broke the silence, saying, "Not tonight, my little beauties. We are either too early or too late, but let's sing Away in a Manger." My mother led, we followed, singing this lovely carol. Across the meadow from where we were standing at our back door, the night was crisp and cold and a single yellow light shone from Ford Hall farmhouse. My mother closed the door and said, "Off to bed with you, now – it's Christmas!"

She gave us a stocking each which we hung on our bedrails, and we slipped down into the sheets. I thought of the night sky, so cold and mysterious, with its thousands of stars. Beyond them was heaven where God lived, and the angels. I knew all this because my teacher told me, and here is where I drifted off to sleep, dreaming of things that always had no answer and always frightened me.

Then we were all awake. I grabbed my stocking, and ran down the stairs dragging it behind me. I sat on the hearth rug with my sisters in front of a blazing fire, unwrapping our Christmas haul – apples, nuts, oranges rolling all over the floor, with always a star prize in that stocking, right at the bottom – a tin tractor, or a tin motor car for my brother and me. My sisters had all sorts of dolls, some black, some white. We were allowed to play with our presents and then the hearth had to be cleared. My mother washed and helped to dress us, then all of us – except our older sisters, who were working – sat down for egg and bacon breakfast. Afterwards, the table was cleared and my mother got busy preparing and cooking the dinner.

Us children played with our toys, and read stories from our new books, until at one o'clock sharp the great and beautiful white tablecloth was spread over our kitchen table, and Christmas dinner was served: chicken, yorkshire pud, brussels sprouts, carrots, parsnips and delicious gravy – but only water to drink. After this course – the Christmas pud, with a piece of holly on the top. Inside, somewhere, was a wrapped silver thrupence. We would all get excited as portions of pud were put on our plate with a warning to watch out for it, but none of us ever found it. My mother always got it – she had that one worked out.

With everything washed up and put away, my older sisters would start arriving home to spend the rest of the day with the family. I suppose there would be about nine of us as two of my sisters were married and with their own families, they did not come home for Christmas. We would all be excited, showing them what Father Christmas had brought us. They would hug and kiss us and we lapped all this up.

And now the afternoon lull. By now, the confusion of their arrival had died down, and my sisters had taken over most of the supervision. My mother retired to her bedroom to wash and change and reappeared looking, as always, like a queen. My sisters ordered her to sit down, and they would make the afternoon tea.

Then their boyfriends would start to arrive, making thirteen or fourteen of us – big chaps, these boyfriends. The old cottage was getting a bit full, and they were shown into the front room where a fire blazed up the chimney and reflected from my mother's highly polished brass fender. They were given tea and they sat around talking.

At about six o'clock, my sisters and mother started to lay the table, all best china of course, with cold meats, pickle, Christmas cake and chocolate log. Us children sat on stools, with makeshift tables. We thought it was great fun and we loved the cakes.

After tea, my sister's boyfriends would offer cigarettes around. My father, who smoked a pipe, always took one to be friendly but so he didn't burn his fingers, he stabbed the cigarette with a needle and used it as a handle. This always pleased us and we would gather round to watch him, and I'm sure my sister's boyfriends were astonished at this way of smoking.

Then the girls cleared everything away and we played on the table with our toys until one of them shouted, "Time for bed!" Our great day was over. We were all worn out and up the wooden hill we went, under the thatch and beams. Our Christmas, which we had looked forward to for so long, was now just a dream.

On Boxing Day, my mother would turn us out of our lovely warm beds and after breakfast we would run down the path to meet our friends. Beyond the floodgates of the mill, hundreds of birds were feeding off the mill sweepings thrown out of the swill-house door.

We would walk along the footpath towards Hall Meadows, where young men of the village were ferreting for rabbits. One man stood nearby with a gun at the ready, and he quickly told us to 'bugger off'. We obeyed instantly. It didn't bother us, there was plenty more for us amuse ourselves with, and there was a whole fortnight before we were back at school.

All the working men of the village would be back at work after Boxing Day. I would go with my brother Jep who worked at the mill on deliveries, with a horse and miller's cart painted yellow with a semi-circular board which was higher than the original front board.

It was painted red with cream lettering: 'W.J.Ruffle, Miller and Corn Merchants, Alpheton.'

The cart itself was almost a work of art. It had special wooden spoked wheels and iron centre hub. The buck was a combination of flat and lattice-work boards, decorated with wrought-iron strengtheners. The backboard was full height to the sides, adjusted by chains so one could make a platform to stand sacks on. Its paintwork was that of a gypsy van, scroll-lines here and there, and little flutes cut into the woodwork, not too deep so as to damage or lose its strength. It had two oil lamps up front with copper fittings, two rein guides, one each side of the front board. All iron work was painted black, main body yellow, scroll-lines and flutes bright red, wheels yellow-and-red scrolls – quite a gay looking cart. It even had round steps for the horseman to mount up onto the cart. No other cart in the village looked like this one.

We would start off from the mill on a journey up Cold Hill to Alpheton, delivering small amounts to cottages who kept poultry or pigs. My brother, who took the cash, also had a little red book to take orders for next week's delivery. He would have on board Midland's bran, mixed corn, kibbled maize and so on. It was a slow job. At most cottages they wanted him to see their pigs and tell him how they were getting on as they were very proud of their animals. The journey would take him right through the village, up to Simpsons' at The Nest on Shop Hill, then on to Greyhound Cottages at the Warbanks at Cockfield.

On the return journey, he would pick up sacks of corn from Clapstile Farm to be taken to the mill for grinding into meal and some of this would be delivered the next week.

The horse and cart was later replaced by a two-ton Morris commercial lorry on single wheels, rear brakes only, and a roof ladder fitted to carry the tarpaulin. It was quite smart, decked out in the same gay colours as the former cart. I think it was mostly well overloaded because when it was climbing Cold Hill or Highcross we would only be going at walking pace and the steam would rise from the radiator. As I sat on the bench-seat beside my brother, he had great difficulty getting the right gear. Nevertheless, it was better than his horse and cart – he was in the dry while travelling anyway, with a place for his order book and a second coat. In the lorry, he would deliver to a shop in North Street, Sudbury, that was fitted out with corn and meal bins – I think it was run by a Mrs Beevis – and then on to Baker's Mill to pick up different types of meal. Sometimes he would drive to Hitchcocks in Bures, to Pauls in Ipswich, and on to the docks for different meals. He would deliver to farms in Stanstead, Long Melford, Shimpling, Lawshall and Alpheton, so I had great, enjoyable rides around the Suffolk countryside.

But my play days and freedom, those that I had so much enjoyed, were coming to an end. In the autumn of 1938 my brother Harry, who worked at Alpheton Hall farm, came home one day and said to my mother, "They've asked me if Jim would like a job Saturday mornings – just feeding and cleaning out chickens and collecting the eggs."

My mother looked at me and said, "Did you hear that?"

I nodded my head.

"Well, it won't hurt you to do a little job. It will help to buy your clothes."

So my mother agreed I should go on the coming Saturday.

PART TWO

"We'll Make a Man of You, Jimmy."

Saturday Job

Though I did not know it, this was the greatest step I ever took in my life. The farm had everything from ferrets to fine Suffolk horses. The workers were some of the toughest people you ever saw. They would and they could tame anything from wild horses to mad bulls. They feared nothing and showed every animal who was in charge, but they were gentle giants.

On my first Saturday at work, I cycled from my mother's cottage with my brother at a quarter to seven to arrive at the farm at seven o'clock. It was dark as we cycled along in the cold morning air to arrive at the cart shed, the meeting place for all the labourers.

They called out, "Brought your brother with you, today?"

"Just Saturday mornings," Harry replied. "He's still at school."

"How old is he?"

"Just turned thirteen."

"Christ! He's a little'un, ain't he?"

Everyone looked at me and my brother agreed I was very short.

At that moment, a man appeared out of the half-light and gave all the men their orders. On this Saturday, Harry, who worked in the cowshed, took over the work in the cowshed and dairy while the men had their breakfast.

I followed him. Hurricane lanterns hung here and there. The cowshed seemed to go on forever. It was a very narrow, L-shaped building, smelling of dairy cows, dung and mangolds.

"You can help me start by releasing the cows' neck chains – just slip the T-piece through the ringle," said Harry. "Let them know you're going up between them – and mind your fingers. They're very thirsty and they want to get to the pond for a drink."

Here I was, standing knee high to a grasshopper and scared as hell, but I got the courage from somewhere to go between the first two cows. I had a heck of a job to reach the ringle, and I got the T-piece half-way through when the cow tried to run off. There was a heck of a bang on the ringle as the T-piece tightened up with great force. The cow was stopped dead in its tracks. My fingers tingled from the force on the metal, but no damage done.

At the second attempt, I was faster and off went the first cow. It wasn't long before the cowshed was empty. Then we went into the dairy, where all the empty buckets stood. The milking machine equipment all had to be washed up and steam sterilised. My brother lit the coal fire under the copper, as this was the only way to get hot water.

Then we went into the stable, where Harry harnessed up a horse. In the middle of the yard, twenty yards in front of us stood a tall, big man. He was smoking a pipe with one side burnt down, a cap that showed all the contours of his head, long white eyebrows and a mouth that curved into a lovely smile. He wore a pullover but the neck-piece hung halfway down his chest and was full of holes and pipe tobacco burns. His trousers were also burnt, full of holes and covered in cow dung, dried milk and meal dust. His wellington boots were covered in mud.

He looked down at me with a lovely kind smile and said, "This your little brother, Harry?" His eyes met mine and in that instant I knew I had met George E. Colson, known as GEC, boss of Alpheton Hall. He was the greatest and kindest man I ever met and it was he who laid the path down in the direction I was to follow.

"Come with me, Jimmy boy. I'll show you where the chicken feed is." We went in the direction of the granary.

By now, it was daylight and I took note of my strange surroundings. There was mud and cow muck and water a foot deep everywhere. GEC ploughed on through it. It was splashing all up his legs and mine. "Plenty of mud about here this time of year, Jimmy boy, but take no notice of it. Where there's mud there's money."

He walked so fast, I had to run at intervals to keep up. We left the farmyard and walked for three hundred yards along the public lane. At a bad bend at the bottom of the hill was a meadow with six or seven horses all trying to find a place so they could look over the five-bar gate.

"We go up this meadow, my old beauty. Generally climb over the top of the gate. Take too long to open it. It's tied up with barb-wire along the top rail so lift your legs well up – don't scratch your arss. Don't worry about the horses, they won't hurt you. Shout at the buggers – hee-up there! Out of the bloody way! Lean into them if they crowd you in."

He was much, much bigger than me and much stronger. He went straight through the middle of them pushing on one then another. There was mud everywhere and deep hoofmarks. With my short legs I had to jump to get through and keep close to GEC for fear of the horses crushing me, but he ploughed on like a tank. At last and with great relief we reached the grass and the going was easier, thank God. We walked on up the meadow, over a stream that ran through the middle. A chicken shed came into sight. When we reached it, it was surrounded by posts and barb-wire.

"Git under the wire, Jimmy. Just chuck the wheat on the ground well away from the wire so the horses don't get it. I'll collect the eggs this afternoon – they lay all over the place: in the fields, hedges, some in the nest boxes. These lot of chickens are a long way from the farm but the old shed has been here for years. May as well use it. They lay well and it uses up the tail wheat. There! You got an idea now about this lot. You don't want to be too fussy. We never clean them out. They have got acres here to shet on and they'll be a long time filling the old shed up to the top."

We walked back down the meadow and crossed back over the stream. He didn't wade through the water but walked with the same gait as he did on the meadow. Result: water splashed up all over his trousers but he took no notice. Nothing seemed to make him uncomfortable. We walked on, followed by the horses – 'colts' he called them – as they had followed us back from the chicken shed. When we reached our five-bar gate that didn't open, he stopped and looked at me.

"Now, Jimmy," he said. "Every time you feed the chickens, these colts will follow you up and back. Now try not to be scared of them. They are young and boisterous and want to play, but don't play with them. They're strong as oak trees, but you must shout at them and show them you're angry and that you are the boss. If you play with them, they'll come back for more and then it could get rough. They're not broken in yet so they're a bit wild. Next time bring a nice springy stick. If there's any trouble, use it. They will soon learn. Now, one more thing on safety – and remember this! Never, ever get behind them. If you ever see one manoeuvring to get its arss facing you and with its ears lying back, get up near his head fast, for they can kick a gnat's eye out. Remember that. Now, let's go to the others."

We went on along the road and through a gap in the hedge. "Now this is where the ducks sleep. Shut up every night and let them out in the morning." The ducks ran off down to the pond in the farmyard. "Now in all this mud there are eggs somewhere, so look hard and we'll find them." We did indeed, covered in mud and mostly frozen.

"Do you know, Jimmy boy, they always lay very early in the mornings and early in the spring most of the eggs get frozen, but it don't seem to affect them. But we feed them down at the pond when we feed the geese. If you don't pen them up they lay all over the place, drop eggs anywhere until they want to 'set'. Then they build a nest with straw and feather down, lay a clutch of eggs and set on them for about one month, when they hatch off. The duck goes really bloody daft. She walks them all over the place. A lot die of exhaustion. Others are caught by rats and birds of prey. So if ever they start to make a nest, take their eggs – they'll soon get fed up with trying. The missus puts them down under an old setting hen – she makes a better mother than a duck."

Satisfied that we had found most of the eggs, we made our way back to the farmyard, up to a shed called 'the giggers'. Out came about twenty geese, running like hell with wings outstretched, making an awful noise. I had to run like the wind to get out of the way of these half flying, excited birds.

"You want to stand well back when you open the doors, 'cause they can knock you arss-over-head."

Up the granary steps we went, filled two buckets with tail wheat, down the steps, across the yard to the pond, scattered the wheat in a long line on an area of grass outcropping here and there to one side of the pond where neither cattle nor horses came. There was an almighty rush as ducks, geese, chickens and moorhens appeared.

"Haven't undone the turkey shed yet. Forgot about that. Stand back, Jimmy. They'll be in a hell of a hurry this morning."

He opened one door on the double-door shed and there was an immediate sighting of strange looking objects with two-foot necks, a wingspan of more than three feet, long thin legs – some flying at three feet just under the top of the door-frame, others just about midway and some still running for take-off. Some crashed into the woodwork and were in the process of recovery. There was wind, dust and turkeys everywhere. When the turkeys and dust had all flown away, I saw GEC laughing and looking at me.

"Take no notice, Jimmy, you'll soon get used to it all. We keep the turkeys for hatching eggs. They lay all over the place, so that will be your job to watch where they go and hunt out their nests and take their eggs. Now where are we? Let's go and meet the missus. She'll like you."

Up to the farmhouse we go, both of us covered in mud. He opened the door and walked straight in.

"Don't worry about your shoes. We're not fussy here."

From the hall we turned left into the huge kitchen, a great pine table, scrubbed white, is all I can remember seeing. Mrs GEC came into the kitchen from another room.

"This is Jimmy, mother."

"Good morning, madam," I said rather nervously.

"So you're going to look after my chickens."

"Yes," I replied.

"Well, I hope you'll like it here with us. There are hundreds of jobs we can find you to do, but at the moment, we'll just stay with the poultry. The master will show you my little chicks out back. Now at twelve o'clock, you walk into the kitchen, and I shall leave your wages on a plate on the corner of the table. So everything on the plate, no matter what it is, you take."

She wished me goodbye and left the room, and GEC took me out the back door to where small chicks were being raised.

"Her baby chicks are in here, under 'foster-mothers'." These were galvanised dome-shaped things with green pieces of baize hanging around it. Chickens' heads appeared in and out of the baize. It smelled warm and looked quite cosy. There was chaff all over the floor.

"The missus always fills the lamps, so you won't have to worry about them. What I would like you to do this morning is take the old chaff out, scrape it into a bag and dump it near the pond. Ducks and the others will soon sort that out. Get fresh chaff out of the chaff house inside the big barn, next to the churchyard. You can't miss it. Then see they have chick food. It's in the outhouse next door. Make sure they have water, as they get very thirsty with the heat from the lamps and the dry meal. Never touch the 'foster-mothers', Jimmy, because it could upset the paraffin lamps and it could cause a fire."

By now my head was spinning, and it seemed a long morning.

"I think that's all for now, Jimmy. Go and have your 'nineses'." That was the nine o'clock snack. "You brought some drink with you and something to eat?"

"Yes," I replied.

"Well, go and find your brother and sit with him while you eat. All the workmen stop on this farm for nineses, Jimmy boy. They usually stop for fifteen minutes to half an hour. They also manage a puff or so from their pipes. I don't stop none of them any money nor ask them to work extra time. We give and take here. They help me, they are all very good. So I like to help them. But you must remember if you ever get to be a boss man that nobody can work on an empty gut. Nor can't horses either. Cows won't give milk if you don't give grub and that's the same with your chickens. They won't lay eggs if you don't feed them. Is that correct, Jimmy?"

"Yes," I replied.

I found my brother and another man, Ron 'Ganty' Andrews, and we went to the cart shed. It was warm in there, with a copper standing in one corner. We got our grub bags off some nails, hammered into a post out of the way of rats and mice, and all three of us walked towards the copper. It was surrounded by coal and wood, drainpipes here and there with bits of board on top, and old chaff bags.

"We sit on these pipes," said my brother. "Bring one up

close." He produced a toasting fork, cut from the hedge. "Pork lard sandwiches this morning. Lovely toasted. I'll do yours first."

He opened up the copper door, revealing a lovely red bronze [fire]. We ate, with hot tea from our flasks. Ron sat in the corner enjoying his bread and cheese, cut with a shut knife as most farm workers do. He said very little and he was a quiet man, but he did ask me if I knew his young brother Lionel, known as 'Barney', who was my age and went to the same school.

"Oh, yes," I said. "He's a good friend of mine."

"You may see him a bit later. Sometimes he comes down here to see me on a Saturday."

I hoped he would. Now, Harry was telling me to get back to work. "You know what you have to do?"

"Oh, yes," I said with confidence.

"Good. If you need help, come and find me in the cowshed."

As we got up to walk off, we came face to face with two huge young men. They looked like giants to me, both dressed in expensive clothes that were covered in mud, oil, meal and cowdung. They both had flat-type hats on their heads and they were without doubt two fine-looking chaps. Both had newly lit cigarettes in their mouths, and they had the look of confidence of boss men.

"Hello, Harry," they said. "This your brother, Jimmy?"

Harry introduced me to Master Dick and Master Len. They both stepped forward and shook my hand, saying, "It's Dick and Len. You can drop the Master bit. That's not needed on this farm."

Len said, "The Guv'nor took you round this morning to show you what to do?"

Then Len gave me some extra advice. "The chickens that run around here in the farmyard go round and lay eggs in the churchyard, too, so make sure you search there – but go when the sun shines, it's a lot more pleasant. You don't want to be going into the churchyard at dusk. By the way, Harry, you'd better show your brother all round the farm. Show him where it's safe to go, and the danger areas, so he can be on his guard."

Dick added, "We've got to work now, but don't you worry yourself about nothing, Jimmy. If you get in a muddle, or want to know something, come and see us. We're here to help you and if you feel like a rest or a sit down, you do so. We're a rough lot, but we're human."

Harry took me to see the corn barn, which had the stockman's area and the chaff house at one end. It was a huge area, partitioned off with flat boards. The chaff was so high it stood up straight like a rock face. The stockman was chipping away at this hard, compacted surface.

My brother said, "You watch."

On went the stockman, working away at the chaff face. All at once, the stockman ran like hell towards the chaff house door as an avalanche of seven or eight tons of chaff followed him right up to the door. He looked at my brother with a smile on his face.

"Dangerous bloody job, this, Harry boy."

"It smells lovely," I said.

"Yes," said the stockman. "When it was put in here, it was sprayed with molasses. Good grub. The cattle love it."

From there we went to the stables. "These are the working horses' stables and horse yard." He showed me the right-angled pieces of wood, cut from the hedgerow. "Each horse has its own harness, so it's important they go on the right place." He showed me the corn hutch and the racks fixed over the mangers, for hay or straw. There were some in the horse yard, too.

There was another yard, next to it. "These are for show horses and their foals. If they have a foal, they don't work. They spend some time in the yard, and some time out on the meadows, even at this time of year."

Then he took me to what he called the 'access area', with yards around it for cattle and pigs. There were boxes at the back for calves that had been weaned, and then we went through to the oat barn, and saw about twenty heifers which were in there for fattening. On the other side was the calving area.

We walked through the big L-shaped cowshed, and out the other side to another shed. Harry said, "This big place here don't appear to have a name, but it's got an overhead tank and pump. The water in the tank is free-flowing to the milk cooler, but the water has to be pumped every day by hand."

This was almost the end of my tour of Alpheton Hall farm.

Harry said, "You've seen in the dairy and cart sheds, and you've seen the shed under the granary – that's where you let the geese and turkeys out this morning. So you get the idea – there's livestock everywhere. But there's one more thing. Come with me to the cowshed."

Tied up at the end was a lovely looking bull. He must have weighed a ton, he was massive. He was all muscle, a fearful-looking creature. Over his eyes, and strapped around his horns was an aluminium mask.

"This is Herk. Treat him with great care. Rum fellow, he is, not two days alike. He can't see you because of the mask but he can smell you, and he'll make a run for you. Don't trust him. We take him down to the horse pond twice a day for him to drink, but we use bull handles clipped to his ring. Don't touch him, nor go near him. You heard that?"

I'd heard. "Yes," I nodded.

"Now go and clean your chickens out, and don't touch those lamps."

I completed cleaning out the baby chicks and walked to the barn with my empty chaff bag. The stockman was still there, mixing up big heaps of chaff, mangolds, meal and linseed cake. It all looked good and smelled lovely.

"Lot to do, Saturdays," he said, "mixing up feed for Saturday afternoon, all day Sunday and Monday morning. If I didn't, I wouldn't get any time off at all, but there you are, he pays me well and they're good people to work for, so I can't complain, really. Mind you, they're bloody good workers themselves. Start milking at five o'clock every morning and they're still working at five o'clock at night, the old man and all. Got some bloody stock about here, boy, I can tell you, hellish good."

He went on, chatting away to me as he worked. "Farmers! Sin all them grut stacks in the stackyard, they can't be short of cash. Don't, they would've thrashed them by now. Some bloody work about there in the next couple of months. There's all the thrashing to do, pulling down and spring drilling. He'll soon have to get some of this muck out of the yards and all. Don't, they'll fall over the bloody walls – but there, he got some good strong hosses and he don't half feed them and all. They have some oats into them, but once they start on suffin they soon make a hole in it. I said to my missus, it's no place here for the meek-an-mild, there is cow-shet, horse-shet, pig-shet, chicken-shet – mixed up with mud and slurry everywhere and it's no place for a parson's son, either, I can tell you. Well, must get on. Don't, I'll be late for dinner. Farewell, my little old beauty!"

I put my chaff bag on the heap of empty bags and walked towards the cowshed to see my brother and I found him in the shed-with-no-name, pumping water into the overhead tank for milk-cooling.

"Want a go?" he asked. I grabbed the handle, and Harry went to clean out the copper hole and re-lay the fire for tomorrow. I must have been doing about eight strokes a minute, and I don't suppose the pump had ever gone so fast. My arms soon began to ache and water started running out of a pipe high up on the tank. I ran round to the cart shed and told Harry.

"Don't worry," he said. "It's the overflow. The tank's full. That didn't take you very long." Then he noticed the time. "It's past twelve, made me late showing you around this morning. Never mind, go and get your money."

I walked through the mud and slurry to the farmhouse back door and opened the great door as quiet as possible. Sure enough, a plate was nestling on the corner of the big table. I moved from the door to the plate as silent as a mouse in the night, and sure as God made little apples, there lay a shilling piece – and two walnut whips!

I wondered if they were mine.

I didn't know whether I should take them or leave them. Oh! for the taste of a walnut whip. The temptation was too great. I grabbed my shilling and both walnut whips and made haste to the door.

A voice broke the silence. I am sure the bricks sank under my feet, for I felt smaller than ever.

"Did you find your walnut whips, Jimmy?"

"Yes, madam," I replied in a faltering voice. "Thank you very much. I didn't know if they were intended for me, but you did say everything on the plate, madam."

"Quite correct, Jimmy dear, but one is for you and one for your brother. Such a hardworking boy. The master thinks the world of him, so I like to give him little treats now and again. And by the way, Jimmy, it's not necessary to take your hat off every time you come into the kitchen. I know you have been taught to do it, and it's a very polite and dignified thing to do and I admire you for it, but this is part of your workplace. You will be coming in and out with eggs and so on." I listened politely as she chatted on, and eventually, she said, " Now off you go and have your dinner and I'll see you next Saturday."

I went back through the mud to the cart shed, where my brother Harry was waiting. "Where the hell have you been? Everybody has gone home except us. Our dinner will be spoiled and I've got to be back at three o'clock to help milk."

"The lady kept talking."

"What the hell about?"

"All sorts of things."

"A long time talking about allsorts! Come on, for Christ's sake."

"The lady of the house sent you this."

"Caw'd a hell she did? Have you got one?"

Within two minutes they were gone.

"Bloody lovely," he said, and we were soon cycling home via Alpheton Hall private track to Aveley Lane, up Tippet's Hill and back down to our village. My first taste of work was over.

Rosettes In The Dust

After that, every Saturday I cycled to Alpheton to feed the chickens, ducks, turkeys, geese and so on. I had my fun with the colts on Long Meadow. Instead of climbing the five-bar gate with two pails of wheat, I would walk up the field on the other side of the hedge trying to fool the colts, who were a persistent nuisance.

When I ran, they ran. When I walked, they walked. They would push me in the back with their heads and blow slaver all over me, try to push their heads into my pails of wheat, bearing me down to the ground, and this is where my stick came in. I would lash out and shout at them – they seemed to love this. They would all jump around and face the way we had come from, throwing mud and turf all over me with great force.

The combined force and strength of these six colts was tremendous. They would turn and come back at full gallop, pass me, but cut in close in front of me, kicking their back legs high in the air, plastering me with lumps of mud and turf. Oh yes, they knew what they were doing, and they were enjoying it. And now they knew how to work as a team, I had no defence whatsoever against the weight and force of these gallant chargers.

I knew I had to outwit them, so this Saturday, instead of climbing over the gate, I went straight past and into the field on the opposite side of the high hedge to the meadow. I walked on until, opposite the chicken hut, I reached the place where I had already made a small hole in the hedge I could crawl through.

So far so good. I now had three hundred yards to go, to get to the chicken hut on the opposite side of the meadow and over the stream. It was the longest three hundred yards I've ever walked, but hurray! I made it. It was the first time I had walked six feet tall.

Now this meadow was three hundred yards wide by one mile long, so I had another idea. I would go back through the hedge behind the chicken hut and back along the field on the opposite side from where I'd come, so I didn't have to run the three hundred yard gauntlet.

So the colts' fun and games were over, but I used to walk up to the gate and give them a friendly pat sometimes.

I hunted out all the chicken, turkey, duck and geese nests in the great and ancient hedgerows on Long Meadow and Back Meadow, and areas in and around the churchyard. I marked every nest with a piece of rag tied to the hedgerow, so others knew where they were. I enjoyed all this. It gave me the chance to explore every hidden corner, ditch and building of Alpheton Hall – and of course I enjoyed the freedom I had to do it.

I climbed onto old and ancient machines left here and there in the hedges and buildings. I would also wander into the churchyard, where chickens loved making nests on the sunny side of the tombstones in the long grass. It was such a quiet and sacred place and so peaceful, yet somehow it seemed forbidden. Over time, I must have read every epitaph on every gravestone and could almost remember them all by heart. If I felt brave or more adventurous, I would walk into the church porch and open the great door into the church. I would just have a peek inside, then close it as gently and quietly as possible, then disappear back to the churchyard and farm buildings.

Spring came, and one Saturday GEC said, "It will soon be Easter. We'll be showing our Suffolks at Saffron Walden Agricultural Show. I'd like you to come, Jimmy. Would you like that?"

I agreed without hesitation. "Good," he said. "Your job will be to hold young Peggy's foal and look after all our tackle on our stand to see no-one takes it while we're in the ring."

I wondered about feeding the poultry, and my other jobs.

"We won't bother to feed them on the Saturday. They won't take no harm for one day. After all, they've got the whole farm to shack on. If they haven't got enough, they can always go for a walk and find some – they're free to go where they like. I'll tell you what. You can come into work on Easter Sunday and Monday to feed the chickens and help in the cowshed and dairy. Master Dick and Master Len will want some time off to see their girlfriends, I expect."

So on that Easter Saturday, the day of the show, my mother got Harry and me out of our beds at half past four in the morning. Tea and toast awaited us, all laid out on the pine-scrubbed table. We were both dressed in our second-best clothes, with bib-brace overalls over the top, all washed and clean at a quarter to five. We walked out of our cottage door with my mother warning Harry about some of the perils that could befall me if he didn't keep a strict eye on me.

It was very dark and quiet as we cycled up the hill out of the village to Aveley Lane, standing up on our pedals and taking in great gulps of fresh, Suffolk air. A few lights were shining through the tiny cottage windows but the hamlet was still and peaceful, just the lonely chained dog barking here and there to break the ghostly silence on our journey to Alpheton Hall.

When we arrived, the little Lister Stationary Engine was

hammering away, hard at work driving the milking machine vacuum pump. Paraffin hurricane lamps hung everywhere, giving off their yellow, haunting lights. Looking through the early morning darkness, one could see cows everywhere – some in the yard, some drinking from the farm pond, the whole area awash with mud, cowdung and water.

We walked into the cowshed – there was a heavy odour of milk, cowpat, cow wee and cow breath. A sparkling golden wonder of light hung in the roof of the building where the hurricane lamps' yellow rays were caught on the misty vapour of the cows' breath.

The boss was hard at work. "Morning, Harry. Morning, Jimmy. If you two can finish the milking, we'll go to the house for a cup of tea. We won't be long. Don't muck out – I've arranged for that. Just finish milking, wash up the machines and get the milk ready and labelled for the lorry. You can turn the cows out onto Back Meadow and leave everything else. Ron will finish off in the dairy."

So I helped Harry complete the milking. Harry used the machine, and I sat on a two-legged stool, stripping the last drops of milk from each teat. We moved on to the stable, where the show horses had spent the night. Harry lit the lantern and fed the horses some crushed oats. They stood calm and still as Harry and I combed their golden manes and tails. The stable door opened and in came GEC with his two big sons.

"Well done, Harry. You're a good'un, you are. I'll braid the mane if Dick braid the tail. Len, you get the harness ready. Jimmy, if you get that tin off the shelf with the paint brush in, you can paint the hooves."

This I did without question. Harry curry-combed them all over, rubbing an oil substance onto their glossy coats. At last, GEC was satisfied and everything was ready.

A trunk was packed with curry-combs, brushes, hoof-black, little bottles with all sorts of chemicals, whose secrets were known only to the boss. There was also a tin of leather polish, Brasso, various rags and brushes, two small nets of hay and second nosebags, plus half a stone of crushed oats.

GEC checked everything off on a list, all seemed to be in

order. Now, by some magic, it was daylight. We had all been so busy working, the dawn had crept up on us. The sun was shining and birds were whistling in the stackyard. It looked like being a great day.

At a quarter to eight, a Bedford cattle truck arrived, sent down by Fred Elliot, the haulage contractor in Alpheton. All our equipment was loaded first into the piece overhanging the roof, some straw was shaken out onto the tail ramp and floor of the lorry, then it was the horses' turn to walk up the ramp.

Two Suffolk horses appeared from the stable – Alpheton Hall Peggy I and her daughter Alpheton Hall Peggy II and her foal. Len led one, Harry led the other and the foal followed its mother. They walked straight into the lorry and Fred gave the foal a push up the ramp. Dick gave Harry a parcel neatly wrapped in brown paper, and Harry put this in the luggage compartment over the roof. I walked up the backboard to join Harry. The tailgate was shut very gently, and Dick rode in the front with the driver. The lorry fired up and we were on our way to Saffron Walden.

The little 28hp Bedford lorry rocked and rolled, especially on sharp bends. Our average speed was about 20 miles an hour. The horses stood rock still. They were used to being transported to shows. The foal laid in front of his mother's legs, and every now and then his mother lowered her head and nudged her son and blew warm air over him, the equivalent of a human kiss.

It was very draughty riding in the back of the lorry, for this was not a purpose-built horsebox. This was a cattle lorry with slatted wooden sides, which were removed from the back of the lorry when it was used for general haulage. After what seemed ages, we arrived at the show site, the lorry going very slowly over the rough park turf, looking for our stand number and at last we came to a halt.

The backboard was lowered, Peggy I was reversed out, Peggy II was turned round in the lorry and led down the ramp by Harry and the foal followed its mother. Everything was off-loaded, horse food, the wooden trunk with its mystery veterinary cosmetics and the mystery parcel Dick had given to Harry as we departed from Alpheton Hall.

Our stand was quite good, under the shade of a huge chestnut tree. Harry was holding both horses and Dick was already grooming them. It was my job to hold the foal, who now had a halter on his head and he did everything he could to protest. He reared up on his back legs, threw his front foot out and kicked me on the leg, then spent most of the day coming after me, trying to bite. In other words, he was a little bugger.

The mystery parcel was opened by Dick, its contents revealed: two beautiful white horse rugs, edged with orange ribbon and on the two front corners in orange ribbon were displayed the initials of my great friend and father figure, GEC. Though only a humble schoolboy, I felt very proud to be a small part of this show team, and I thought – how on earth did this wonderful spectacle manage to come out of the cowdung, water and slurry of Alpheton Hall?

People came to the stand to visit the horses. GEC arrived at the stand in his tweed suit and cap. He looked very, very smart and was smoking his burnt-down pipe. He was still wearing that lovely friendly smile, and he came over and had a word with Harry and me. Accompanied by his two sons, he looked and was a true professional farmer and horseman.

The horses were led into the ring by Dick and Len. Peggy I: First Prize; Peggy II, with foal at foot: First Prize. The Champion Suffolk Horse was Alpheton Hall Peggy I – GEC had won the top prize!

After this, the horses were brought back to the stand under the chestnut tree. Dick, Harry and I stayed on for the Grand Parade. GEC and Len left in the car for home to milk the cows.

After the parade, Fred arrived with the cattle truck and we rolled and swayed our way home, gearbox whining and groaning on the hills. We were back at Alpheton Hall around seven o'clock and the horses were put back in their special yard, fed and watered.

There was no celebration, no fuss, no drinks for this remarkable success – only one of many over the years. Rosettes were pinned on the stable walls in great clusters, covered in cobwebs and dust. Two or three more would now be added to the collection – if Harry found the time to do it. If not, they would lie on a sill in the cowshed, covered in dust and cow dung and in the end, thrown out onto the dung cart destined for the muck hill.

GEC and his sons didn't value pretty things. They lived in the real world of muscle, and muscle meant power. Power was all that farming was about and GEC knew it. He kept a stable of twenty working horses and followers, and they were well fed and cared for. And they were obedient. No horse stepped out of line on this farm. If it did, it was soon put back in its place. These horses were so big, with huge muscles moving all over their bodies, they could do all the farm work without wilting and still carry their heads high after a day's work.

Going to the shows was not really my scene, men strutting about in bowler hats all looking important, flags flying, dressed-up horses and, to me, the stupid sport of horse-jumping and dressage. Like my great friend GEC, I also believe in the world of reality. I was quite content with my job at Alpheton Hall on Saturdays – and now, even some Sundays.

Harvest 1939
As harvest approached and the long summer holidays, GEC said, "Come and work up here on your school holidays, Jimmy boy. I have some jobs lined up for you." As the corn reached its golden colours, GEC and his sons fetched the binder out from winter storage and pulled it onto Church Field where forty acres of golden oats stood ready to harvest. The old International 10-20 tractor was manoeuvred into the cutting position on the binder, and off it went for the start of the 1939 harvest.

That evening, the boss said, "Jimmy, feed the chickens in the morning, then go to the binder in Church Field and I'll meet you there. You can drive the tractor round the field and I'll see to the binder. We'll make a good pair, you and I."

The next morning, I fed the chickens and went to Church field about half past eight. The binder and tractor stood sheeted up. It smelled rather good – paraffin oil, binder grease, blue cross binder twine and the tarpaulin covers, mixed with the smell of newly cut oats. In the distance, some men were standing the sheaves together to make shocks [stooks]. The great hedgerows and tree boughs overhanging the headland made a picturesque scene on this late July morning.

I undid the ropes securing the tarpaulin to the binder and tractor and laid them out to dry. There had been a heavy dag [dew]. Now the dag was disappearing fast as the sun rose high in the sky. I filled the grease guns from the grease bucket and started to work on the important moving parts of the binder.

"Well done, Jimmy," came a voice from behind me. GEC had arrived. He helped finished greasing, then called me to the platform of the binder. "These canvasses have to be slackened off every night and tightened up before we start in the morning. We'll stop and give them a final tightening after we've done the first half hour, because they'll get hotter – they're affected by temperature and dampness."

He walked over to the standing corn, which was beginning to move in the gentle summer breeze. He grabbed the corn with his great hand. "Not quite ready, yet. We'll give it another half hour. Had your nineses, yet?"

We sat on the binder platform and I ate breakfast while the boss drank tea from the flask he'd brought with him. There was no sign of the workmen I'd seen earlier. We were all busy with our nineses.

GEC gave me some advice. "Now, Jimmy, when you grow up, if you want to get that little bit better off, you must try to keep money flowing in, day and night. When my workmen stop working at the end of the day, their money stops, so they have no income while they're at home or asleep. Now, while I'm asleep and tucked up in my bed, I have money coming in. Do you know how I manage that?"

"No, I don't," I answered truthfully.

"Simple, Jimmy. My cows are making milk, my pigs are getting fat, my chickens are laying eggs and my corn is growing to reap at harvest. So that makes me a bit better off every day. So, as you get older, you must do the same because it's a wicked world to survive in, my boy. Now, come on, let's go and feel the corn, see if it's dry enough."

We walked to the standing corn, the stubble cracking under our feet. He grabbed a handful, then put it to his nose for a smell. "Here, take this, Jimmy," he said, handing me the corn he had plucked from the straw. "What do you think? Is it dry enough?"

He said it with a beaming smile. What advice did this old-timer want from a fledgling like me? I looked up and said, "Yes, that's okay."

"Well, then. We'll make a start."

He moved on to where the tractor stood, turned on the petrol and tripped the mag, cranked the starting handle and after a few swings, the engine fired up, with a few misfires and bangs in the manifold. As it warmed up, it settled into a smooth run.

GEC looked at me and laughed. "I'll drive the first round and show you how it goes. Sit on the mudguard and watch. Right, first things first – power drive to the binder. Clutch down, then pull this little iron back – you can feel it go in gear. Let the clutch out: tractor stays still, binder drives. Clutch in: binder stops, but don't forget, it's still in gear. Anyone working on the binder, and you let the clutch out, could get hurt. So listen, Jimmy, always take it out of power drive gear and drive gear. Never sit with your foot on the clutch while the tractor's in gear. Right, I've got to get off now and turn onto paraffin, she's hot enough now."

He came back to his seat and continued the instructions. "Now, this long stick of iron, here, is the gear lever – three forward gears, one reverse. You only want one gear, second, and that's to the left and back. Right, we'll move off. Now watch me: clutch in, power drive, lever back, drive gear left and back. Nothing's happened because I've got the clutch in. Now we'll go – let the clutch out, steady and smooth and........ here we go!"

The binder sprang to life, the sails – or flyers – spun round like a huge propeller. The connecting rod and cutting knife were working overtime, the canvas running round sweet and lovely on the rollers, and the sheaf packers were making an awful noise, screaming out to be filled with straw.

As the tractor and binder reached the standing corn, the tractor engine tightened up and the clatter of the binder became less. The golden corn fell, as if by magic, onto the platform canvas with a gentle touch of the sails.

It was then taken up in between two canvasses to the packers, tied by the knotter and sheaves were thrown to the ground by the sheaf tines, triggered off by the weight of the sheaf.

GEC looked at me and gave me one of his big, friendly smiles. Then he shouted above the noise of the machine, "Watch how I turn at the corners. Cut all the way out, then turn and come back, cutting full width all the way in."

We completed our first round without trouble. On the start of the second, he stopped. "Well, there you are my little friend. On the tractor seat!"

He climbed onto the binder seat. I looked round and he held up his hand to give me the okay. I selected both gears, opened the throttle, and now the worst bit. I gradually let my foot off the clutch, and with a slight chuck we were off. I had to work like hell to get the tractor on the right lock. I was all hands, first one way, then I overdid it and had to come back the other. Oh, what a hash I made of that, but mind, they did steer very, very heavy in those days. And bear in mind, I was only thirteen and very small indeed, but as GEC always reminded me, "We'll make a man of you, Jimmy, not to worry."

After that incident, I got on quite well. I took the first corner perfect. Here I was, feeling quite confident, sitting on this great iron tractor seat with this huge iron steering wheel in my hands. It had iron wheels in front, spade lug iron wheels at the rear. I would look to the rear every so often to make sure GEC was still with me and there he sat, high up on his binder seat, smoke rising majestically into the clear summer sky from his pipe. But he was very alert, watching everything on that machine.

Round and round and round we went, and I really did feel a great little Jimmy Mott. All at once there was a loud shout, and banging on the tin cover of the packers. I stopped the tractor, put both gears into neutral, jumped off and went round to where the boss was scratching his head.

"Bloody string broke. It's chucking out loose sheaves." He went down under the binder to re-thread the needle. "Well, there's no string here. Look in the string box, Jimmy."

"It's empty."

"Oh, well, I never thought about that. The spare string lay down on the bottom headland, near the tarpaulin, don't it?"

I ran and fetched a ball of the string and was back in no time. GEC was quick with praise. "Well done. You're the sort I like."

I put the string in the box, threaded it through the lid and into the eye loop arm that held it tight, threaded it into more guides and handed the loose end to GEC.

"Come under here with me, Jimmy, and I'll show you how to thread the needle. You got to learn, and besides, I'm a bloody old man, my boy. You can get under there better than me."

That done, he said, "Up on your tractor and into power drive. Drive the binder, only stay on your seat and watch me as I throw the loose corn onto the platform. That will tie the loose into sheaves, but don't take your eyes off me in case I fall on the canvas. If you see anything going wrong, stop the binder at once. Safety first all the while with machines, Jimmy."

The loose corn made a couple of sheaves, which he made into a stook, then we stopped the binder and he leaned on the mudguard. "I reckon we've enough string for a couple more rounds, then it'll be getting on for dinner time."

We completed the two rounds without any breakdowns or stops of any sort. I stopped to take the tractor out of power drive and slipped down to where the tarpaulin lay and our supplies of string, petrol, TVO, grease, and so on.

GEC said, "Before we go to dinner we'll fill the string box, then it's all ready when we start again. We've not had a bad morning – mind you, the weather is good and that is our master. We won't be back here directly after dinner – it will probably be after five o'clock, so come round to the farmyard after dinner and you can feed your chickens first. Then you and I will do the milking this afternoon, but bring some food and drink back because we'll be cutting after tea."

I cycled home to lunch with Harry, who had been busy working with other men on the farm setting up sheaves into stooks and preparing straw bases for corn stacks, greasing up the harvest wagons, cutting round fields of wheat with scythes and tying it into sheaves with straw binds to make way for the binder on its first round. Everyone was busy, the reapers were out and the sun was high in the sky on this late July day.

Harry and I raced down the two hundred yards or so of main road from Aveley Lane to the gateway of our cottage, leaning our bikes over with our feet out, making sparks on the hard flint surface with our hobnail boots. We raced up the path, applying our brakes hard and skidding our tyres as we came to a halt.

"Just as daft as ten year-old kids," said our mother. "Grow up, for God's sake. Wash your hands. There's a bowl of lovely soft hot water all ready for you in the back'us."

My father, my brother Jep, Beryl and Iris were already sitting eating their dinner. Within seconds, ours was on our plates – rabbit, potatoes, runner beans, lovely rabbit gravy and afterwards, jam roly-poly.

"Mind your tongues, that dinner's come from a hot place," warned mother. "I've packed your fourses and flasks of tea, and bottles of tea for you to drink."

"Thanks, Mum," said Harry. "Give you a bob or two extra on Saturday for a little present."

The conversation over dinner was all about harvest work. Some farm workers 'took the harvest on', that is, to see the harvest in for a weekly wage plus five pounds bonus at the end of harvest, regardless of how many hours they worked. It was a fiddle, but if you lived in a tied cottage, you had no choice. The head horseman usually took on the position of 'Lord of the Harvest' – in other words, the harvest foreman. At Alpheton Hall, the head horseman was my father's cousin, Tom Mott.

Then it was back to work. Harry and I picked up our grub bags and bade farewell to our family. "Look after that boy," my mother called after us.

"He'll be all right. Don't keep worrying," said Harry as we leapt on our bicycles and pedalled off like the clappers, up the main road, westward along Aveley Lane, down Tippets Hill, round the corner and across the little bridge over the Chad, turning up the private track to Alpheton Hall.

Here, on this gorgeous summer day, was a sight to behold on both sides of this dusty, sandy track. The ditches and verges were covered in seedy grasses of all kinds and I would think that every wild flower God ever made grew here, and to complement this, the magic and music of the honeybees, bumblebees and grass bees. Hundreds of butterflies, all colours, all sizes, floated along with no effort on the heat haze of the midday sun – midsummer's day magic and I knew that only our Maker could put on a show like that.

We rode straight into the cart shed together, brakes applied, hard tyres scorching and wheels locked, making the dust fly high in the air. The cowdung, urine and mud had now dried hard like plaster, but any surface disturbance would cause the dust to fly.

"Silly young buggers," said the old workers, still taking their dinner break in the cart shed surrounded by dust of our making. "Can't sit comfortable for five minutes." Bloody cranky buggers. "Bugger off and feed the bloody chickens."

With that outburst, I made haste to the granary to collect my bucket of wheat and headed for Long Meadow. There was no way now of taking my new route along the fields. The corn, grass, nettles and all sorts of vegetation was so high and covered in flies, bees and a myriad insects that it was almost impossible for a little fellow like me with two buckets of wheat to get access through it. But those bloody colts. Could I hold them off, I wondered.

I tried to sum it up. Against me, outnumbered six to one and their great strength and power. My strength was very little up against theirs. On the other hand, my brain power was not good, but better that theirs. Six young horses versus one young human.

Well, you've got to go, I told myself. They make men of you on this farm. I placed my buckets of wheat near a gap in the fence adjacent to the gate and my sporting colts were all milling around. I climbed up to the top of the gate. They all started to close in tight, but I dropped down on their side. I lashed out with my open hands, shouting, "Get back you buggers, I'll show you who's boss."

With my arms outstretched, they were giving ground. Moving back, in a second, I dropped my arms and ran to the gap in the hedge and grabbed my buckets. Now I had both hands full, I had no defence, but I quickly put down my buckets and scattered some wheat on the ground. Immediately they went for the wheat and I, and my two buckets, were gone like a flash, heading for the chicken hut, half a mile up Long Meadow.

I crossed the stream and took a glance back and couldn't

believe it. They were heading my way, full gallop and ears laid back, dust flying around their hooves – an awesome sight.

Could I make it to the hut and safety? I ran like hell, but with two buckets of wheat and no use of my arms to pump air into my lungs, I was out of breath and slowing up. In the same instant, I felt hot breath on the back of my neck.

I stopped and turned to face them. I had no choice. I was out of breath and out of ideas. I put the buckets down and stretched out my arms. They all turned, some to the left and some to the right, galloping past me.

I quickly picked up my buckets and made once again for the chicken hut. They had gone on, out of sight. I reached the barb-wire fence surrounding the hut and crawled under the bottom strand. I scattered the wheat out for the chickens, collected the eggs and made my way back to the farm.

I was almost to the gate and I looked up. Here they were, coming flat out towards me again.

I pushed the two buckets, now full of eggs, through the gap. I had no time to climb the gate, they were there, blowing wind round my behind. So I went through the gap with the eggs, covered in dust and horse slaver around my bottom end. I grabbed the stick that stood near the gate and climbed over it.

"Come on, you buggers, if you want a fight!"

They moved in towards me and I moved towards them. I lashed out with my stick, caught one or two on the nose, and I went for some of the others, shouting and wielding my stick. They moved some distance off and stood looking at me, but made no attempt to approach.

I climbed back over the gate. Thank God that run was over for today!

I went on feeding and egg collecting around the farm. My last call was to collect the eggs from behind the tombstones in the churchyard. It was so very hot as I walked from nest to nest and the pollen from the tall grasses drifted like blue clouds slowly to the ground. It was quiet and peaceful.

There were no birds or wildlife of any kind to be seen, only look-out birds sitting on top of the tallest trees, ready to shout out their warnings of approaching danger during the summer rest time in the heat of the long, hot days.

I walked back through the long grass, disturbing the butterflies that flew off lazily. Reluctantly, I took the buckets, filled with eggs, and placed them on top of the great pine kitchen table and went off to find GEC in the cowshed. He had a problem.

"We're going to be late starting the milking, Jimmy. See this cow that calved this morning? She's ill and I think it's milk fever."

He sent me to the cart shed to fetch a valve from my bicycle tube and my bicycle pump, and take them to the oat barn. I did this and when I got to the oat barn, the sick cow just laid there looking a sorry sight. The calf came up to me trying to suck my fingers, searching for a teat to drink from, but there was no sign of the boss.

I wondered, of course, what he could possibly want with my bicycle valve and pump. Surely it had no connection with a sick cow? But this was Alpheton Hall and GEC was a remarkable man. He was a farmer, horseman, cattleman and a vet, and wonders never ceased. One never stopped learning.

Eventually, GEC walked into the barn, smoke coming out of his pipe, saliva flowing freely from its stem. He was trailing a lovely smell of Three Nuns tobacco and a streamers of white ribbon, which turned out to be strips of white rag.

"Bloody calf's a nuisance," he said. "Let the little bugger out into the middlestry [centre aisle], Jimmy. It won't go far away. Got your valve and pump ready?"

I handed these to him. He stuck the valve into the teat, then tied a strip of white rag as near to the bottom of the teat as possible to help keep the valve in place. Then he screwed the connection to the valve and then to the pump, and pumped away. The part of the udder connected to the teat began to swell up. GEC kept on pumping, watching the swelling on the udder. All at once, he stopped.

"Now, hold that pump handle down, Jimmy, while I tie another strip of rag higher up on the teat." When he'd done that, he said, "Take the valve out of the teat and I'll tighten the bottom strip. There! That's off and no air coming out."

He went on, doing the same to the other three quarters. When he'd finished, the cow had quite an enormous udder, decorated with white rag strips to the teats – an amazing sight, and it looked out of place.

"Let the calf back in, so its mother can see it. Push it into the corner and I'll put a couple of hurdles in front of it, so it can't get near its mother and try to suck when we start to milk. I'll give it a bottle – cow body heat – so it'll be the right temperature for it."

Its mother lay there, breathing heavily. GEC placed a bag of straw under its head to stop it laying flat. "There, that'll make breathing easier for her. Right, that's all we can do for now, Jimmy – we must get on with the milking. Now, you've finished your chickens. What are you going to do?"

I just said, "Whatever."

"Right, then. You put the bridle on Kit and go down to the Lower Meadows and get the cows up."

The Things We Didn't Tell Mother

Kit was the farm pony. I had never ridden her before, but I went to the stable, collected Kit's bridle and walked into the horse yard, where Kit was enjoying her afternoon in the shade of the open-ended shelter.

Kit saw her bridle and approached me with her head lowered to assist me. I put on her bridle and adjusted it. There was no saddle. Kit was always ridden bareback. I led Kit up to the five-bar horse yard gate, let go the bridle rein, climbed up the gate and jumped with my legs wide open onto Kit's back.

This was my first mistake and I learned a hard and painful lesson from this as the water poured from my eyes. Nevertheless, I was astride Kit and I gathered the reins into my hands.

"Gee up, Kit," I said, and Kit moved off immediately.

We turned left and out of the yard, through the back gate into the stackyard, then out onto the private track towards Aveley Lane. So far so good. Kit turned into the open wheat field on her own accord. She knew the way, and where she was going. She had done this journey hundreds of times.

Once on the field, she began to trot. I bounced up and down and from side to side and knew I was coming off. I was just hanging all to one side, clinging to Kit's mane – I had no control over her whatsoever.

When she broke into a fast gallop, the bouncing stopped and the ride was much smoother, but I was still hanging to one side and Kit seemed to be going like hell. I made one great effort to get back to the correct position and nearly made it, but to get back to the centre of Kit's back was impossible and now Kit was slowing up fast. She came to an abrupt stop with her head down, and I went forward, along the side of her neck, with one leg passing over her ears and I finished up in a heap beside Kit's front feet, with wheat ears all around me.

Kit turned and lowered her head to look at me. She just stood there and didn't move. I was saying to myself, "Come on, get up, we all have to learn."

I jumped up, grabbed the rein and patted Kit's nose as a friendship signal. She had stopped right on the edge of the ditch leading from the field out onto the road, where there was a down-and-up ramp on either side, giving easy access onto Aveley Lane. We walked the hundred yards or so along the lane to a five-bar gate, which I opened, ready to drive out the herd. Then I drew Kit up alongside, this time doing a gentle slide onto her back.

The cows were grazing along a distance of several hundred yards, up the long valley meadow which was split in two by the Chad. Back in control and sitting up high on Kit, I called to the nearest cows, "Come on, come on."

We made our way to one of the river crossings using the earth ramps made by cattle grazing these pastures for centuries. We went down this steep ramp, me holding the reins tight to prevent Kit putting her head down, and to keep things on an even keel. We crossed the clear, flowing water then I gave Kit her head as we climbed the ramp up the other side, still calling, "Come on, come on."

With the cows forming up into a close, compact herd, we rode some way down the meadow and turned to drive the stragglers down the ramp. Then we turned again, going back down the meadow to a second ramp, a quarter of a mile further down the river. This time, we turned left onto the riverbed. Kit and I walked upstream, driving the cows out of the river where they had taken refuge from the hot midday sun and the swarms of flies that torment these poor creatures in the summer months.

Tall trees on both sides of the riverbank provided excellent shade, and the cool, slow trickling water running over their feet was an added bonus.

Kit loved it as we proceeded upstream, me shouting "Hi, up! Move on! Get up!" It was hard work to drive them out of this lovely, tranquil place. Kit was putting her feet down hard, so the cool water was splashed onto her belly.

The cows at the head of the line were now leaving the river and moving up the ramp and onto the meadow, me still shouting, "Get up, get up, move on!" Kit moved along to the last cows in the line, and I nudged them up with my feet. At last, all the cows were on the ramp, and Kit and I followed.

The cows were now stretched out for about two hundred yards. The lead cows were going along Aveley Lane and here we were, still way back on the meadow. I hustled Kit up, but she knew what to do better than me. She could herd them up, if I could stay on her back. I nipped my knees in tight to Kit's fat belly and held onto her mane. This was it.

"Come on, Kit," I said. "Gee up." Kit moved fast, right up to the tail-enders. "Come, on! Come on!" I shouted. The lead cows were stopping to pinch mouthfuls of grass from the roadside, and were now just loitering along, with me and Kit moving the back-enders up fast.

We soon had the whole herd under control. From now on, it was easy. The leaders turned off Aveley Lane and up the private track, with Kit and me following at the rear.

Somewhere mixed in with the herd was Herk, the bull. So far on this drive I hadn't spotted him, but I knew he would be there somewhere. He wouldn't leave them, but he would be wearing his alloy mask over his eyes, that's for sure, because Lower Meadow had a public footpath running through it and Herk, like all bulls, had strange moments.

Suddenly, one cow broke from the herd and went up the bank onto the wheat field. Kit spotted this and without warning, broke into a trot and jumped from the road to the top of the field, clearing the verge and bank in one leap.

In an instant, I was lying flat on Kit's back with my feet way up in the air and I had to let go of Kit's reins. The next moment, I was sliding over Kit's tail and onto the wheat field. I got up instantly, and there was Kit with no rider driving this loose cow back into the herd. My God, she was experienced at driving cow herds. I think she could fetch the herd up for milking on her own if she could open gates.

Kit fell in again behind the herd and I walked up to her and took hold of her head. There was no means of getting back on her back so I had to walk, leading Kit into the farmyard. The cows all went to the pond to drink. GEC appeared at the cowshed door and he was laughing.

"Doubt you fell off, Jimmy boy?"

"Twice," I said.

"It will probably be three times tomorrow, but stick to it, Jimmy boy, it's best to learn the hard way. You can take her bridle off, and hang it up. She won't go nowhere. She'll sleep with the cows on Back Meadow tonight."

The cows made their way into the cowshed without being driven. They knew their food was in the manger ready for them. GEC went on explaining, "They always go to the same stall every time for milking. All cows have a name – it's written on the wall in front of them. They can't read, of course, but they will mostly obey simple instructions, if you use their name."

With the cows all in and their neck chains secured, GEC used the machines and I stripped the last drops of milk from their teats, sitting on a three-legged wooden stool. Everything was going well. The boss flicked his ear to dislodge a fly and said, "Bloody flies are sharp today. Keep your head tight into the cow's groin, Jimmy. They can lash out in a second, especially when the flies bite. It makes them ill-tempered."

The boss disappeared into the dairy with two buckets of milk to put through the cooler when the cow I was stripping lashed out with a kick. I held most of the force, but almost instantly, the second kick came with much greater power. Off balance from the first, I had no time to recover or get up and move out of the way. The foot caught the milking bucket, the bucket hit my stool, and I fell over backwards into the gutter. I scrambled onto my feet, covered in cowdung and wee – my trousers, shirt and hands were covered in it – but the worst thing was, the cow in question had got its foot caught in the handle of my milking bucket. The more it rattled, the more it kicked.

It went mad. It jumped up and down, came back full on its neck chain and went forward again. It jumped up and down with its back legs, but still the bucket stayed on, making a hell of a clatter on the concrete floor. Its tail was up straight, and droppings were pouring from it.

Two or three cowshed cats went past me at great speed, running for safety. GEC appeared and could see what had happened. He walked past the cow and me, down to the bottom of the cowshed, and came back with a two-tined fork. After a few attempts, he caught the handle of the bucket onto the fork tine and gave a push at the right moment and the bucket fell off.

He laughed like the clappers, went off and came back with a clean bag, and wiped the rear of my trousers and the back of my shirt. He said, "Go to the dairy and wash your legs. And your face. And your arms!"

I cleaned myself up and returned. The boss said, "I've cleaned your stool and washed the bucket out. You'll be okay. Now keep your head well in tight. You mustn't give up. You got to learn to face up to things – it's far too easy to walk away."

I continued to strip the milk from the teats, and pushed my head so hard into the cow's flank I made my neck ache. GEC watched me. "It does help to push your head in hard, but they are big, strong animals and nothing will stop them if they're determined to let their foot fly out. It's not the most comfortable seat in the world, you never know when you'll be ejected."

After milking, we washed up the milking utensils and released all the cows onto Back Meadow for the night. Kit, our lovely pony, who had spent the last hour or so wandering around the farmyard eating choice pieces of new hay and pickings from the hedgerow, went with them.

GEC and I washed down the cowshed floor with buckets of water from the horse pond – there was no pipe water anywhere on the farm. Then the boss said, "That's it, Jimmy. Now we'll go to the oat barn to look at our sick cow. You take this bottle of milk for the calf." He gave me the milk and a rubber teat to slip over the neck of the bottle. "You can feed the calf, and I'll take a close look at the mother."

We walked from the cowshed to the oat barn side by side, GEC talking about the weather and the farm and the harvest. The sick cow lay in the barn, in the same position as we left it. GEC went down on one knee beside it, looking at its eyes. I went over to the calf in the corner, behind the hurdle.

I held the bottle to its lips and it immediately started to suck, but sometimes it let go, then it seemed to forget where it was and grabbed my finger by mistake. I would have to continually keep offering the teat up to its lips, then halfway through the bottle, it appeared to fall asleep and swayed from side to side. Then it fell on its knees and rolled on its side.

"It's fell asleep, Jimmy. They get very tired when they suck and they're very young. We'll leave them for now and come back later. It's just after five o'clock. I'll go in and have a cup of tea and a mite of grub with the missus. If you take your grub bag down to the binder and sit there and have your flask and something to eat, you'll be there when I'm ready – about twenty minutes, I should think."

I collected my grub bag from the cart shed and strolled out through the stackyard and into Church Field, past the church. It looked a fine feature out here, the ancient structure standing tall and majestically lovely surrounded by the great, golden cornfields.

I walked on towards the binder. It was a lovely summer evening, the sky a high and beautiful blue, with just a whisper of wind to keep the evening fresh, carrying the smell of newly cut corn. I sat on the binder platform and ate my fourses and it was so peaceful I almost fell asleep. I thought of my friends and playmates. By now, on an evening like this, they would be bathing in the cool clear water of the Chad. At times, I missed them and their company, but I also knew that I was slowly falling in love with Alpheton Hall – its great cornfields, its lush green meadows with its ponds and streams running through them, and the great hedgerows that surround them offering cattle drinking water and shelter through the seasons. In truth, I was happy as a pig in straw.

Then GEC was walking towards me, smoking his pipe and surveying part of his kingdom at the same time.

"Had your tea, Jimmy?" he said.

"Yes," I replied.

"Right, we'll knock off a round or two, then. It's a lovely warm evening."

He lifted the bonnet of the tractor and tripped the mag, cranked the starting handle and it fired up instantly, smoke rings blowing from the exhaust.

"On your seat, Jimmy boy. Remember the do's and don'ts and stop at the next corner and switch off the petrol and turn on the paraffin."

He climbed onto his seat on the binder, I opened the throttle, let out the clutch and we were off. I stopped at the standing corn, pulled in the power-drive gear and looked at GEC, who smiled and put his hand up. The flyers and canvasses turned and into the standing corn it went.

The corn fell like magic onto the canvasses. Hundreds of swallows flew just above stubble height in front of the tractor, taking in a fine supper of insects before retiring for the night. The sun was starting its descent in the western sky when the boss rattled his stick on the packers cover and pointed towards home. I stopped at the corner nearest to the farm, took out the power-drive gear, turned off the paraffin and within a short time, the tractor had come to a halt. Oh, it did seem so quiet after the noise had all stopped.

GEC slackened the canvas and we covered the binder with a tarpaulin and put the store of binder twine underneath. "I'll get someone to bring down twenty gallons of paraffin and some more binder twine in the morning with the horse and cart. We'd better have a look at our sick cow, Jimmy, and remove the air from her udder. She should be better and up in the morning."

We walked through the great corn barn, into an open yard, then into the oat barn. The cow was still lying down with her head resting on the bag of straw. GEC pulled her eyelids down and up, looking at both eyes closely. "Not right, but not too bad. Her breathing's a lot easier."

He stood and thought for a moment. "I think I'll give her a drench of some sort," he said, "but first of all, I'll remove the air."

He untied the rag ribbons around the teats and took the whole lot off completely, but nothing happened – nothing at all. Oh dear, I thought, the air won't come out, now. What will he do? But nothing worried GEC. He knew all the answers. He grabbed a teat in each hand and commenced a milking action, and as this released the air pressure, it sounded like a thousand tin whistles with a trombone thrown in. Oh dear, I had to laugh out loud.

GEC could see I was tickled pink and he also broke into a hearty laugh. After GEC had completed all four quarters, he then started to milk her, with all the milk falling onto the muck floor. As the cow was lying down, it was impossible to catch it in a bucket. This done, GEC said, "Go to the house and ask the missus for a small bottle of beer."

Off I went and knocked on the kitchen door.

"Yes, Jimmy?" she said.

The master would like a small bottle of beer," I said.

"What does he want that for?"

"For a sick cow, I think."

"Cows don't drink beer, Jimmy."

"I think this one does, madam."

"I'll come with you, Jimmy. It do seem a strange request."

She went back into the house and came back in a minute with a bottle of beer in her hand.

In the barn, she took it to the boss. "Jimmy say you needed a small bottle of beer, George."

"Yes, that's right. Going to make up a drench for this cow. It's gone down with milk fever."

"Oh, I see. I thought Jimmy had got it wrong. I didn't know cows drank beer."

"They don't usually. You have to force it down their throat."

"All right, then, George. I'll be off back to the house."

GEC got hold of the beer bottle. "You go to the dairy, Jimmy, and bring back one pint of milk out of the churn. And pick up the drench bottle from the cowshed. It stands on a beam down in the bottom corner. You've probably never seen one, but you can't miss it. It's got a milking machine teat rubber pushed over the neck."

I went to the dairy first, then to the cowshed. I returned to the oat barn with both items.

"Hold onto that milk for a bit, my old beauty, while I pour the beer into the drench bottle. Right, now the milk, please." Then he shook the bottle vigorously to get the two liquids to mix. He replaced the rubber teat over the neck of the bottle and shook the bottle, holding it upside down to make sure the mixture ran out.

"Now my little friend, I'll hold the head up and force her mouth open, and you hold the bottle and get the rubber in this corner of her mouth. Got that? Yes, here we go."

He grabbed the head, held it up with fingers in the nostril, the mouth partly opened. "Right, now stick the rubber in. That's it." Some went down the cow's throat and some went down its neck.

"Shake it backwards and forwards to let the air in, it'll run better."

After about five minutes, the bottle was empty.

"Well, Jimmy boy, it's time to call it a day."

Just as we were leaving, Master Dick and Master Len arrived at the oat barn with my brother Harry. Master Dick said, "How's that cow, Gov'ner?"

"She'll be up in the morning. Jimmy and I gave her the air treatment this afternoon and we have just stripped her out and given her a drench of beer and milk."

Dick looked surprised. "How did you do that on your own?"

"I held her head up and Jimmy tipped it down her throat."

"Learning you something, isn't he, Jimmy?" He turned to the others. "We all had a good laugh, didn't we, Len. We've seen people fall off ponies sideways and over the head, but never seen anyone come off backwards, over the arss before he went all the way down with both feet high in the air – but he bloody soon got back up on his feet."

GEC said, "He tells me he fell off a couple of times. Stick at it, Jimmy boy. Get your knees well in and lean well forward. You'll soon learn to ride bareback."

It was getting dark and we decided we'd better go home. Harry and I went to the cart shed. He helped me insert the valve into the tube housing and pump up my tyre. "Here," he said, "you're covered in cow-shet. Look at those trousers and shirt – it's even in your hair. What have you been doing?"

"Bloody cow kicked me in the gutter when I was stripping."

"So, you fell off Kit twice and got kicked in the gutter. You have had a great day. Let's get home. We'll have to light the copper and have a bath. You're not sleeping with me in that state. You'll stink like a bloody polecat."

We arrived home safe, anyway. Mother said, "Wash your hands and have your tea."

Harry said, "I'll put a match to the copper, first."

"It's already alight, so you can have a bath after tea."

"Jim must go now," said Harry.

"Why's that?"

"He's covered in cow-shet."

"How did you manage that?"

Harry answered quickly, "He fell over in the cowshed gutter, playing about."

"Course he was," agreed my mother, and went to look for clean pants, shirt and trousers for me.

"Leave your dirty clothes down in the wash house, and don't forget to wash your neck and your hair."

I was drying myself when Harry came in. "Get dressed, and go and have your tea."

"Hey," I said. "You told her I was playing around."

Harry looked at me and said, "You don't let them know everything, so don't tell her you got kicked by a cow, nor that you fell off that pony twice. Keep your gob shut."

Off I went into the house. Mum was waiting. "You look lovely and clean. Now come and eat your tea." It was the cooked meal of the day, lovely cottage pie, with apple pie and custard to follow.

While I ate, my mother talked. "You be careful up that farm. Don't go near those tractors or binders, nor get too near them horses. They're a lively lot at Alpheton Hall. You just look after your chickens, then you won't get hurt."

Harry came in and said he had filled the copper from the pond, which was behind the row of thatched cottages, opposite the Rose and Crown.

"Well done," said our mother. "It will spare me a job tomorrow."

Harry had spotted the boys down the road, so we went to join them, talking and playing around until ten o'clock, then we walked up the long path to Rose Cottage. It was a gorgeous night with a light, warm breeze and a beautiful harvest smell hanging in the air. In the dark, half of a harvest moon lit Rose Cottage with its gentle, silver light. The cottage looked as though at some stage, many years ago, it had just risen out of the ground with faded painted doors and windows, the colours not now distinguishable, and its long, low-slung weather-beaten straw thatch and its whitewashed walls had long ago settled to an antique yellow-white patina, but it held many unsolved secrets.

Many a night, when Harry and I lay in our lovely feather beds, when all was still and quiet, a rustling noise would be heard in one corner of the bedroom, then soft footsteps. I would lie there with my head covered and my heart pounding and then, whatever it was, or if it was anything at all, would gently press on my bed covers. I could stand it no longer. I would shout, "Mum!" in a loud voice, waking up the whole household.

My mother would arrive in our bedroom in seconds, telling me there was nothing there and go back to sleep. Harry said he never heard a thing, nor did any other member of the family, but this would happen to me perhaps on five or six occasions in one year. Although I always called out to my mother and it woke most of the family, it was never discussed in the household the next day, nor never mentioned in the house. Not even Harry ever said a thing and this always seemed strange to me because we pulled each other's legs, given an opening. I always thought my mother knew the real answer and had laid the law down that this was never to be mentioned to me nor talked of in the house, but this is only one of many secrets that Rose Cottage held.

Harry and I would jump out of bed at six in the morning, when our mother shouted, "Come on you young buggers, time for work!" Very often, I would have a wrestling session in the mornings when we got up. Harry always won but I loved to have a go, hoping one day I could manage to win. We rattled and lumped on the bedroom floor and I would shout out when he hurt me. Suddenly, all hell would be let loose. Our mother would arrive, slapping us both around the ear-hole for making such a noise so early in the morning and telling us to get downstairs immediately.

My father and older brothers would be eating their breakfast when we arrived in the kitchen, our mother following behind, still telling us off. "The trouble is, in this house there is no-one to take you two in hand. You're half wild. Now have your breakfast and off you go to Alpheton Hall."

My father and brothers would just smile, but took the hint from our mother. On this summer morning, Harry and I finished our breakfast, collected our grub bags and cycles out of the shed and headed off as fast as possible.

"I'll beat you to the farm," said Harry.

"I bet you won't," I said as we pedalled along Aveley Lane and down Tippets Hill, laying our cycles well over on the sharp bend at Tippets Bridge. I was close to Harry's back wheel at this stage, and now the test – the steep incline up the private track to the farm.

Pushing with all my strength on the pedals, we overtook the old farm workers on their way to work.

"Mad buggers," shouted one as we went past. We ignored that remark because we had not got the wind to answer but, alas, Harry left me struggling.

"Told you I could beat you," he said, as I arrived at the cart shed, puffing and blowing. I had to concede he had won but I had enjoyed every minute of that race. It was, of course, new energy – in a new dawn, in a new day. As one old man said, "Any old cock can crow first thing in the morning, but you want to crow at night when you have been pitching wheat sheaves all day. You won't be so bloody cocky then."

Harry and I went into the cowshed to help finish the milking and to wash and clean the milking machines, buckets, and so on.

"Morning, Jimmy," said GEC, "Your sick cow is much better

and up on its feet and nuzzling up to its calf."

"That's good," was my reply.

"If you go off now and feed the chickens, you can go down to the binder afterwards and take off the tarpaulin and grease up."

A Kick Under The Table

It was going to be a good day for cutting corn. The dew wasn't too heavy, and the boss wanted an early start. Ron was bringing the paraffin down in the tumbrel.

GEC said "Those cans are very heavy and you may hurt yourself, so Ron will fill the tractor up."

But first, I had to feed the chickens. I collected my buckets of wheat from the corn bin up in the granary and made my way off to Long Meadow and my friendly, playful colts were already waiting for me. This was the worst job in my working day, running the gauntlet from access gate to chicken hut and chicken hut to gate.

I know, I thought. I'll say a wee prayer, but changed my mind as I knew God was too busy for such a trifling matter. We must handle small things for ourselves. And then it came to me like magic. I wouldn't climb the gate and give them the satisfaction of moving in close and nosing me and roughing me up. I would go back to Wood Drift, a cart track leading to Alpheton Wood with fields to left and right. It had a bridge where it crossed over Long Meadow stream.

I climbed down the embankment and into the stream and walked upstream in the water. Because of the long grass and rushes the colts didn't see me for a while and when they did, they didn't move, just stared in my direction but stayed near the gate. So I had an easy there-and-return journey and the clear, shallow water running over the outside of my wellies was a great foot cooler on this lovely harvest morning.

All poultry fed, I made a quick trip around the tombstones and long grass in the churchyard to collect yesterday's eggs and deliver them to the kitchen in the farmhouse. I picked up my nineses bag from the cart shed and made my way down to the binder.

I removed the tarpaulin and laid it out to dry, then greased all the moving parts, checked the string box and oiled all the chain-driven parts. At that moment, Ron arrived with the horse and tumbrel, with the paraffin in five-gallon old oil cans and a square-top funnel. A big young man, Ron was powerful as an ox, but very few words. He placed the funnel in the top of the fuel tank, picked up the two five-gallon drums, lifted them up and poured them with ease into the fuel tank.

"May as well have my nineses with you, Jim." He had a huge piece of bread and cheese and a raw onion, which he whittled with his pocket knife. He finished eating, put his hand in his pocket, pulled out his tobacco tin and rolled up a cigarette. Ron didn't belong to the old school of farm workers. He didn't wear a wrapper around his neck, nor dog collars below his knees. He didn't plough with horses, though he would use one on odd-job days as today, but he was more mechanically minded and did most of the tractor ploughing on the farm. At haysel and harvest, he worked as the farm thatcher as well.

He got to his feet. "Well, must go, Jim boy, lots of work to do, a busy time of year, this." He went off with his horse and tumbrel.

It was so hot, I moved into the shade of a well-spread ash while waiting for GEC, when suddenly the area seemed to go so quiet it was as if a sudden peace had descended on the spot where I was standing. It also seemed that I was not alone and so, half-scared, I quickly moved off and went to the tractor where I spotted some labourers picking up sheaves to make into stooks. So I went over and quickly joined them and I was very glad of their company.

In a short while, GEC arrived at the tractor and binder, and I walked back.

"You thought you would give the labourers a hand, Jimmy? Good lad, it all helps. Are we all ready here, then?"

"Yes, if you think it's dry enough."

He gave me that lovely friendly smile and rubbed his big hand over my head. "We'll finish here by dinner. Dick and Len will pack up the binder and move it onto Eighteen Acres. Right, off we go, then."

Once again, we were away, with GEC on the binder and me on the great, iron tractor. Round and round we went and the area of standing corn got smaller and smaller. Rabbits and hares ran out in dozens as they lost their cover. Swallows swarmed around us as the turning of the sails put thousands of insects to flight.

The swallows would come up from the back of the binder, drop down to stubble height in front of the tractor, skim along for fifty yards or so, turn left over the cut corn, then fly past us and again swoop over the machine. All these birds kept to the same flight path and kept with us all day long. They were part of the binder scene, as seagulls are to the plough.

At around one o'clock, we did our final lap and Church Field's standing corn was now tied into little sheaves, lying ready for stooking. Then the sun would finish it ripening and depending on the weather, in another three or four days it would be ready for carting and stacking in the stackyard.

I put the binder out of power drive and slipped down to where our string and tarpaulin lay. The tractor stopped and once again there was a pleasant silence after the noise of the machine. After lunch, we were moving on to Eighteen Acres.

GEC and myself walked up to the farm, side by side.

"Well, Jimmy, that's forty acres arss-over-head, we should pull a fair hole into Eighteen Acres this afternoon. Rare lovely weather, Jimmy boy. Couldn't be better for harvest time, hot sun and warm wind – good for drying and ripening."

I collected my cycle from the cart shed and when I arrived back at Rose Cottage, the family were eating dinner.

"You're late," said my mother.

"Yes, I didn't know the time." I quickly went out to wash my hands in the back'us. My mother dished up my dinner and I joined the others up at the table.

"You'll have to have a watch, Jimmy boy," said my father. "No need to be late looking after chickens."

This remark alerted Harry and I received an almighty kick to my leg under the table, so I made no reply to my father.

The family, as always, were talking about farming matters and the weather, which, of course, played a big part in their working lives and they believed in old sayings and customs like:

– It's going to bloody rain. That old mare I was using this morning shook in her harness.

– Is that true?

– Yes.

– Then you'd better keep your eye out and cover up those onions. Pity if they get wet now when they're lovely and dry.

Dinner over and back at work, I cycled straight up to the gate at Eighteen Acres, stood my bicycle up near the hedge in the shade and hung my fourses bag on a nut stub in the hedge. Ron walked into the field, and Dick and Len had already knocked off two rounds with the tractor and binder. It wasn't long before GEC arrived, and we took over. We started the tractor and switched onto paraffin straight away as the engine was still hot. I opened up the throttle and we were away.

It was so hot, one could hardly bear to touch the steering wheel or the mudguards, but round and round we went, accompanied by the swallows who weren't long in finding us, filling their bellies with insects.

Men appeared in the field, standing the sheaves up together into stooks. Dick and Len had run through the corn, throwing the sheaves onto the brew of the field and some had gone right into the ditch. These sheaves had to be moved to make a clear way for the tractor and binder. At that time, men usually cut the first round, around the outside of the field, with scythes and bundled and tied it into sheaves by hand, because farmers thought too much corn was lost by running over it with the tractor, but this method was beginning to die out as too costly – better to lose a bit of corn.

Then GEC hit the packer's guard with his stick. I looked round and he held up two fingers, meaning time for milking. I rode my bike to the farm, went to the horse yard, slipped onto Kit's back, no high flying act, far too painful. Off we went, Kit and I, making our way towards Alpheton Hall private track.

I felt quite proud sitting up here on Kit's back, and despite all my previous experience, quite confident – but at the moment, Kit was only walking. It was not really comfortable up here. There were two factors which made it so: Kit's fat belly and my short legs, which had to open so far to straddle this kind little animal. Nevertheless, there was no adjustment possible, so on we went till we reached the wheat field leading to Aveley Lane.

Kit had a well-worn path through the wheat. She turned left onto the wheat field and began to trot. This was it. Hold on, Jimmy boy, push your knees well in, lean well forward. I began to bounce up and down and from side to side, when Kit decided she had enough speed to break into a gallop. It was much smoother now, we seemed to be going like hell, and the wind was blowing through my hair. I had lost my cap some way back. Kit's mane was flying up and down in front of my eyes. We were now approaching the ramp onto Aveley Lane and I decided to pull Kit up and try to make her walk instead of trotting. It was the trotting stage that grounded me. Kit obeyed the rein, we trotted for a short distance, then she slowed down to a walk.

Kit walked down the ramp onto Aveley Lane and along to the meadow gate, almost adjacent to Tippet's Bridge. I slipped off Kit's back, opened up the meadow gate wide to let the herd through, then climbed up the gate and slipped back onto Kit's back.

I started to call the herd up, making for the ramp over the Chad. Kit loved rounding up the herd. She would gallop at full speed, then turn suddenly, so – hold on tight, Jimmy. Don't and you'll hit the turf. It was all great fun for a boy of thirteen. Falling off, whether over the ears or over the rear, became part of the job – or it was with me, anyway. Of course, one is very flexible when young.

We moved on down to the second ramp, down into the river and drove the cows out of their shady area. It was a very hot day and I wore only short trousers and singlet, so I jumped off Kit's back and splashed the cool, clear water over my head and body, removing my vest first and putting it in my trouser pocket. I also cupped handfuls of water over Kit's face and ears. She loved it and lowered her head for more.

We walked and drove the herd up to Aveley Lane and I climbed the gate and remounted Kit. Then I drove the herd along Aveley Lane, up the private track and into the farmyard in triumph.

GEC was there. "Well done. You're still astride your charge today, Jimmy. But where's your vest and cap?"

"My vest's in my pocket and my cap lays somewhere in Sunnitch wheat field. It fell off when Kit trotted. I took my vest off to throw water over my head and belly to cool off in the Chad. It was lovely. You'd have liked it too, I'm sure."

"I would," he said with a smile. "Now come on, put that vest on. Don't, you'll get terribly burnt. That's a good lad." He looked hard at me and said, "It's lovely to be young."

We tied up the cows, then after milking, GEC said, "They can all go out onto Back Meadow, except one, and that's Mary. I noticed she's walking lame, but leave two more in with her for company, with a space about two stalls either side of her. It will give us room to work because she'll have to be put down on the floor."

So I drove the rest of the cows, and Kit, out onto Back Meadow, which was adjacent to the farmyard and much nearer for early morning milking.

Long Meadow stream fed the ponds in the farmyard and the surplus water fell over a waterfall, continuing through Back Meadow. Big earth ramps ran down its banks, where cattle and horses had gone down to drink for hundreds of years. Over on the south side was about three acres of pasture, great areas of blackthorn either side of the river and the occasional ash tree. It was an ideal place for cattle or any animal. Hundreds of rabbits lived in great earthworks among the blackthorn bushes.

When I returned, GEC was standing there with a strange looking knife and various ointments. "Right, Jimmy boy, we'll put her down first."

He made a loop in the end of the rope, over the cow's horns, threaded the loose end through the loop and centralised it between the horns. Then he ran the loose end along the top of the spine for about a yard, then turned it around the cow's belly, holding it with his left hand, then slipped the end through the straight. Still following the spine, he made the same sort of loop around the body, just in front of the udder.

"Hold the loose end, Jimmy." Then he put hessian bags under the rope, where it passed under the cow's belly, and straightened the rope up. "Right, now pull steady."

The cow's head came up in the air, the middle of the spine started to cave in, and she fell gently to the floor. "Hold it now, Jimmy, with the minimum of pressure."

He grabbed his knife and cleaned out all the hoof. Just at the top there was an area of sorry-looking flesh, discharging here and there. He washed it with warm disinfectant.

"There must be something in there," he said. He got his knife and went deep into the swollen area. This must have hurt as the cow struggled to get up.

"Put a bit more pressure on, Jimmy. That's it, now hold her tight because I'm really going in there." And he did. The cow blared out and struggled. "Well I be buggered," he said. "Would you believe it. Look at this, Jimmy."

A rubber ring from a jam jar lid had somehow managed to go over the hoof and lodge tight around the fleshy part just above the hoof. As the leg had swelled, the tighter it had become. He lifted it out of the wound, held it between his fingers and cut it.

"Well, we've found the trouble, that's the good thing. Now, what about this wound? The flesh is rotten and discharging everywhere, stinks like hell. You hold onto her, Jimmy. I'll get some hot water from the house."

When he got back, he poured something from a bottle into the water and bathed the area. By now it looked clean but very raw. "Right, let her get up, now."

He removed the plough cord and I ran and opened the gate to Back Meadow so he could drive her, and the other two cows, through for the night.

"It's difficult to know what to do with a wound like that, but the air is a good healer and it's a dry night, so there will be no mud but we'll have to bandage it tomorrow because the flies will go for any open wound. Poor old bugger must have suffered the last day or two but it should be easier for her tonight. We put her down a couple of days ago but could find nothing wrong. Thought she'd sprained it, but I noticed when she came in the yard this afternoon, it was worse. Right then, Jimmy, we'll have our tea then go and knock a bit more down."

The labourers were busy carting and stacking wheat in the stackyard, so I thought I would sit with them and have my fourses. Three harvest wagons stood there, with shaft horses. I joined head horseman Tom Mott, Dick Talbot and the other four labourers.

"Come and put your arss down here, boy," said one. "We won't eat you." They were all whittling their half-loaves of bread with a dab of butter in the middle, and a lump of cheese and onions. I poured myself a cup of tea from my flask and proceeded to eat my jam sandwich, made from hedgerow fruit.

"What the hell have you got there, boy?"

"A bullace jam sandwich."

"My Christ, that'll put some lead into your whistle."

"Would you like one?" I offered.

"No thanks!" he said.

"Only I thought it might put some into yours."

"Cheeky young bugger," he said.

"You ask for it, Dick. Leave the boy alone."

"Only a joke, my old beauty," he turned to me. "You're sharp as that bullace jam."

You cannot write or tell it. It must be experienced to capture the atmosphere of having harvest fourses there, with the smell of new-cut sheaves mingling with the flowers of the mayweed which cover every stackyard, and the aroma of the great oiled tarpaulins laid out to dry, the heat from the sun drawing all the wonderful smells out, lingering in the heavy air of the warm, still evening. We sat there enjoying our tea and the welcome rest.

Children who had brought their fathers' tea sat with their dads enjoying their picnic. The wagons stood here and there, the horses given their heads. Half a dozen two-tined forks with their hand-polished ash handles lay against the quarter-built stack.

In this scene of peace and tranquillity, with harvest only just beginning, nothing could put these old-timers under stress. It took more than harvest to excite them. They sat enjoying their fourses as contented as a pig with its belly full. They knew the art of how to relax and enjoy it, for all the hard work that stared them in the face.

"Hello," said one, here comes the governor looking for you, Jimmy boy." He came straight up to the workmen and head horseman, who was always in charge of the harvest men.

"How's it going, then, Tom?"

"Quite well," said Tom. "It's a good bit of wheat."

"Not bad at all," said the boss. "Are you using a trace horse?"

"No, we're clearing the top end, first. It's nearest to the stackyard and it's all down hill. We'll use the trace horse on the bottom end of the field. It's a hell of a pull from down there."

"Well, I can see you have got it all worked out. What time do you leave off?"

"About eight, I should think."

"Men and horses will all have had enough by then," said GEC. "Come on then, Jimmy. Let's get your old tractor going. Bloody good men, that lot, they don't need a boss, only Friday nights."

We walked on up Wood Drift. GEC seemed relaxed and happy, puffs of smoke were leaving his half-burnt pipe at an alarming rate, and a fair rate of slaver trickled down his pipe stem and onto his shirt. He looked down at me and said, "I don't think things will be this peaceful much longer. I was listening to the news on the wireless while I had my cup of tea. That bloody Hitler man keeps shouting his mouth off."

I made no comment. I had never heard of Hitler.

"I Wonder He Don't Break His Neck."
We reached our tractor and binder, and after our usual routine, we set off for another evening's corn cutting. All went well until suddenly, GEC's stick thrashed onto the packer's cover and he was shouting, "Whoa, Jimmy! Whoa!"

I stopped immediately, put both transmission and power driver gears into neutral and knocked down the throttle. I jumped off the tractor and saw GEC thrashing at something in the middle of the platform canvas. There also seemed to be smoke rising in the air. I grabbed a sack off the tractor seat and ran round to the back of the binder. GEC took the sack from my hand and thrashed at the area of smoke and smouldering canvas.

When it was under control, he stood up, looked at me and said, "There must have been some lighted bacca fell off my pipe. That's a fair hole in there, but I think we can finish the season with it. Bloody good job you brought that bag round or I shouldn't have had a hat left. You and I make a fine pair – what one don't think of, the other does. Right-o, my little friend. We'll have another round or two. Take your sack to sit on, but make sure it's not alight.

Don't, it'll burn your arss and that will never do."

At the end of the run, we covered the binder with the tarpaulin and made our way back down Wood Drift together. There was just half a sun left, showing in the western sky and its dying red beams seemed to light up the very surface of the Earth.

"It's rare and lovely weather for harvest work, so we must keep the wheels turning while it last, so tomorrow we'll have a change of plan."

I was to take Kit and drive the cows down to the meadows after milking in the morning, and when I'd seen to the chickens, we would be spending most of the day cutting corn. Then with a smile, he said, "Tom and the harvest men will move the colts off Long Meadow tomorrow and put them in Top Meadow, so they won't torment you any more."

Tomorrow came with the sun high up in the sky as I cycled to work at six-thirty along Aveley Lane. I must have looked quite a sight with my big cap, no shirt, short trousers held up with braces, socks – probably one up, one down – big boots covered in dried cowdung and no muscles in my arms, chest or belly, legs like matchsticks. I was straight everywhere, just like a pea-stick.

"Hello," said a voice. An old-timer approached from the allotment gate, dressed in heavy cords. I recognised George Day. His trousers had a stable-door flap and dog collars just below his knees. He carried his jacket on his arm and his frail basket was slung over his shoulder, his trilby hat just a bit askew, his wrapper twisted and tied round his braces. He had a two-week growth of beard and signs of barley avils lodged in it from yesterday's harvest work.

"What are you going to do today?"

"Harvesting," I said.

He eyed me up and down and said, "You'll have to eat a bloody lot more suet puddings afore you'll make a harvester. You take it steady, my old partner. It's going to be a bloody scorcher."

I cycled off along Aveley Lane, its grassy banks now turning brown under the heat of summer. The high, wide and blue Suffolk sky seemed to be miles – and thousands of miles – above me. The wild flowers of summer had taken their drink of midsummer dew and on them huge bumblebees stood on tiptoe, their engines at full buzz and wings at full flap, straining for take-off into the sweet, light air of this heavenly morning. Here I was, this thin brown nut stick boy making my early morning journey to work, not a care in the world and when I put my hat on, it covered all I owned.

At Alpheton Hall men were arriving for another hard day of harvest work. They were all smoking an assortment of clay or wood pipes, some rolling cigarettes. The small amount of skin that was exposed on their faces was heavily tanned, either by the sun or pickled by tobacco smoke or both. The rest of their faces was covered in several days' growth of beard. It did not appear to be hair, it looked more like thousands of little bushes and the outstanding thing about them was the whites of their eyes, which seemed to stand out like jewels against their pickled brown skin.

Their hands were enormous, with extraordinary thick fingers. I think, because of their heavy work over generations, nature or evolution had designed these men for the work they were doing. I don't know whether they were Anglo-Saxon, Roman or a mix of many Europeans but they all had a similar stocky build, especially their heavy bone structure.

I first noticed their big fingers when they lit their pipes. They seemed to have difficulty selecting a match out of the box. They could not have threaded a needle to sew a button on their coats. This is why they always used string to keep their clothes together.

Harry and I went into the cowshed. GEC was anxious to get the cows out of the way, to make way for the harvest horses which were coming out of the stable any minute. I had to get on Kit fast.

In the stable, Tom already had the bridle on Kit. "Hold your foot up, Jimmy. I'll give you a leg up." He did, but he pushed so hard I went right over the other side and landed on the horse muck.

Tom laughed. "Let's try again." This time I landed square on Kit's back, and I was off, geeing up the cows and we had the yard cleared in no time. I felt very honoured and very proud to be sitting up here, driving this forty to fifty-strong cow herd to their lush pastures.

Two labourers stood on Church Field in the shade of the two enormous chestnut trees which stood by the track, waiting for the harvest wagons to arrive to take them to their long day's work pitching the sheaves.

"Hello, boy. I had to look twice to see if there was anyone on the pony's back."

"Get yourself some glasses," I said.

"And another thing," he called. "Put your bloody shirt on. You'll be burnt to a cinder, silly young bugger."

Kit, the herd and I mardled on down the track. Herk, the bull, was in fighting mood this morning. He was driving his horns into the ground and making strange noises. He scraped the ground hard with his right foot, sending grass and dirt flying high in the air. He would shake his head vigorously so the safety chain, threaded through his nose ring, thrashed his eye mask. Herk was a massive beast weighing around a ton, quite capable of putting me and Kit in the dust so we never gave him the chance. We kept well back, never putting ourselves between him and the herd. That way we had three escape routes should he try to have a go at us, but he didn't. He seemed quite happy to play his war games alone.

We completed our journey without further incident. I dropped off Kit's back and shut the gate leading into the meadow. Then I remounted and sat on Kit's back for a few moments, surveying the herd making its way down to the river, as all good cattlemen do, looking for lame or sick animals. We had a leisurely walk back to the farm, obeying Tom's instruction not to trot or gallop now that the ground was midsummer hard. Everything by now had dried off and got airborne: bees, moths, flies, butterflies, grasshoppers and dragonflies all humming or buzzing different tunes. 'A Midsummer Night's Dream'? No, early morning opera acted out in all the grassy banks of England without an audience.

When I'd got Kit out on Back Meadow and my shirt on my back against the sun, I fed the chickens and collected the eggs. Today, I was accompanied by the farm sheepdog, which had been trained to herd cattle. She was a lovely friendly dog who really knew her job, but we never worked her too much in hot weather. Her home was a little straw bed under the manger in the cowshed. She rounded up the herd every morning and brought them up to the cowshed soon after five, ready for GEC and his sons to do the early morning milking, but she loved to have a walk round with me as I saw to the chickens.

From then on, GEC and I worked steadily through the harvest, moving from field to field. As the weeks went by, we finished all the cutting but there was still some carting and stacking to do. On this day, the cart was from a field named Shimpling Dodsers, a long way from the stackyard, perhaps a mile or more. Because of the distance GEC wanted four wagons and a trace horse, with four men in the field and four at the stack.

Tom asked, "Who drives the wagons?"

"Jimmy," he said.

"Is he big or strong enough?"

"Well, no, not really, but his [he's] got a lot up top and his bloody nimble. One thing we must not let him do is come down the steep hill off Back Meadow into the farmyard. That's the most dangerous place, especially with a trace horse. So, Jimmy, you stop at the top of the hill until the empty wagon comes along and tie the trace horse behind it and go back to fetch your loaded wagon."

I was to do this work between working with the herd and the chickens.

"Right you are," said Tom, and took me to meet my first wagon at the top of the hill on Back Meadow.

An old farm labourer there tied the trace horse behind and said, "Be bloody careful of this one. Prince is a big, wild bastard. He used to be a whole hoss, you know, until they cut him two years ago. I don't reckon they cut him clean. His a rum bugger at times."

In my innocence, I only understood parts of his conversation but his last warning as we parted was, "Keep out of the way of those bloody great wheels, then you'll be okay." I was to ride the empty wagons out to the field, but you never burden the horses with extra weight when pulling heavy loads. On the way back, I would be walking.

I climbed up on the shaft horse's back, gee'd him up and off we went down Back Meadow, following the tracks of the other wagons, through a narrow gateway that straddled a three yard ditch, leading onto Shimpling Hatch, then we turned right and on to Shimpling Dodsers.

I seemed to be doing quite well, sitting up high on the shaft horse's back between the collar and the saddle, open legged. But it was bloody uncomfortable with the saddle to collar strap buckle chafing my behind.

I arrived next to the loaded wagon where the men were roping the load up tight. I led the trace horse up in front of the shaft horse, when a voice said,

"I'll couple that up, boy. Now, remember, all hooks face inwards – like that – never leave a hook sticking outwards. It could catch in your clothing and pull you arss-over-head and the wheels could go over you. Always remember that. Now this bloody horse, he is a rum bloody animal, and they should never put a boy like you with bloody powerful horses like these. It's a man's job. Someone with strength has got be matched with strength. Now, if he buggers you about, zig-zag his rein. That will twist his head one way, then the other, but you will have to pull hard. That will give him something to worry about. When you get to Shimpling Hatch gateway leading onto Long Meadow, pull out three hundred yards or so onto the field and plumb that bloody gateway and pull out quick enough."

He gave me the reins.

"I'll start it off for you. Get up there, Prince!"

There was an almighty bang as Prince leapt forward and the trace chains tightened up.

"Mad bastard," he said. "I'll set you on your bloody arss, you bugger."

And he did. As he zig-zagged the reins, he got Prince up in the air and then on his rear.

"I'll show you who is bloody boss," he said. "Now, come on, let's do it right." And Prince walked off with his pride damaged. "There you are, boy. Look after yourself as you go through that gateway and bugger the wagon."

It did seem a great responsibility. Everything seemed so big, the length from the trace horse to the rear of the wagon and the height of the load. Nevertheless, I was jogging along quite comfortably on foot, the wagon was creaking and rolling from side to side. Now for that gateway.

The field entrance was in sight, to my left. I would have to steer my load in a big curve to line up to it. Pull out quick enough. I pulled Prince's rein gently to the right. Prince obeyed and the shaft horse followed. We were now making our way wide, out onto Shimpling Hatch. That's enough. I pulled Prince's rein to the left and plumbed up to the gateway, coming on lovely, but not there yet. I could see there would be little room for me, so I moved up nearer the trace horse, out of the way of the wagon wheels, holding Prince back tight on the rein. Then we were through and heading onto Back Meadow.

It was homeward bound for him and he wanted to go like hell. I zig-zagged him gently and he slowed up. The old-timer had done some good by putting him on his rear. I felt very relieved. We were going at normal pace and on the home straight. The great harvest wheels were sliding from side to side on their stub axles – no ball-bearings in those days. I felt so proud of what I thought was a great achievement.

I stopped on the top of the hill and waited for the empty wagon to arrive. I went up to Prince and patted him on the nose and plucked him a handful of grass – a peace offering. I thought it might just help to calm him down and be my friend, as Kit was.

I pushed him two or three steps backwards and unhooked his trace from the shaft wherries and waited for the empty wagon. When it arrived, the old farm labourer tied Prince to the rear and said, "Git on your hoss, boy."

I climbed up the front wheel of the wagon, walked along the shaft and sat between the saddle and the collar of the shaft horse again.

The old labourer shouted, "Caw'd a hell, boy! You can't sit there. You're in the wrong bloody place! Come back here, you, and sit behind the saddle, sideways. Put your fit [feet] on the shafts, if your legs are long enough."

I obeyed.

"There, that's better, my little old beauty. You can lean forward and reach the rein so you can steer it. You mustn't sit between collar and saddle. You're too big for that, now. You'll do yourself an injury, if you know what I mean and you mustn't do that. You got the best part of your life coming. Christ, I wish I were your age. I'd look after things better than you do. Right you are there, my old beauty, off you go."

Back to the field gang I went, with the empty wagon. It was great, sitting up here sideways on the back of this huge Suffolk Punch. Prince, my trace horse, was marching along behind, picking his feet up high, head held well up. A proud horse was Prince, his neck was massive and at the end of the day it never sagged, not even under the weight of his great collar. He was built like a mountain of muscles and his feet were as big as barn shovels. As one old farmhand said, "Mind your bloody toes, boy. If he stamp on them, that'll be mincemeat."

All morning I went backwards and forwards, driving the great harvest wagons from field to farm until I was told to stop.

"Don't come back no more, Jimmy boy. By the time we get this loaded, it will be twelve o'clock and that means dinnertime. One of the men from the stack gang will see to your shaft horse. You lead the trace to the pond to have a drink. He'll make his own way to the stable, but stay there with him until the horseman arrives. Don't, he'll lift the lid off the corn hutch with his nose and make himself ill. Oh no, he's not bloody daft. He knows where the pantry is and how to open the door."

So off I went home to dinner, in hot pursuit of Harry and very close up to the rear wheel of his bicycle. He was not in the mood. "I'm not going to play around. It's too hot. Come on, ride properly and let's get home and have our dinner."

As usual, most of the family were sitting around the table when Harry and I arrived. "Wash your hands," said my mother. "Be quick – I've got suet pudding and rabbit gravy for you. That's the stuff for harvest men."

My father said to Harry, "Carting wheat up at Alpheton Hall?"

"Yes," said Harry.

"Three at the stack, three in the field?"

"No," said Harry. "Four men stack and field."

"Christ, they got some labour up there, then."

"Four wagons and a trace horse. Long haul, nearly a mile from field to stack."

"Who drive away?"

Harry pointed to me. "He drive them wagons and with a trace horse."

My father looked at me. "Some farmers would have a fit putting a boy like him driving wagons."

"He's all right," said Harry. "They turn boys into men at an early age up there. Anyway, he knows how to handle a bloody horse. He rides the farm pony to get the cow herd from the lower meadows barebacked."

"I wonder he don't break his neck."

"Not him. He's slipped over the pony's ears scores of times."

Harry looked at the clock and decided we had to get back. We picked up our fourses bags, loaded with sandwiches and a couple of bottles of cold tea and cycled off.

That afternoon, I carried on driving. The field gang taught me how to rope up a load – on what hook to start and what hook to finish on. At three o'clock, I left my heavy horses and put the bridle on Kit and off we went. It was a joy to be pony-riding down this familiar old track. Golden stubble and stooked cornfields were all around me, women and children scattered here and there, gleaning the last remnant of corn from the stubble left behind by the harvest men. It was more out of pleasure than gain, a few ears of wheat for their cottage chickens, a lovely afternoon out for these ladies with little financial reward but great contentment and happiness.

I reached the Lower Meadow's gateway off Aveley Lane. Two old men from the village were leaning on the brick parapet of this quaint little bridge, looking down into the trickling water of the Chad. I jumped off Kit's back to open the five-bar gate, the old men raised their walking sticks in the air and I waved back to them. I pulled Kit up to the gate, climbed up and slipped back onto her back, when I heard one of the old men shouting and waving his stick. I turned Kit and went up to him.

"Hello, Jimmy. I hope you don't think we're interfering, but on that second meadow near the stile there's bin an old cow laying there for ages. She's out there on her own and if my mind serves me right, there's suffin wrong with her."

I thanked them, and decided I'd better take a look. "D'you

think you could stop the cows from coming onto the road, while I go and see?"

"Course we can, boy. There's two on'us. None of us are much bloody good, so I'll shut the gate and watch for you coming up with them, then we'll open it for you."

"Thank you, sir," I said, and moved Kit up into a faster walk, crossed the river and made my way to the sick cow. On reaching her, she looked at me in a pitiful way. I knew immediately what was wrong, and I knew exactly what to do. I jumped off Kit's back and walked up, talking to her in a kind, low voice and took a look to make sure things were the right way round. Within fifteen minutes, she had a lovely bull calf. I cleaned its airways and dragged it by its front feet to its mother's face, where she licked and kissed it. GEC and I had done this before.

When I got back to the gate with the herd, the old timers opened it for us.

"What's wrong with her, Jimmy boy?"

"A calf."

"Is she all right?"

"Yes, I'll come down with a horse and cart later for them."

"That's it," said the old timer. "Put the calf in the tumbrel, the mother will follow behind."

On reaching the cowshed, I told GEC what had happened. "Well, keep on your pony and go to Harry," he said. "Tell him to take his horse and tumbrel down to Lower Meadow and pick up the calf. Harry will know what to do. I'll have to take some milk away from the mother. She'll be in full flush. Then I'll tip it in the pig swill tub, they like that mixed in with meal. It mustn't go in the churn for three or four days, it's yellow and too rich."

That long summer of 1939, I carried on with the cows, the chickens, driving the wagons and then, August over, it was Friday night. Payday, we always walked up to the kitchen door to collect our wages. GEC handed the men pound notes, silver and copper.

When he got to me, he gave me my money and said, "So, you've got to go back to school on Monday, Jimmy. You keep coming up Saturdays to feed the chickens, won't you. And when you leave school at Christmas, don't go looking for a job. You come up here and work for me – I don't want to part with you."

So my long summer holidays were over and I had enjoyed every moment of it. It had been a glorious summer and I had learned a lot. But it was also great to be back in the fold with all my playmates again. Armed with a piece of soap and a towel, we all went to the Chad for our Friday night scrub and had great fun wallowing in its clear, warm water.

Three To A Seat, Three To A Seat!
There we all stood on the Monday morning, outside the thatched cottages opposite the Rose and Crown. Most of us had some new article of clothing, with our hair groomed and pan-shine faces. I suppose we looked quite a smart lot for 1920s or 30s models.

Around the top corner came Theobald's Thornycroft bus in its green and white livery. The driver was Mr Theobald himself, a huge man. We all clambered aboard, the driver shouting out in a gruff voice, "Three to a seat, you're only matchsticks, and sit bloody still. No clambering about on the seats."

Off we went, over the bridge at the river Chad, up Cold Hill. I had done this journey so many times over the years, and I recall those young people who waited for the school bus in those long gone days. Then, usually at the end of the term that they reached their fourteenth birthday, they disappeared into the world of work.

From Bridge Street, there were nearly a score of us attending Shimpling School at one time or another, including my brother Harry, my sisters Beryl and Iris, myself, and my cousin Dorothy Mott. Also around our age were Herbert and Peter Newman, Ernie and Margaret Bugg, Dusty, Will, Albert, Winnie and Charlie Frost, and Betty Levett.

At the top of Cold Hill, Joe Wright would be standing on the corner named after him with Jean Ranson. At our next stop, the council houses, we would pick up Barney Andrews, Bob and Evelyn Pawsey, Ronny King, Joan King, and my second cousins Evelyn and Beryl Mott (Tom Mott's children), with the bus driver still shouting, "Three to a seat and sit still."

On we'd go to the thatched cottages near the old Alpheton school, picking up Ernest Long, and on past the Red Lion up the

"My father..... served as a soldier during the First World War." [page 2]

"I was the ninth child and youngest son of John and Lizzie Mott...." [page 1]
Jimmy, aged 3, with father and brother Wally

"Our home was Rose Cottage in Bridge Street.....[page 1]
...... a good soul lived there named Liz." [page 149]
Top: Rose Cottage, on the left-hand side
Below: Jimmy's mother, Lizzie Mott

Fun On The River Chad

"The miller and his friends had skates and glided along." [page 9]

*"One summer treat was boating on the Chad......
Mr Ruffle's son Dick sometimes did the rowing."
[page 31]*

The Hamlet Of Bridge Street

Above: Mr Goldsmith, outside the Smithy and Post Office
"Sparks would fly across the traverse, and us kids would try to catch them.." [page 11]

Below: The old main Sudbury to Bury road through Bridge Street
"..ancient Elizabethan houses......... my mother had had a sweet shop there." [page 17]

Top *"One boy stayed behind..., sitting straddle-legged between the saddle and the collar..."* [page 35]

Below: Horse and tumbrel along the Suffolk lanes

Bottom: Fred Long collecting water for Lodge Farm in summer *"Lots of Suffolk villages became short of water."* [page 37]

Bringing In The Harvest
Above: (left to right) Oscar Simpson, Jimmy Mott, land girl Barbara, Sam Eady

Below: (left to right) Charlie Reeman, Bob Pawsey, Harry Fuller, Wally Mott

Field Labour
Above: Tom Moss, Tom Mott, Ron King, Chummy Mathews, Dusty Frost, Bill King, George Last, land girls Doreen and Barbara, Joe Wright.

Left: Vic Simpson, Horseman, Lavenham Lodge

Below: David Alston
"The stock at Alpheton Hall were all beef cattle" [page 177]

Above: Alpheton and Bridge Street Home Guard.

Left: Harry Mott

Below: Men of the USAAF 487th Bomb Group, Lavenham Airfield

"...we shall be forever grateful for their sacrifice and the support of the American people." [page 213]

old main road, stopping to pick up Cynthia Mitchell. At the top of Shop Hill we'd pick up Ann Elliot and Dot Long, then up to Elms Corner where Sam and Rosemary Eady would be waiting. Pam Warner would be at the cottage beside the road on the turnpike and the last stop would be Midway Farm, picking up John Jackson. Now, this was to be the last few weeks of my journey to Shimpling School.

We arrived just before nine, laughing and chatting, satchels loaded with sandwiches and bottles of cold tea or lemonade. It was just one great, great buzz of excitement when all at once the great bell tolled out, ordering us to our classrooms. In we marched, still talking, when a huge shout rebounded from one wall to the other.

"Silence!"

Miss Fisher! A great hush fell immediately and we were almost afraid to breathe. It reminded us that we were really and truly back, our freedom gone. We would now do in school hours what our teacher and the parson ordered. If we did not obey her, she would dish out her punishment, which was very severe, and the parson would preach to us to love our enemies.

We were back to the Lord's Prayer and "All Things Bright and Beautiful", followed by lessons. Then at playtime, out came our football and up the school meadow to our football pitch. It was great to be back with all my friends. I don't suppose I had really realised how much I had missed them.

Mr Theobald was driving the school bus on the way home. Most of the boys were shouting, "Three to a seat, three to a seat, you're only bloody matchsticks, three to a seat." Our driver pretended not to hear them, but those famous words lived on for the rest of the term.

Back at Bridge Street, my sisters and I ran up the path to Rose Cottage. Our mother was standing by the door to greet us, and as always we were starving hungry and we tormented her for something to eat. She would disappear into the back'us and come out with something like a wedge of jam tart each and say, "You little buggers will eat us out of house and home."

Then she would make us get our school clothes off and change into our old play things, saying, "I know what you are. You'll go out there and come home covered in mud and ruin your school clothes. Come on, get them off."

I thought I would go down the Lower Meadows.

I crossed Serpenpan Meadow, down towards Dark Lane. This walk had everything I loved, but I loved to walk it alone. It had broken stiles, lichen-covered five-bar broken gates, crooked footpaths, an old unkempt grassy cart track, lush water meadows and reeded dykes, but everything was as nature intended with fallen trees at different stages of decay, huge ant-hills and broken riverbanks.

I had only time for a quick survey of the area, admiring its tranquillity, then did a fast walk back to my mother's cottage. As I lifted the latch and saw all the rest of the family were home, my mother greeted me with her usual, "Wash your hands and get up to the table, tea is almost ready. I must light the lamp before I dish up, the evenings are pulling in sharp, now."

Here we all sat, eating our dinner, all seven of us, eight including my mother, chatting and eating, when Harry said, "What did you go down to Lower Meadows for?"

"Just for a walk down Dark Lane and beside the river. It's lovely down there."

"How do you make that out, Jim boy?" said my father.

"Well, it's wild, lonely and beautiful and I just like it."

"Keep going if you like it, boy," said my mother.

After tea we'd do homework, or my sisters and I would play games like snakes and ladders. We had to be in bed by seven o'clock during school term.

My older brothers and my father would light their paraffin hurricane lanterns and go off to feed the pigs, muck out and litter them up, feed about sixty or seventy tame rabbits, close up the chicken huts for the night and mix up the middlings in a wooden butt for feeding the next morning. All this was at Rose Cottage. Then, this done, they would go to the allotments and make their way to the potato patch. They would hang their lanterns on crotch sticks and work to dig up the potatoes, leaving off about half past eight most nights.

They would be up again around half past five in the morning to feed all the family's livestock before starting their regular farm jobs at seven. Nothing was neglected, clean water always in drinking troughs, clean and warm beds for all our animals.

My mother would walk around the livestock at about ten o'clock in the mornings to see everything was in order, for the welfare of the stock was most important. Then she would move to the vegetable garden and pick sprouts, cabbage, or whatever there was in season for the family dinner.

On top of all this, the men of the family would cut down great hedges on the farm on Saturday afternoons in return for the wood and a horse and cart to take it home. In those days, the winters were severe and a good stock of fuel was essential.

It was, of course, work, work, work, but it never seemed to be a burden to them – it was a way of life. We were almost self-sufficient except for meat, but the wild rabbits filled that gap, and the odd pheasant and our own cockerels and old hens that were past laying.

The lady of Rose Cottage was our mother, our cook, our cleaner, our washerwoman, our ironing woman, our supervisor, foreman – the boss. She was also our doctor and she had all the ointments, potions, elixirs for cut fingers, grazed knees, runny noses and scabby ear holes. When occasion demanded, she was village midwife and assisted with the sick and dying. She also found time to work in the fields, pea-picking, knocking sugarbeet and loading mangolds.

We were not totally self-sufficient, and with very little in the way of transport, we relied on the tradesmen of the district. In Bridge Street we had the services of Mr Goldsmith, the blacksmith, and his wife Mrs Goldsmith, who ran the Post Office. Also Fred Bugg, the wheelwright, and Mr Ruffle at the mill. Tradesmen who supplied us from Long Melford were the baker, Jess Adams, Mr Ruse, the butcher, and Mr Stanhope, the grocer. Mr Wash had a couple of hardware stores and drove his van, all hung with saucepans and other items, out to the villages. Clothes we bought 'on tick' from the tick-tack man, Mr Palmer in Sudbury.

This was my last term at school and from our bus windows I watched the dark and dying last months and days of 1939. England was now at war with Germany. We had reached Michaelmas, the start of the farming year and the Smythe drills were out in the fields, drilling winter wheat. Clamps of sugarbeet appeared on the roadside verges, waiting for transport to the sugar factory at Bury St Edmunds.

From the rain-lashed windows of the bus, I would watch men in the fields struggling to earn a crust, getting the last of the remaining beet out of the wet, sodden soil, and I was glad I was going home to a blazing fire and the comfort of home.

Then men came to Rose Cottage to fit us all with gas masks. My mother had to register for poultry and pig food with the Ministry of Food. We learned that most food would be rationed and clothing coupons issued. There would be a blackout, no lights to be shown. Wooden shutters were made for our cottage windows.

"We shouldn't take too much harm," said my mother. "We must grow plenty of fruit and veg. As for meat, it will be mostly rabbit. Keep all the chickens we can for eggs. The worst things for us will be sugar and butter, but if I can get the milk, I can shake the butter up in a jar."

Mr Goldsmith, the blacksmith, was appointed as A.R.P. warden in Bridge Street. Special Constable was Fred Bugg, the village wheelwright. A Home Guard Company was formed for Bridge Street and Alpheton.

All cars and lorries had to have their lights subdued, with a special mask fitted. Petrol was for special and emergency vehicles only. All private cars had to be taken off the road. Men were busy painting the bricks white on the bridge near the blacksmith's shop, and white lines were painted in the middle of the road. All signposts were dug up and put in store or broken up, and all place names were removed.

Posters appeared everywhere, warning people to be careful, making them aware of all sorts of things. I saw posters that said, 'Careless Talk Costs Lives'; 'Use Your Loaf, Don't Waste It'; 'Dig For Victory'; and 'Cut Your Gas And Electricity'. Both gas and electricity came from coal.

Farm labourers at Alpheton Hall were working overtime putting up rough-cut poles on Church Field every four to five hundred yards, to help deter gliders landing on these big acreage fields.

Then a Pill Box was built at the junction of Lavenham Lane and the main road, next to the bridge. A line of defence was erected along the railway track, with huge concrete Pill Boxes built along its banks and inside Lineage Wood. Some were disguised as hay or straw stacks. They did the disguise with a wooden frame and nets, with straw and hay stuffed into the squares of the nets. The end product was brilliant and really did look like stacks.

Draglines were used in the railway cut areas, on the south-west side, making the sloping sides vertical and then shored up with a type of pit prop. These were supposed to be tank traps.

Purpose-built holes were dug and boxed out with covers at Lavenham railway bridge for explosives to be placed in, if it became necessary to blow the bridge.

Searchlights appeared everywhere in the night sky.

At school, we practised fire drills by forming up in our classroom, led by our teacher, marching outside and up the school meadow, well away from the school.

I still did my Saturday work at Alpheton Hall, looking after the chickens and helping Harry in the cowshed. Master Dick would talk to us about the war, saying that things did not look very good. Hitler's Panzer divisions and squadrons of dive bombers were driving their way through Poland and nothing could stop them.

I thought, 'Panzer divisions'? What the hell are they? By listening to him, I began to realise the danger of war. No, they won't come here. They're miles away. I tried to dismiss it from my mind, but it continued to keep coming back. It put me on very high alert.

I had almost forgotten all about it until one day, while out with my dog right in the middle of a twenty acre field, I happened to look around and there, before my very eyes, not half a mile away were three aircraft in line, just jumping over the hedges.

This was it! Dive bomber! I was off like a shot. I ran like hell to the nearest hedge and ditch. Their wheels were hanging down on stalks and their engines were making a heck of a noise as they rose over the last hedge between me and them.

Twenty yards to go and panting for air, ten yards to go..... I made one big leap and through the bushes I went, into the bottom of the ditch. Scared and fighting for breath, I passed through the woodwork of the hedge and there they were, skimming along just above the ploughed field. Christ, I was scared, even the dog was shaking.

At school on Monday, some boys said, "Did you see those aeroplanes on Saturday?"

"No, I didn't," I replied.

"Well, I don't know where you were. You couldn't miss them."

I was not going to tell them I had been scared as hell.

At home, the family listened with great interest to the news on our K.B. battery accumulator crackling wireless. We would hear of great British ships being sunk, such as the aircraft carrier, Courageous, and lots of British merchant ships. Poland had fallen to the Germans' well-trained and equipped army. Nothing seemed to be in our favour.

"Always the same," said the old men of the village. "Half the men of our country on the dole, and they knew bloody well the Germans were re-arming with modern equipment. What have we got? Stables full of horses and artillery guns, still with wagon wheels to face these crack German divisions. Wake up, old England! Well, they will have to get rid of this bloody lot and bring in some young modern men."

There was one bright spot which came out of the gloom, and that was the Battle of the River Plate. How proud we were when the Exeter, Ajax and Achilles, from their action and daring forced the great German battleship Graf Spee into Montevideo Harbour.

We listened to the radio every night to hear of her plight. We all thought there would be a great sea battle, but we were disappointed. The great ship scuttled herself rather than face the British cruisers.

At Christmas 1939, I left school and with others walked up to Miss Fisher. For the first time in nine years of my schooling, she shook hands as friends, and slipped one shilling into my hand and wished me well, as she put it, "for the long, long road ahead", and how right she was. I had left the protection of my school and, up to a point, the protection of my parents. The battles that lay ahead would have to be fought by me – and fight them I did.

Young, Wild And Dangerous
So I stepped into the world of manual workers. I was poorly equipped in stature and strength, but my old farmer friend GEC must have had some faith and hope in me because he gave me a job as he promised he would, looking after the chickens, geese, turkeys, ducks – and the colts.

I would also be helping in the cowshed, and walking horses down to the blacksmith at Bridge Street forge for shoeing. I liked the latter, for Mr Goldsmith was quite a character and he loved young people.

"Hello, Jimmy," he would say. "Do you need five shoes put on that horse, or just four today?"

"Just four today, sir, please."

And when he'd finished, he'd say, "Now mind how you go when you go back, my lovely lad. Always face the oncoming traffic when you've got a loose horse."

Though only fourteen, I brought many a calf into the world if the going was easy. I pumped up many an udder with my bicycle valve and pump when a cow had milk fever. I also stabbed a few cows and inserted a wooden peg in the wound to let out the gas when they got blown on early spring grass with a fair amount of clover in it, then pumped her belly with my foot to help it escape. The cow could put up with the treatment if I could put up with the stink.

Alpheton Hall was a remarkable farm, and because of its very location in a shallow valley beside a tributary of the Chad, all water drained off the roads and fields into the farmyard. It was mud – mud – slurry. Men waded in it, the cow herd, the yarded cattle, the horses, in fact every farm animal had to go through it to get to the drinking pond, but this did not worry GEC or his men. They could handle most of the difficult situations that occurred and the cattle were well looked after and given warm straw beds to lie on during the long and cold, wet winters.

Then the day came when Tom, head horseman, said, "You can come with us this morning, Jimmy. We're breaking in the colts. Master Dick and Master Len will be there, too. It'll take us a week or more to break that lot in and into the shafts, then we'll have to take them to the blacksmith's to have their first shoes fitted. Their days of chasing you up Long Meadow are over."

The colts were all on Back Meadow and one by one they had to be caught – and they were young and wild and dangerous and could kick out a gnat's eye. Tom, the horseman, secured a rope to the gatepost and Dick had a halter in his hands, attached to the rope.

Dick said, "Now your turn, Jimmy. Get your chicken bucket half full of wheat and walk up to the gate as you always do. Let the colt put its head down in the bucket so it knows there is food in there. If it lets you pat its head and fuss it, I'll take the halter off the post and hold it in my hand, then I'll steadily move towards you and join you in stroking its head, very gently. When I see the opportunity, I'll get the halter onto its head – then all hell will break loose. Tom, Len, and a couple of the men here will run up and catch hold of the rope and pull it towards the gate – then we've got him." Then he smiled. "Well, that's how it's supposed to work."

Dick did get the halter on and immediately the colt tried to run off, but it soon took up the slack in the rope and knew it was trapped. It kicked and reared up in the air but four powerful men were on the rope, reeling him in like a fish on a line.

They let him play for a while to get rid of his energy. When they had his head tight to the gate, the horseman slipped a bridle over his ears and buckled it up. The iron bit, which hung loose one side of the bridle, was slipped into his mouth and connected to the other side of the bridle.

"Got him now," said Dick. Tom had attached two leather leads either side of the bridle, two men each side, holding the leads.

They called to me to open the gate to let them through. I shut it behind them. Over in the corner of the meadow was a tree trunk on the ground, equipped with hooks for pulling. Tom picked up the huge horse collar and slipped it over the bridle and onto the horse's head.

Next came the plough trace. Tom put it on the colt's back and buckled up, keeping in tight against the animal in case the colt tried to kick him. It was rearing, kicking, jumping, shaking and sweating. It did not like its harness.

The plough trace was hooked up to the log. Long reins were fixed to the bridle and all the men moved behind, with the colt now on its own up front. It thought, 'I'll be off', and then realised it wasn't so easy with the tree trunk in tow. It started to run but this took the wind from its sails, so it walked round and round pulling its heavy load.

Sometimes it lay down and I was told to crack the whip to make it get up. Then it would jump and rear up and walk backwards.

"Catch him round the arss with the whip when he walks backward, Jimmy. Go on, harder, sting his arss."

The colt would then jump forward, tightening the trace up with a bang. On and on he went, walking and kicking, running a bit, and in the end he gave it all up. Sweating heavily, he hung his head and just stopped. Tom and Master Dick moved forward and patted his neck and spoke to him kindly. He had, after a hard fight, surrendered.

He was led off with his head low and his pride hurt, to the pond for a drink. Then he was tied up in the stable where he had never been before and given a meal of crushed oats and chaff, but he would hold his head high again tomorrow. He had not given up yet.

So the six colts were broken in one by one. Except one that we could do nothing with. He wouldn't walk, he just lay and kicked like hell. Nothing would make him walk. They tried and tried to no avail, and then the boss arrived on the scene.

GEC stood, sucking his pipe, talking to his two powerful sons and Tom, the horseman. They shouted over to me.

"Jimmy, go over to the tool shed and fetch a slasher."

Master Dick took it from me and made for a great mound of blackberry bushes. He cut off the longest strands of briars he could find. GEC wound them into a tight bush ball.

"Right," he said to Tom, "lift up his tail."

In a second, GEC stuck the thorny ball up his rear end and

clamped his tail down tight. It was an instant success. The colt shot up in the air for two or three feet, then shot off at full gallop – but two mighty men already had the reins in their hands and had him under control in seconds. Then the colt took up the weight of the tree trunk and they let him have his head.

He went like hell, pulling this great load with his tail clamped down hard. They always clamp their tail down if you put something like that under it – they haven't got the sense to lift it to ease the pain.

Now GEC stepped forward. "Enough is enough," he called to his sons. "He could collapse if you let him carry on." His sons moved to stop the colt pulling. GEC moved up to the colt's head and rubbed his nose and patted his neck.

"Give him a handful of grass, Jimmy. He knows you, he chased you up Long Meadow many a time, and you never had any bushes up your arss."

Then it was dinner time, and the horse was taken for a drink. "Not too much, mind. Don't, he'll get gut ache. Then he can have just a handful of crushed oats, and when he's tied up take out the bush ball. He'll have a sore arss for a day or two, but it's much kinder than the whip."

It was a cold, wet, miserable day as Harry and myself cycled home to dinner at Rose Cottage. Smoke from field fires was rising slowly into the heavy atmosphere, as farm workers were busy cutting field hedges on neighbouring farms. The sugarbeet season was all but over. Teams of horses were struggling to plough up the last of the wet and racked-up sugarbeet land to benefit from the winter frosts that lay ahead, steam rising from their bodies mixing with the damp air. The ploughmen themselves struggled to hold their ploughs in this racked-up, waterlogged field, dressed in farm workers' wet-weather clothing – hessian sacks caped around their shoulders and tied with binder string around their necks, hessian sack putties tied around their legs to knee-high, and on their heads their battered hats.

Harry and I cycled along viewing this scene, which was Bridge Pastures, a field next to Aveley Lane. The horse and plough teams belonged to GEC's eldest son, Edward, of Rowhedge Farm.

As they worked their lines, each team produced a halo of ghostly mist and into this mist of horse-sweat, hundreds of seagulls rose and fell like white angels. These lovely Suffolk scenes were everywhere throughout the year, but alas, try as I might, I could not master the art of painting so all was lost to me, except in memories.

After dinner, back at the stable three colts were harnessed up, led to the cart shed and each one backed into the tumbrel shaft – with some difficulty. Some kicked like hell, others did a kind of tap or ballerina dance. My job was to have the old yard horse on a lead in the area, to give the young horses confidence.

"Right-o, Jimmy. You lead off with your old mare. Go up Wood Drift, where the ground is soft." We had to keep off the hard ground until the colts were shod, or it could have ruined their feet.

Off I went with the horse and cart, leading this line of tumbrels. Our friend who had had the bush ball under his tail was being a bloody nuisance. He seemed to hate the saddle on his back, and the noise of the harness chains and tumbrel wheels. Master Dick was his handler, so the right man had got him.

"Right," said Dick. "Load this tumbrel up with good wet, heavy muck off the heap. Leave your horse there, Jimmy, she won't go far. And hold the colt while we load the tumbrel."

So I left the old mare, who was called Matchet, and patted the colt's head and ran my hand up and down its nose while the tumbrel was loaded. Then it was time for me to lead off again, with Dick following. "Make your old mare step it out. It's uphill all the way to the top of Wood Drift, it'll take the wind out of him."

Off we went, downhill at first. This was the first time he had had weight on his back and Dick had him up close to the tailboard of my cart. This really worried our young, active horse. With the weight on his back and the load pushing him along, he was sitting well back in his britchons to control what was behind him. He did not think about kicking, his mind was on his own safety.

Down the hill he did very well. Now the long, heavy pull up Wood Drift. Before we got half-way up, Dick shouted to me to stop. I walked back to him.

"Must give him a rest, now. Mustn't do too much to him."

Dick rubbed the colt's face and patted him all over. He just stood there with his head down. After a while we moved on and after three or four stops, we turned at the top. Now it was downhill all the way back.

We reached the farm with no problems. There, the tumbrel was off-loaded, the colts and my old mare were stripped of their harness and a halter was placed over their heads and tied to the cart shed posts for them to get used to mechanical noises. There they all stood in line, with my old mare Matchet acting as step-mother.

"Right, here we go then. Start her up, Harry."

My brother started the oil engine that drove the milking machine pump. Bang, bang, bang.

The colts' ears stood up straight and they stood at full alert, then round the corner came Ron with his old 10-20 International tractor, driving past their rear. They could see the tractor as they had no blinkers, they just turned to get a better look, but there they stayed until the milking was finished.

The next dry day they were put into tumbrels carting muck from around the gateways of the yards. All the tumbrels were loaded light to make it easier for them as it was an uphill pull when fully loaded. My job was to hold the colts at the muck hill while the horsemen off-loaded. Dick drove the tumbrels between yard and hill, and all the while they were being looked at by GEC, Dick and Tom, to see if they had sore shoulders or chafing anywhere.

The next step in their breaking-in was the blacksmith's. So early one morning, we set off from the farm. Tom was in front with two colts. I was leading Matchet, with one colt tied to her nearside. All went well until we reached the top of Tippets Hill, near Rowhedge Farm driveway. There we met the Tar Pot, with smoke billowing from its chimney and council workmen patching the road.

A workman's shovel may have scraped along the hard road surface, making an unusual noise, or perhaps they didn't like the black Tar Pot with its tall chimney. The leading colts went absolutely mad. They rose up in the air, slewed across the road, out at full length of their leads, doing a frightening act.

Council workmen disappeared from the scene as if the curtain had dropped on Act One. There stood Tom, his trilby hat lying in the road, looking up at his two chestnut chargers high up on their back legs. I thought for a moment they might break away.

He shouted at me to move up in front. I obeyed straight away. My old mare Matchet and the colt by her side walked calmly past the two rearing colts. When I dared to turn to look around, there they were, following calmly behind as if nothing had happened. The horseman even had his trilby hat on.

We arrived at the blacksmith's without any more mishaps. There was Mr Goldsmith, standing smiling at us, his cloth cap on his head and his leathers hanging down each leg. "Hello, Jimmy. I'll take the horses. You go up to your mother's and sit in the warm for half an hour. We can manage here."

So I left Tom and had hot tea and buttered toast for my breakfast, sitting by my mother's old kitchen range. Then I walked back down to see how the blacksmith was getting on.

"Just in time, Jimmy, my little old beauty. I've put the twitch on this bugger, his a bloody nuisance. Hold it like this. If you watch me working and he starts to mess around, wind the twitch up tighter. That way it'll worry him and he will think at what is going on with his nose and forget about his feet. It just fools him."

Now a twitch is a piece of wood cut from the hedge, with a hole drilled about two inches from the bottom. A piece of sturdy leather shoelace is threaded through the hole and tied at both ends, leaving a leather ring. This is twisted over the top lip of the horse's mouth and the more you twist the more it hurts.

By twelve o'clock, all three colts were completely finished. They hadn't been too much trouble, but of course, our blacksmith was very experienced and knew how to handle young horses.

Then we had to face the return journey.

Mr Goldsmith said, "I'll see you out of the travis, onto the main road." I led off, with Matchet and the colt. "Be careful, Jimmy, the main road's busy with army lorries, armoured cars, sand lorries, all sorts of military vehicles. These days it's hardly safe for experienced men, let alone a boy of your age. You keep in tight to the side."

So off we went, myself leading and Tom Mott following. We were really clip-clopping along, the colts feeling strange with iron shoes, lifting their feet high in the air and coming down hard on the metal surface.

We arrived back at Alpheton Hall with no more trouble and the colts taken to the pond for a drink. Tom tied them up in the stable and fed them. "Well done, Jim, well done boy. Have a bit longer for dinner, it's well past twelve o'clock."

The family were all seated around the old, planked pine table in the kitchen, talking about the war as I walked in. Russia and Finland were now at war with each other.

"Hurry up and wash your hands, or your dinner will be cold."

"Have much trouble with the colts, Jim?" said Harry.

"No, not really," I replied. "Tom's were a nuisance especially when we met the Tar Pot at the top of Tippet's Hill, but Tom held onto them, with his knowledge of horses."

It was a gloomy, wet, late December day as Harry and I cycled back to work. From now on, my job was to help Harry with the dairy herd and all the yarded cattle and pigs and poultry, and the colts running loose on meadows with their huge shelter-belt hedges.

The Trouble With Teats

We started at seven in the morning and finished at five o'clock at night, or at any time if cattle were ill or calving. Time didn't matter, but the welfare of the cattle did. As always, we had good back up from GEC and his sons, and also from the workmen on the farm.

In our severe, cold and snowy winters, the health and welfare of all the cattle was of first importance and because it is really against livestock's nature to live herded up in yards and cowsheds, they do, of course, find it claustrophobic and restricted. They love wide open spaces, and yarded cattle and milking cows very often went off their food or were generally ill and miserable. Their coats were dull, they lost weight and milk production fell rapidly.

So GEC, with his great knowledge of cattle, gathered perhaps from his forefathers, knew the simple answers to most cattle ailments, and in this case, GEC turned them out onto Back Meadow. Harry and I took loads of good barley straw for bedding onto this meadow, in lovely sheltered places surrounded by areas of blackthorn, on GEC's orders. They would be fed on mangolds, not minced but just cut with a spade, and a generous forkful or two of good hay. He selected all off-colour cows and cattle, perhaps four or five, maybe more, and we would drive them onto the meadow.

"There you are. They'll soon pick up. Winter blues and lack of soil in their diet. There is something in dirt that do them good. They'll sleep out all night, whatever the weather. Keep them well supplied with barley straw, they'll live for a week or two as nature intended. You will have to bring the milking cows in twice a day. Drive them to the calf area in the oat barn and let the calves suckle – there again, as nature intended."

He had, of course, put them back to their wild beginnings. Every day GEC would visit them and stand there with his pipe on for ten to fifteen minutes, just watching. After a week or so camping out, there would be a great improvement in their health and behaviour. After a few weeks, they would be back to full health and back in their respective places.

Now you may say, rightfully, why herd them in yards and cowsheds with fattening cattle, whose sole purpose in their final year before slaughter is to put on weight? Beef cattle would take too long for the weight to go on, the farmer would lose out on profit and the butcher don't want old, tough meat.

As for dairy cows, they are kept in because it would be an awful job rounding up the cows for milking at four o'clock on a wet or snowy morning on a dark winter's day. The meadows would poach up to slurry, ruining the rich meadow grass. The cows' teats would get covered in mud and dry on hard, causing them to crack and get mastitis. Then again, the farmer needs his straw stamped up for manure or muck, to spread on his fields. Without it, he would be a very poor farmer indeed.

There were, of course, problems to overcome. Almost every day, they would lay down to rest and when getting back onto their feet, some cows would accidentally stamp on their teats – mostly ones with big udders. This would cause the teat to split, leaving a wide, ugly gash the length of the teat. It would be so sore the cow could not bear us to touch it – but we had to take her milk. It was one of the most dangerous of all jobs connected with cow herds.

So sore was the cow's teat, she would tremble when we were

near her and she would use every bit of her defence system to keep us at bay, but it had to have treatment. The wound had to be treated, and it was especially important that the milk was taken away from that damaged teat quarter twice a day. If not, the cow would get severe mastitis and die.

So first, we would have to make room for ourselves to work by releasing her stall mate. A rope was placed around the cow's belly, just in front of her hip joints, and tied to her separation stall rail. All the while, GEC would talk to the animal to keep her calm. Then he would produce a siphon needle from his medics box. It was a stainless steel instrument, a hollow tube inserted so the vent hole of the needle was just below the teat.

This occasion, Harry and GEC leaned in heavily to the cow's flank to prevent her kicking out. Then he gave me my instructions. "Take the needle, Jimmy, put one hand gently on the uninjured side of her teat for support, then with the other, insert the needle very slowly into the cow's teat. She'll object for a bit when you first touch her, but be gentle, don't be frightened, and keep calm. Harry and I have got her penned in tight."

Right then. Down I went, with the needle in my hand and my heart pounding like a blacksmith's hammer. Apart from shaking hands, I did exactly as GEC instructed. The insertion of the needle was easy and the milk soon started to run from the needle vent onto the ground, but what a relief it was when I finally stood up beside Harry and GEC. As always, the boss had that lovely smile for me and said, "Well done, Jimmy boy. Now, how about that teat wound? Is it clean? Is it worse than we thought?"

"I don't know," I replied truthfully. "I didn't stop to look."

He laughed at my answer. It was fifteen minutes or more for the siphon to drain all the milk from that quarter, and it took the pressure off the damaged teat. Then I was told to remove the siphon, pulling it gently, straight down, until it was clear of the teat. This I did with no problem.

"Now lean on her with Harry while I go to look at the damage." He was there for a minute or so, then got up, went to the medics box and came up with something in a tin. It looked like Vaseline.

"Are you going to dress it with this, or shall I, Jimmy?"

"You can," I said.

"Thank you," he said. "Harry, hold tight, and Jimmy, get up there close with him. This is the sore bit I've got to touch."

The cow hated it. She pushed and jumped and rocked from side to side. GEC was talking up to us. "Stick to her, Harry, shove hard against her." When he had finished, he said to Harry, "She's got a nasty gash there, full length of the teat, but that stuff I just put on will help to remove the soreness. Oh well, we done quite well. She was quieter than I thought she'd be. I'll tell you what, Harry, cut down on the bedding straw. Too much straw cause these type of problems, the teats and feet get too mixed up in deep straw. We never get these problems when they sleep out, though they do get teats caught on barb-wire or other things sometimes."

GEC inspected all the cows and yard cattle every day, looking for any sign of illness or injury. He could spot anything wrong in a second, such as lameness, dull coat, coughing, off their food, or unusual behaviour. On one occasion, a cow's eye continued to water and the animal just kept on shaking its head.

GEC took a quick look. "It's got an oat flight in its eye. Right Jimmy, go to the stackyard and bring back half a dozen bits of long straight wheat straws."

I returned and gave them to the boss. He went to the medics box, took out a pair of scissors, held the straw up to gauge the length he required and trimmed the ends to his satisfaction.

"Right, Harry, grab hold of her horns and press her head slightly down and hold her tight. Jimmy, you watch that oat flight and tell me when it gets to the bottom of the eye. Right, here we go. Got her tight, Harry?"

He lifted the straw, held it quite close to the oat flight, put the straw in his mouth and blew air down the straw. The oat flight glided down to the bottom of the eye like magic, where I gently wiped it onto my finger.

"Well done. You got it. Hold onto her for a minute, Harry." GEC bathed the eye in warm water on a cottonwool pad to wash away the pus. "That'll ease her discomfort. I never use oat chaff, but this is coming from the wild oats in the corn."

Some of the treatments would go on for three to four weeks, taking up our valuable time. We also had calving cows to see to, some births were easy, some difficult and some very difficult. We had calves to wean from their mothers and learn them to suckle our fingers and suck the milk from the bucket through little bunches of hay we used to make, to save time so we did not have to stand with them. The work was endless and it went on for seven days a week.

Harry and myself weren't the only ones getting to grips with this new way of life. Most of the boys from Bridge Street went on to farm work after we left school at fourteen, and remained my friends throughout my life. Our friend William Frost worked on a farm nearby, Ernie Bugg went to join his father at Ford Hall and Barney Andrews eventually joined his brother Ron. Only Dusty Frost tried something different, working in Sudbury as a delivery boy, pedalling an 'International Stores chariot' round the town, which was what they called those bicycles with a basket on the front.

He didn't stay very long, it wasn't in his blood and eventually he came to farm work. The thing was, he used to get home from Sudbury so late at night. At the farm, you left off at five, we'd had our tea and were back out soon after six o'clock. We didn't go to town, we went to the fields and places, taking the dogs rabbiting in the moonlight. That's where we learned to love all these things – the different shadows. It is light and shadow that make the world, really, isn't it? So that's how we spent our time after work, until the weather stopped us.

The Only Snow White Around Was Me
That winter, our mother would wake us up at five-thirty some mornings, saying, "Come on, you had better get up now. It's been snowing heavy overnight and there's a strong east wind, so no doubt there'll be deep drifts."

Harry and myself would jump out of our warm beds, dress, go down the old twisted staircase, out to the bowl in the back'us to wash our faces, then back in the kitchen for hot tea and toast.

That dark, snowy morning my mother said, "I'd leave your bicycles at home and walk. You'll never cycle through it. It's a blizzard, and it freezes like hell. I've put extra food in your grub bags in case you can't make it home for dinner."

"Okay," said Harry, "off we go, James." He opened the door and there it was, the wind howling round Rose Cottage. It was dark and snow was twisting and twirling in the wind.

My mother said, "It's not fit to go out. Look after that boy and keep hold of him down the path."

We went forward onto the main road, towards Aveley Lane. The roads were blocked with deep drifts and it was bitterly cold. Harry said, "We'll have to go back and try Spring Meadow. We'll keep to the fields, but we must get to Tippets Bridge to get over the Chad."

Harry walked in front and I just followed him. We did not talk very much, as the bitter wind took our breath away. We reached the bridge and looked over the parapet. It was just full up with snow, and so was the road ahead, four to five foot deep.

"Now what?" said Harry. "I know, I'll just keep near the hedge. You follow me." We were now walking in very deep drifts, up to our thighs. Harry said, "You stay where you are. I'll try to cross the ditch. It's only a matter of yards, now."

Harry tested his footing through the ditch and reached the field, which was clear. The wind had blown all the snow onto the road. "Now walk in my footmarks, and hold your hand out and I'll drag you over." After he'd done that, we had to tip the snow from our wellies, and Harry gave me a good brush down.

We stood and took stock of our position. It had stopped snowing, and the stars were shining high up in the early morning sky. We set off again and we were making good progress, the way ahead was clear. Now and then we had to stop as strong gusts of wind whipped up the fine powdery snow, causing a white – or rather a blackout. The wind howled around our bodies so strong, we had to lay into the wind. The east side of our clothing was covered in ice, my feet were frozen lumps. The higher we got up the hill to Alpheton Hall, the more exposed we became.

Harry fell back and walked beside me to give me some protection from the relentless blast. "Keep going," he said, "another ten minutes and we'll be going down the hill and then we'll be into the farmyard."

I didn't answer, for the uphill walk and the cold wind had taken my breath away, but I thought encouraging words. We plodded on and reached the shelter of the farm and into the cart shed we went.

"Well, we made it," said Harry. "Let me brush the snow and ice from your clothing, then you brush mine. Take your cap off and thrash it on the post, that'll knock the ice off. We'll have a rest before we go into the cowshed."

Harry poured a cup of tea from his flask, and we had half each. "Feel better now? Hell of a pull up that hill in the snow and wind. Right, let's go."

Into the cowshed we went, the lanterns hanging on the beams swayed vigorously as we opened the doors, and the pulsators on the Alfa Laval milking machines were ticking away in tune with each other. It seemed quite cosy in here after coming in from the blizzard.

GEC and his two sons were busy stripping the cows and keeping an eye on the machines. "Morning Harry, morning Jimmy. Christ, you did well to get here this morning so early. What's it like right out in the open?"

"It's a bugger," said Harry. "We had to walk by the fields, the roads are blocked solid."

"It is bad, then. Well, thanks for making a great effort to get here, Harry," Dick said. "How did you get little brother here, then?"

"Bloody dragged him through the snow in some places."

"Well Harry, you and Jimmy can carry on now. We'll go to the house for breakfast. Tom has been here for orders. I've told him to send two labourers to the pond to break the ice, so all the animals can drink. Four labourers to load muck onto the tumbles from around the cattle yards and gateways and spread it onto the ice in the yard. They'll muck out the cowshed and litter up for you today."

Then GEC said, "Don't, Harry, please, turn no cows out into the yard for drinking until I'm satisfied that the muck they put over the ice is thick enough. If any of those cows slip and fall, we shall have dead calves on our hands, or broken legs. The milk lorry will be late, or he may not get here at all, but the milk won't take any harm while it's freezing like this. If it's too long, we'll run out of churns, but there, we must take one thing at a time. All the labourers will stay around the farm today, so you can have all the help you need. Jimmy, I would like you to go up to Mrs Sylvester's and get two gallons of petrol and a two-ounce tin of Three Nuns tobacco. Since the war started, tobacco is getting very short. I'll give you the money when I come out after breakfast."

Mrs Sylvester's garage on Tye Green held the wartime permits to store and sell petrol. The petrol was required for the milking machine engine, which drove the air compressor. The tobacco was for GEC's pipe, of course.

As the dawn gradually broke and the sun came up red in the eastern sky and the bitter east wind blew relentlessly, the landscape was stark and desolate. Harry and I completed the milking and washing of all the dairy equipment.

Harry said, "I'll keep the copper fire going today, we can sit around it and have our dinner – we'll never make it home today. If it was me, I'd go and feed your chickens now and give them a bit more while the weather stays bad. Feed them in their huts, no good throwing it in the snow."

Off I went, with two full buckets of wheat. First, the long walk up to Long Meadow. Looking ahead, I could just see fencing posts around the hut, sticking out in the snow. I picked my path through the deep drifts and found a suitable place to cross Long Meadow stream and wade slowly through the water and snow. It was level with the top of my wellies and some water went over the top when I pushed to get out the other side. I now had very cold, wet feet.

I managed to enter the hut and put one bucket on the floor. It was immediately occupied by a dozen or so hens fighting to get the biggest share. I dived my free hand into the bucket I was holding onto and scattered wheat all over the hut. There was a hell of a stampede of chickens flying in all directions. I emptied one, and scattered the rest from the second bucket. Then I filled my bucket with snow and emptied several bucketfuls at different points in the hut – I mustn't leave them to dehydrate.

I walked back down the meadow, ploughing snow furrows with my feet. I had not a care in the world and not a worry. I had a feeling of being a supreme human being, but of course we do not really live in the real world when we are young, we mostly live a life of fantasy.

The virgin snow lay thick on the ground and that cold east wind continued to blow snow from the tall hedgerows when all at once, ahead of me in a snow flurry, I thought I saw something. It appeared to be a deeper white, in the form of something stretched, elongated. At that very moment, everything went quiet and peaceful and it seemed to be just the area around me. The wind still blew, but I could not hear it and I knew I was not alone. My heart pounding, and so scared, I ran and ran heading for Harry and the cowshed, when all of a sudden I heard a voice as I was passing the cart shed.

"What are you running like mad for? Come and have your breakfast." To my great relief, it was Harry. "Here, come and sit near the fire. Here's your grub bag. Are you cold?"

"My feet are. The water went over my welly tops crossing Long Meadow stream."

"You must take them off or you'll get frostbite in this weather." I took off my wellies and drained the water from them. "Give me your socks." He wrung them out and laid them on top of the copper. He went to an old coat that hung in the cart shed, whipped out the lining and gave me half. "Dry your feet with this and hold your feet in front of the fire."

Then he went to the stackyard and came back with two small scuds of hay and levelled that out in my wellies. "Tear this old bit of lining, and wrap a piece round each foot when we're ready to go back to work. Your socks should be dry by dinner time. Now let's eat our breakfast and get warm. There's one man in the barn putting mangolds through the mincer for us."

After bread and cheese and a lovely warm, Harry and I went back to work. There was no sign of GEC, though he would be around somewhere. Harry was worrying about the cows.

"I'm sure they need a drink by now, but we mustn't turn them out. GEC said he wanted to inspect the yard to make sure it was safe for the cows to walk on. Never mind, he'll be here in a moment or two. We'll go to the barn and start mixing up the food for feeding this afternoon and tomorrow morning."

We mixed up six or seven heaps. They all had different ingredients but all had sweet chaff and mangolds. There was something there for all the cattle: some for dry cows; some for steaming up cows near to calving; some for heavy milkers; some for normal milkers; some for bullocks in their final year of fattening and some for those which had another year to go, all worked out by GEC.

Harry said, "Where do you think he is? You go to the kitchen door to find out."

I knocked on the door, GEC opened up. "You said you would like to inspect the yard before the cows were released for water."

"Good God, I forgot, Jimmy. I'll come straight away."

GEC took one look and said, "Let them out, Harry, very steady. Let them take their time, don't rush them." He inspected every one as they came out of the cowshed. "Stand near the pond, Jimmy. There's only room for about six to drink at any one time. Don't let them go on the ice, whatever you do."

It took Harry and myself the rest of the morning to get all the cows watered. They would have to go out for water again this afternoon, but each cow would be released after it had been milked and the men working on ice-breaking would continue to make a longer drinking area, so this would stop bunching and pushing and prevent accidents.

We had our lunch – again bread and cheese – by the copper fire. Harry said, "You can put your socks on now they're dry." One or two labourers joined us around the fire for their lunch.

"Bloody weather, Harry. It makes a lot of hard work. That pond ice we're breaking is a good six inches thick. It takes a lot of muscle to break it. It'll freeze like hell again tonight and we'll have to keep on breaking it day in, day out, while the weather's like this. With all the cattle and horses there is on this farm, it's a hell of a job keeping them all supplied with water."

"Then there's the colts wintering out on Top Meadow. They usually have the water cart filled and left on the meadow."

"They drained the water out yesterday so it shouldn't burst the tank. The young bosses fed them and broke the ice on Top Meadow pond."

We stirred ourselves, and Harry sent me off to see to the poultry. "No sense sitting around here for an hour, may as well get on. We've a hell of a lot to do. You'll have to get over Long Meadow stream as best you can. Pick the shallowest spot you can find and shut the chicken hut door if they're still in there. Mr Fox will be around tonight looking for a dinner."

I filled up my buckets with wheat and off I went up Long Meadow. Lots of chickens came running down to meet me and followed me back up to the hut. They had found their way through the snow. I scattered the wheat on the floor of the hut, collected the eggs and after some pushing and shoving, I closed the door and made a quick dash back to the farm. I fed all the chickens that lived and lay eggs around the farm. I found eggs all over the place – under cattle mangers, some on straw heaps in the stackyard.

I walked through the churchyard but made no attempt to search for eggs as there were only the tops of tombstones just sticking out of the snow. The church and churchyard had taken on a magic look. Everything was white, right to the top of the tower, but I did not linger. I delivered the eggs into the farmyard kitchen and went back to the cowshed to meet Harry.

"GEC's been here. He left the money for the petrol and his tobacco. The empty two-gallon can is near the milking machine engine. Your hands will get freezing carrying that can. I've got a small clover seed bag out of the granary, so slip your hand into it and it'll keep the wind out. GEC is going to help with the milking while you're away and Masters Dick and Len will feed the colts on Top Meadow. Now off you go and no buggering about playing in weather like this."

I put on Harry's seed bag glove, picked up the red petrol can and off I went up the steep lane that led from the church and farm to Alpheton village. There was ice and drifted snow everywhere. It was hanging in great untouched nature-shaped pillows from the lane's steep banks. It resembled the approaches to a magic fairy castle but the only Snow White around was me. The wind howled out its low and high notes but there was only me here to hear its serenade. I marched on, listening to the music of the wild, wild wind.

I arrived at the garage, left the can near the pump and went into the shop to purchase GEC's Three Nuns tobacco.

"Hello Jimmy," said Mrs Sylvester, "the usual I expect." She was very kind and nearly always gave me a chocolate wafer or a biscuit or two, along with my purchases. She also loved to pull my leg about girlfriends and all sorts of things that young people do. She handed me the tobacco, took the money and said, "I suppose I'll have to get my coat and hat on, just to fill your can."

Outside, unlocking the pumps with a big bunch of keys, she put the petrol hose into the can and wound the handle for one gallon, then back and forwards again for two. Then she disappeared back into the warm, leaving me to face the icy blast whipping off the fields here at the top of the hill.

It was snowing hard again on the return journey. My arms ached, my hands were cold despite Harry's glove bag, but I was grateful for it. I arrived back at the farm, covered in snow. GEC was there with Harry in the cowshed. He said, "Hell of a journey getting up there and back in this weather. Come here, let me brush the snow off you. There, that's better. Got my tobacco?"

"Yes, here it is."

"Thank God for that. I don't know what I would do without that. I'll keep here helping Harry if you'll feed the pigs in the yard and the ones on Three Cornered Meadow. Give those in the yard a good shovelful of coal, not big lumps, there's plenty of small dusty stuff around the coal heap. They don't look very sharp to me, suffin' they lack. Their coats don't shine, but there will be a mineral or two in the coal to put them right."

I got ready to go out into the cold again.

GEC said, "Them on Three Corner Meadow are bloody good hogs. They do well despite all the mud and water. They love the outdoor life, as long as they have a good, warm bed they're all right."

Now, with the long, cold day drawing to a close, hundreds of wild birds were taking their place in the cowshed and cattle yard beams. Hundreds of sparrows were making their way deep into the old barn thatch and corn stacks, and tomorrow they would help themselves to food from the cattle mangers. So farming and wildlife lived together and both farmer and birds had to work hard for survival.

The last job was to blow out the hurricane lanterns, one by one. They died out with a puff of paraffin smoke rising up to the cowshed roof as Harry blew out the last one, then it was total darkness. We made our way through the ice and snow to the cart shed to collect our grub bags. We were joined there by the farm labourers picking up their belongings. It was dark, cold and bleak and the wind still moaned around the cart shed corners.

"Hold on," said Bert Frost, "there's someone coming down the road."

We all held our breath and listened. Not a sound.

"Bloody sure I heard someone cough."

"No bugger about here on a night like this," said Dick Talbot. "The bloody cold is getting hold of you, Bert. What you need is a good hot meal and a couple of pints in The Rose."

"Come on, let's get home. Don't, we'll all get froze to death," said another man. As we all started to walk out of the cart shed together, a lone, shadowy figure went walking past.

"Hello, mate, are you lost or something?" called Dick.

The figure stopped immediately and walked towards us.

"Lost!" he said. "Who wouldn't be in this bloody desolate place. I'm the milk lorry driver and I'm stuck coming down the bloody hill, so I don't know how I'll get back up."

"Don't you worry yourself, my old bean," said Dick. "We got enough hosses about here to pull you and your Re-o-speed wagon either bloody way. Go and get the Governor, Harry."

The Governor and his two mighty sons arrived. He decided the best thing was to pull the lorry backwards, so he turned to us and said, "If you chaps wouldn't mind staying on for a bit and get yourselves a shovel each, you could clear behind it, so the wheels can get a grip. That should do it."

Tom was sent to get a horse and tumbrel so the milk churns could be loaded up onto it. There was no chance of getting up the lane to the lorry because it was level full with drifting snow.

"But he can get up the field, easy," said GEC. "Just one thing, we've got to get the churns over the ditch at the top, so we'll need all hands to help lift them over onto the road, and then up onto the lorry. More than one way to kill a cat, isn't there Jimmy boy."

Within an hour, the lorry was loaded and on its way back to London. GEC was happy now he had empty churns for tomorrow's milk.

"Glad that came," he said. "I thought I would have to tip the milk out or feed the pigs on it." We all walked back down to the farm and then GEC turned to us and said, "Thank you all for staying on to help out, especially on a night like this."

We collected our grub bags. Now for the long, cold walk home. I walked behind Harry, following in his footsteps. The fields were dark and desolate, not a sign of any living thing, animal or human. Harry was just a deep, black form I was following. Sometimes the snow was half-way up my wellies and sometimes up to my waist, and I had to form some kind of swimming action with my hands and feet to propel myself along.

Harry had a great advantage on me with his longer legs and I was determined to keep up with him, but it forced me to perform all sorts of actions with my arms, feet and body. Some places the snow was up to my armpits but I ploughed on. I was covered in snow and ice. At last we cleared Aveley Lane and Tippets Bridge and took to the fields, the last leg of our journey home.

"We'll be all right now," said Harry. "Easy going."

There were no lights in the windows of the cottages as we reached the village. The blackout had put them out. The cottages stood stark against the white, cold snow and the main road was hard-packed with it. We reached, at last, the long, narrow path to our dear old cottage. I trudged the last forty yards, still following in my brother's footsteps. We reached the door and Harry lifted the latch with that old, familiar metallic noise and we were home, sweet home.

We knocked the snow off our boots and walked in. All the family turned and looked at us. My mother said, "Christ alive, get those clothes off those boys. They're frozen bloody stiff."

Our older brothers, Jep and Wally, helped us off with our ice and snow-covered clothing. They took them outside and rattled them up against the old hobble door to shake off the worst of it.

My mother brought us clean, dry clothes and said, "Here you are – go in the front room and put these on." To everyone else she said, "Move away from the fire and make room for these two." We emerged feeling better with our warm, dry clothes on.

"Come on, sit on these stools and have a good warm for half an hour and drink this lovely cup of hot, sweet tea," she said. "And I've got just the stuff for this weather – pea soup so thick you can cut it with a knife. I'll soon knock up a couple of twenty-minute swimmers to go in it, so you won't have to wait long." Mother's twenty-minute swimmers were dumplings that stuck your ribs together after a hard, cold day's manual labour. "Put some wood on the fire, Father, and keep them two hot."

"They've been out of this house for nearly fourteen hours, Liz," said my father. "Too long for that young'un."

"Yes, it is," said my mother. "You go to bed as soon as you've had your dinner."

"Don't keep worrying him," said Harry. "He's all right. He don't complain. Sometimes I think he enjoys this weather. The worst part is getting up there and back, but he managed to keep up with me. Where it's too deep for his short legs, he seems to plough through it, somehow. I don't take too much notice of him, but he's always right there behind me. He's walked miles today, through the snow and ice to feed the chickens, and he's fetched petrol from the garage up at Alpheton and lots of other jobs."

"Nevertheless," said my mother, Liz. "It's a long cold, day for a youngster like him. So get up there, Jim boy, deep down in that lovely feather bed with the sheets well over your head – because there will be another busy day for you tomorrow."

Bad News

The British winter of 1939 had its downside, but its weird and wonderful landscape was a joy to behold for those on the right side of the window pane. Of course it was a dead and desolate place stripped of its finery in the dying months of the year, and now the great, great freeze of snow, ice and wind had come to deliver the knockout blow. It had taken everything else from her, even the spirits of the fields and woodlands had gone to the hollows of the earth. She was now alone and it looked oh, so desolate.

For several more weeks, the landscape desperately hung on in her great slumber. As a boy I wondered if nature could fight back. It seemed to me as if nothing would ever grow here again and things were made more plain to me as I saw hundreds of dead pigeons lying beside fields of frozen kale and cabbages and hundreds more too weak to fly.

Thousands of rooks were scavenging the great wheat fields where they had been blown bare by the wind, digging their great beaks deep into the frozen ground to feed off the root and what was left of the mother corn. Lots of these died a cruel death from cold and malnutrition, hundreds came out of the rookery in the mornings, but only about half returned at night. Farmers sent out rook and pigeon scarers to keep them on the wing but it was a hopeless job, they had long run out of fuel and crashed into the cold and frozen fields. I used to give some of them pieces of bread, but could never get them to eat it.

Harry and I continued to struggle to work, as did the labourers. Most of the workmen had to help out, working seven days a week in a desperate battle to keep the cow herd, their calves, bullocks, horses, pigs, colts and all poultry fed and watered. It was a great and what seemed an endless battle and then, as if by magic the Great Thaw came.

The spirits of the fields and woodlands were forced up to the surface from their hollows in the earth by fountains of floodwater, released by the frozen soil. Everywhere was mud and water. The ditches ran, the rivers flooded, it was water, water everywhere, but gradually it subsided and the land began to dry and the sun started once again to warm the earth.

To start the spring of 1940, the birds began to pair off and build their nests like any other year. They would not know or care that in May Germany would invade France and would soon be pushing our gallant troops back towards the coast.

The winds arrived to dry out the heavy Suffolk soils. GEC had his eye on the fields as he walked to inspect the lovely deep tilth that Mr Jack Frost had made for him. He ordered the crab harrows out onto the fields, followed by the old Smythe drill.

Catkins hung yellow in the hedgerows, followed by primroses, violets, peggles, and spring was here. I was riding Kit again, taking the cow herd to the water meadows beside the Chad. As we approached, the sun's rays began to penetrate the silver mist that followed the line of this twisting meadow river. Around us, little streams ran with liquid light over moss-covered stones. We had left the cold and cruel winter behind us, and Kit loved it. She lowered her head to get a mouthful of the lush, green grass. We took a steady ride back to the farm, drinking in the spring sunshine. It was quiet and lovely.

We caught up with Gladys, the char lady who cleaned the farmhouse. I slipped off Kit's back and took her by the lead to walk alongside.

"Hello, Jimmy," she said as she took a long puff from her Woodbine cigarette. "Lovely morning, it's good to be out and aren't you lucky to have a pony to drive the cows down to the pastures every day."

"I am indeed, Gladys."

"But you're a lovely lad, Jim. They all love you at the farm."

And then her next sentence did, I suppose, make me listen harder to what she was saying.

"I don't know how much longer we'll be working here. The missus told me on Friday, when I left off, that the farm is being sold in July. Mind you, I suppose they could buy it, but there you are, that's life. We must wait and see."

Gladys, Kit and I strolled on into the farmyard, talking of 'could be's and 'could not's. As we parted company, she said, "Well, you've got the news. Bye for now."

I put Kit on Back Meadow and walked back towards the cart shed. There was lots of farm traffic standing in the area – the old Smythe drill with horse in shafts and one tied behind; horses and tumbrels loaded with seed corn and artificial fertiliser; another one loaded with harrows and whippletrees. Busy time now for arable workers, around six or seven of them sat around the cart shed, including Harry, having their nineses.

"Here comes the foreman," someone called as I approached.

"Hello, lad," said Dick. "Not a care in the world has he, as free as the birds. It's a lovely life, if only you could keep it that way. Does he know, Harry?"

Harry looked at me. "The farm's being sold."

"I know. Gladys told me."

"So what do you think you're going to do, Jim, if these people don't buy it?"

"Get a light job, I suppose."

"What doing?"

"Bagging feathers, I expect." I could joke, too, especially when the news was serious.

The farm traffic moved off to the fallow fields. No time must be wasted now the east wind was blowing. The sun was high and the little white rag clouds were drifting slowly across a wide blue sky and the March dust was beginning to blow. The great spring offensive had begun.

Harry and I carried on our work, looking after all the livestock on the farm except the working horses. We still got a walnut whip now and again, especially when we went off to shows in Fred Elliot's cattle lorry. We also helped at haysel time, myself driving the wagonloads of hay from field to stack.

Some of the older boys who'd been at school with me had already been called up and gone off in army uniform. As I drove the wagons, I thought about the terrible news that we'd heard. Italy had declared war on the Allies, and by June, our troops were on the beaches at Dunkirk desperately waiting to be brought home.

We were all made more aware that England was at war as occasionally a British Spitfire or Hurricane fighter would chase a lone German bomber across the sky with its machine guns blazing. I would always run and take shelter beside a stack or building. In the evenings, the young men and boys of the village would congregate on the bridge at Bridge Street. Quite often, squadrons of Spitfires and Hurricanes flew in formation across the sky, heading in the London direction. We were watching the great Battle of Britain over English skies, which would rage on above us until October.

Wellington bombers, possibly from Stradishall, flew overhead, making towards the coast. If they were heading for Germany, their chances of returning looked small. They looked very vulnerable and alone, and I would lie in my bed at night and would wonder where they could be and think, was it worth sending half a dozen bombers and their brave crew to such a hostile place? What damage could they possibly do to such a powerful nation?

That summer, the farm was sold but GEC did not buy it. It was sold to a Mr D. Alston of Lodge Farm, Lavenham.

Harry and I helped to get in the harvest. By late September, with the daylight fading fast, Ron and his mate were thatching the great stacks of wheat, barley and oats that were standing in the stackyard, to keep out the autumn and winter weather. Wagons loaded with farm implements were being taken over to GEC's new farm at Rede. The new owner of Alpheton Hall had sent in his crawler tractors and they were cultivating up stubble fields.

A Friday in early October was the last working day for GEC at Alpheton Hall farm. The cow herd was assembled in the farmyard with the farm horses, some pulling tumbrels loaded with our bicycles and miscellaneous farm items. Master Dick was in charge, mounted on a horse at the front, myself riding Kit at the rear just in case a cow tried to break away from the herd, and behind me the farm dog trotting along.

The farm gate was opened and the mixed farm convoy moved off down the private track. On reaching Aveley Lane, the convoy turned right, heading towards Shimpling, no more to head for the lovely Lower Hall Meadows with the twisting Chad running through the middle, where Kit and I had lingered in these old daisy-filled meadows. We would never find them again. It was the end and it was so sad, but gee up, Kit, I got lost in a beautiful dream. Kit responded with a shake of her head. "No, Kit, we are not going the wrong way. This is for real, you are moving to your new home."

We marched on through the winding country lanes to Hartest, Brockley and Rede villages, then on to Rede Lodge. Here we all stayed for an hour or two helping fit cattle and horses into their new home. Those of us whose cycles were on the farm cart cycled back. The older men followed later in the farm car with GEC driving.

He gave us all our weekly pay, thanked us all for what we had done to help him, shook us all by the hand – and that was it.

PART THREE

"Keep Your North Eye Out."

Great Clods Of Moving Earth

The day after we said goodbye to our old life, on the Saturday morning, Tom Mott arrived at Rose Cottage telling us he had been in contact with the new owner. If we needed work, we were to go to Lavenham Lodge on Monday morning and meet in the cart shed there at seven o'clock.

Harry and I presented ourselves in the cart shed as instructed on that October morning, 1940. Out of the semi-darkness, a man came walking towards us. "Morning," he said. "You're Jimmy and you're Harry, is that right?"

"Yes, that's it," said Harry.

"There's supposed to be another man with you, I think. Yes, he's here – Bert Frost. Hello, Bert, I didn't twig you there. Right, you're Jimmy, Harry and Bert. I'm George." This was the foreman, George Eady. "We're going filling beet today, and the next day, and to well after Christmas. Acres and acres of the bloody things about here, big beet grower, he is. You won't see much of him, his allus out. Got some more farms at Old Buckenham in Norfolk and his on the War Agriculture Committee. Well, let's go to the stable and see if Vic have got the hosses harnessed up. Yes, Vic Simpson is the horseman here."

We followed him to the stable. "Morning Vic, got some new men here this morning."

"That's good," said Vic. "We need more manpower about here."

"Can you lead a hoss, Jimmy," said George, "and put it in the tumble shafts?"

"Yes, I can."

"Put it in that tumble over there, then follow me down to the beet field."

I did as I was told. Acres of sugarbeet stretched out around us, towards the great Suffolk sky. George set us working. "Right, bring your old hoss a'twin these two rows. How old are you, Jimmy?"

"Fourteen, fifteen next week."

"Christ, you're a young'un. There's another bloke coming to join you three in a minute, so there will be four of you filling. I'll drive the load back and fore, and Vic will unload and clamp. We've got two lorries carting to the sugar factory all day and every day, so we load them as they come back empty."

The fourth worker turned out to be someone I knew. It was Ron Andrews' brother Barney, my friend from school. George said, "Now, there is just one thing. We have a snack at nine o'clock for ten minutes, dinner is at twelve and we leave off at five......" So far so good.

".....but should one or the other lorry arrive back empty at twelve, we fill it and have a late dinner. Should one or both lorries arrive back empty at five o'clock, we stay on and fill both of them, so they go straight off to the factory in the morning............" Not so good.

".......and you get paid overtime for that." Well, that was good, anyway.

"Right, I reckon we're ready for the fust load. Jimmy, my old boy, gee the old mare up a little, then we can have a heap of beet apiece each to fill the cart."

We soon settled into a quite comfortable routine.

At nine o'clock we had our nineses, just standing around the cart. It seemed so strange after Alpheton Hall, with its rolling fields and lovely twisting stream meadows.

Bert looked up to survey his surroundings and after a few moments of summing up, said, ""Bloody flat and open about here."

"Don't you like the look of it, Bert?" said Harry.

"No, I don't. That north wind will tickle around our arsses before we have finished this job. There ain't nothing between here and King's Lynn. You mark my word, my boy, we're in for a bloody rough time this winter.

"Right, time to get back to work – a new job, a new master and a new leaf to turn over. George isn't back with the empty cart, so Jimmy, take the full cart up to meet him. That'll look better than all four of us standing around one cart."

I took hold of the horse's rein and led it towards the clamp, following in George's tracks. At the clamp, George came over and took hold of the horse. "Glad you came up with the full load. That shows him we're well organised. That's the boss man over there, you know," he said.

"Is it?" I said.

"Yes, that's him, so off you go with the empty cart, and tell the men to keep their north eye out. His sure to come down where you are."

I got back to our filling point and drew the tumbrel between the rows of heaped beet.

"Where did George get to, then?" asked Bert.

"He's up at the clamp, talking to the boss."

"How do you know it's the boss? You've never met him."

"No, but George told me, and he says keep your eye out because he's bound to come down here."

"Did you see him?"

"There was a man there in almost white breeches and check jacket and a cap to match."

"Well, whoever it was you saw don't belong to our class," said Bert. "No, no, because our sort don't wear white coloured breeches in this bloody mud - but I'd say that's who it is, so if any of you see a pair of white breeches coming our way, give us the down."

"Well," said Harry, "here comes George with the empty cart – yes, there is someone with him with white-looking trousers."

"That'll be him," said Bert. "Keep ya backs bent."

At last, George drew up beside us with the empty cart. The man in the white breeches walked straight on without a word.

"That's the boss," said George.

"Well," said Bert, "if he has not got no more to say than that at our first meeting, I don't think we've got nothing to worry about in the future."

George laughed and said, "Well, you'll get used to him. Jimmy, you'll have to drive the carts back and forward for the rest of the day. The light's getting short and I got to feed the old tarkeys afore it gets dark, so I'll leave it to you. Keep an eye on him, Bert, 'cos he's a youngster, ain't he and he ain't very big."

"No, but I think he is 'the chosen one' – well, he was at Alpheton Hall."

Off I went with the loaded cart. On reaching the clamp at the side of Dead Lane, Vic, the horseman said, "Hello, Jimmy, have you had a good day so far?"

"I have, Vic, thank you."

"Lots of difference at Alpheton Hall, wasn't it?"

"Oh, yes. That was all cattle, cows and big Suffolk horses."

"Don't you think our horses are very big, then?"

"Not as big and strong as them at Alpheton Hall."

Vic backed the tumbrel to the clamp and I returned to the field gang. On my next visit to the clamp with a full load, Vic said he would leave off at half past four as he had to go to the farm to feed all the horses and rack up the yard with hay.

"The lorries will be here first thing in the morning, so leave all three tumbrels loaded and leave them on their shaft props in Manse's farmyard. And don't forget one thing, do you know what that is?"

"I do, Vic."

"What is it, then."

"Don't forget to release the belly girt."

Vic laughed. "That's it, Jimmy. And one thing more. Ride all three horses into the pond for a drink and walk them round and round to wash the mud off their legs."

This turned out to be one of the worst parts of my new life. It was now getting dusk so we each led a horse back to Lodge Farm.

"We've got to wash their legs."

"Right," said Harry. "I'll give you a leg up. Take the lead of this one in your hand and then you can walk them both round. Go deep enough so it wash the bellies."

First they both had a drink – ever sat on a horse while it's drinking? It's a short steep slope down into the water, never look down but up. I rode them round and round with the water almost touching my boots.

"That'll do," shouted Harry and out of the pond I came. "Right, jump off and I'll give you a leg up on this one. I'm going to take these two into the stable and get their harness off. Give that one a good drink and clean up and no playing about – don't, you land in the drink. Bring it to the stable when you've finished."

Out of the pond I came, through the stable yard and into the stable. It was very dark, although a lone hurricane lantern was putting out a yellow glow hanging from a beam near the corn hutch.

I unharnessed the horse and George said, "Well, that's about it for today. Time to go home. Come straight to the stable in the morning and get the hosses down to Manse's Farm. We must not hold them lorries up – they're the sacred chariots."

We cycled home to Bridge Street and tumbled into Rose Cottage about half past five for our dinner of cottage pie with a lovely red cheese topping, and rhubarb batter. My mother, Liz, said, "I make these especially for you two. You need good grub when you're out there all day. Must keep your belly buttons away from your backbones, 'cos if they touch, you die."

Afterwards Harry said, "That was a lovely meal, thanks. I was starving. Same again tomorrow, please."

"It gets more difficult every day because of the rationing. You can't get this, you're only allowed so much of that but I suppose as things are, we are lucky we live in the countryside – plenty of rabbits and pheasants down the Lower Meadows, chickens up the garden for meat and eggs, plenty of garden to grow all the vegetables and fruit we need. I'm sure we can keep going with all that. Now come on, get yourselves ready for work tomorrow, there are two bowls of hot water in the back'us and your clean clothes are laying on your bed, so get yourselves moving. And don't stay up late – you got a new boss and a long way to cycle to work. You better be up at half past five to be at work by seven. You mustn't be late. People don't want to employ bloody afternoon farmers, they never were any good."

We continued beet filling all week. On the Saturday morning, our new boss appeared in the field. He came just to pay our wages.

"Hello, sonny," he said. "How old are you?"

By this time, I had turned fifteen.

"Well, in that case, your money will be fourteen shillings a week." He pulled out a wad of notes, selected a ten shilling note then dived into his pocket and came out with a 'Long Melford' cloth bag for small coins. "I'll give you thirteen shillings and stop you one shilling tax. I'll check up what your wages should be and what tax you'll have to pay and adjust things accordingly next week."

And off he went. He must have spent a lot of time working on adjustments, for he never seemed to know the exact tax on paydays.

We learned that the Lodge Farm Estate, owned by the Alston family, comprised three farms at the top end of Alpheton, their farmhouses within around a mile of each other. Lodge Farm seemed to me well maintained but nothing special, with buildings of drab bricks.

Manse's Farm was a lovely moated timber house with character. It had an outstanding thatched cart shed, standing beside the old Dead Lane from Alpheton to Cockfield.

Elms farmhouse was probably a Suffolk longhouse originally. Standing at that time beside the old main road between Bury St Edmunds and Sudbury on a stretch they called the Turnpike, it had the farm pond close to its eastern side access, but modern-built piggeries had spoilt its mellow appearance.

The whole estate stood on a plateau. It was so flat and almost featureless but nothing on the estate was neglected. It was obvious the man who farmed this flat landscape knew his job. George Eady was the farm foreman and he was a lovely character with a heart full of kindness and his greatest hobby was work, he loved it. He also had a great Suffolk accent which I found difficult to understand at times.

George suffered no stress. They couldn't put a man like him under pressure. Day in, day out, for months he would be out with us in those great wet, muddy, slurry-filled, frozen, ice-covered fields. Sometimes you could hardly tell if we were really men and boys or just great clods of moving earth. We would be covered with the stuff. George would look the worst because from driving the horses, they splashed the muddy slime all over him. We could only see the whites of his eyes. His lips were always clean, we reckoned he licked them and swallowed the dirt.

Towards the end of the sugarbeet season, it would get worse and some days it rained all day. We had no waterproof clothing, no gloves, we'd be wet to the skin, our hands just balls of mud.

"We'll have to keep going," George would say. "Don't, we'll never get the bloody things off."

We would have our dinner standing up in the cart shed. We were too wet to sit down. Then, we'd be back to work at one o'clock, still raining under a late November sky. By the end of the afternoon it would be dark, just four lonesome, bedraggled creatures filling beet on this great plateau, not a light to be seen anywhere. It would be absolutely black. We could only hear George returning with the empty cart – we couldn't see him until he arrived beside us.

"Suffin bloody dark, ain't it, Bert. Couldn't hardly find you," said George. "What do you reckon the time is?"

"I'll have a look," said Bert, "if I can get through this bloody lot of pulp bags. Aar, here we are. I can't see the bugger!"

Harry said, "I'll strike a match. There, here we are, just about four o'clock."

"Caw'd a hell, I'll have to go and feed the tarkeys. I shall have to hang a lantern in the shed, for they will be gone to bed. You'll have to drive the next couple of loads, Jimmy. Just follow the tracks, that'll take you to the clamp, and give the horses a bloody good wash, won't you."

Off I went, leading my first load to the clamp but had to keep stopping on the way to give the horse a rest and Vic came to meet me with the empty cart.

"Hello, Jimmy, I came to look for you. I wondered where you were."

"Have to keep stopping, it's hard going now with all this wet. Need a trace horse, Vic."

"Yes, we must have one tomorrow. In that case, just bring what they have in the tumbrel and that will be all for today."

We parked all the tumbrels in Manse's farmyard and led our tired horses home to Lodge Farm stables. I rode them round and round in the pond to remove the mud. When we took off their harness and Vic had fed them with crushed oats and an occasional handful of bean meal, it was five minutes to five. Though we were tired, wet and hungry, with three miles to cycle home in the heavy rain, we would not go until Bert's watch said five o'clock. That is how they were in those days. The boss would not give one minute, but the worker could give twenty-nine, overtime only paid for thirty minutes or over.

That was just one day, and we had many, many days like that. By mid-December it would freeze, severe frosts. It would be so cold and unpleasant, especially at seven o'clock in the mornings in those days. There was no winter working clothing and no waterproof gloves. There was a war on and clothing was on coupons. Before going home at night, we would take off the pulp bags we had wrapped around our legs as protection, and place them in handy rabbit holes to keep them dry overnight, ready to wrap them round us again the next morning.

The fields of beet would be frozen hard. The heaps had to be loosened up with pickaxes before we could load them. Our feet would get so cold each and every day, and chilblains would follow and we would love to rub our feet on the coconut matting that covered most cottage floors. As Bill Eady, George's son, said one day – "Is it work, or is it torture?" I never heard anyone answer that question, but one thing is for sure, I don't think we would have survived the hard work and the inclement weather if it had not been for the extra food our families managed to scavenge out of holes in the ground and branches of trees in the countryside. We could not have made it on wartime rations.

Yet it is surprising and amazing how the older men on the farm stood up to it. Here was Bert Frost and George Eady, well into their sixties. I have seen them in adverse weather conditions looking like two wet rag dolls, soaked to the skin. George would stand up straight to take the ache from his back for a moment, still with a smile on his face, reach up and shake the water from his cap, then shake his hands vigorously to remove some of the cold, wet clay from them. "That ain't no good packing up, is it Bert, 'cos it could be ten times worst tomarra. We're into the wrong time of year. You keep yourself busy, Jimmy boy and don't get cold, whatever you do. Don't, you could get the pip."

It was a desolate scene, the horses with their heads hanging low, their legs and bodies covered in mud and water running from their manes and back. Us beet fillers were in no better shape working in acres of mud and water. It was running in our eyes and squelching under our feet. To add to it, it would be hardly light all day, the rain clouds would sweep low over our heads, releasing their heavy loads relentlessly upon us.

As the day went into afternoon, it got darker and darker and George finally said, "We'll pack up at half past four, get the hosses cleaned up and fed and we'll get home in the dry and warm."

As we arrived in the farmyard and walked past the farmhouse, the Governor stood in the porch. George shouted to the man who paid our wages, "We're going to clean up the horses and feed them and make them comfortable. Then we're all off home – if we ain't done enough today for any master, then so be it!"

The boss man turned and went into his house.

Acres Of Sugarbeet But Not Much Sweetness
We would cycle home in the dark and heavy rain, with dim wartime lighting on our cycles. We could hear the water gushing along the sides of the road, through the gutters and into the ditches. Not a light anywhere, just three lonely, wet beet fillers, making our way home in wartime Britain. Past Elliot's Garage, down Shop Hill, by the village shop and the Red Lion pub, then on past Alpheton Tye and Joe Wright's corner, by Park Farm Drift, down Cold Hill to Bridge Street.

We'd call goodnight to Bert and turn up the path to the little thatched cottage we called home. It wasn't much, but it was warm and comfortable and a good soul lived there named Liz. She looked after all our wants. We tumbled over the doorstep and it was lovely to see the flames leaping up the chimney and the old black kettle with steam hissing from its spout.

"Into the back'us," said Liz, "and shut the door and get your wet clothes off. There's two bowls of hot water waiting. Wash each other's backs and don't forget your hair. Then there's clean, dry clothes, right down to your socks."

Afterwards, Liz went in with the old tin bath and put our wet clothes into it. "I'll wash them tomorrow, but it's a hell of a job getting dry this time of year and if this weather keeps up, we'll run out of dry clothes to wear. Now, come on you two – up to the table and get this hot grub into you. Suet pudding, swede, taters and rabbit pie. I knew what sort of state you'd be in after a day like this."

She turned to my older brothers, who were sitting by the fire. "Come on, you lot, out of the way and let these two have a good warm-up to get the damp out of their bones. Don't, they'll be getting the screws [rheumatism] before they get much older."

In the night, the weather changed. A hard frost penetrated deep into the ground. Back in the stable the next morning, George was there, with that lovely soft smile on his face.

"Hello, Jimmy my boy, we hain't got a lot to look forward to today. Bloody mess out there, I bet, after a day like yesterday and there's a hell of a frost this morning. There'll be cat's ice everywhere on that fild [field] this morning. Vic is going straight to Manse's Farm to load the lorries, so take the trace hoss and tie it behind your tumble, Jimmy, that's a good lad, and Harry and Bert will follow you with their horses and carts."

It was, as we expected, a dismal sight. The racks and holes in the field that filled with water yesterday were now covered with white cat's ice and a strong, bitterly cold wind was blowing from the north.

I set my tumbrel between the beet rows where we had left off yesterday. Bert and Harry joined me, together with our fourth man, Barney. We were all reluctant to touch the white, frosted beet, with our bare hands, but somehow we forced ourselves and the hard, frozen lumps started thumping onto the bottom of the cart.

After a while, Bert said, "Don't put no more on there. Better to load light under these conditions."

George said, "We should get some more lorries today from R.T. Lawrence from Norfolk Lorries and Trailers. They'll take about fifteen ton apiece. As the beet are frozen, they'll have to go straight into the factory afore they turn to mush. Those already clamped are well covered with straw, so they won't take no hut [hurt]."

Flights of golden plovers swirled and twisted high and low over us on this oh-so-bleak morning. "They're doing some hollering this morning," said George. "That's a sure sign of severe weather. They're whistling up the snow showers, they are."

We were coming to the end of the sugarbeet season. George said, "Some of the beet pullers will be finishing their last pieces today, so we'll have more help tomarra. I'll put on another cart or two and perhaps another trace hoss, so we'll have two gangs going then. P'raps I'll go with the new gang tomarra, Jimmy, then you can drive the tumble for this gang all the time. It looks like we'll get them all off by Christmas, now. Bert, the heaps won't be frosted as we move on – the beet pullers are covering them with beet tops, so they'll be able to go into the clamps. Bloody job to know what to do for the best, this time of year."

But learn we did. The cold intensified with severe frost and freezing fog. It would be so dense we couldn't see anything beyond our horse and carts. We had to follow the cart tracks to find our way to the sugarbeet clamps at Manse's Farm, and as the old tracks deteriorated, we had to make new ones on the hard and frozen soil. There was no comfort for man or beast on this fogbound, frozen plateau.

We all worked hard to keep warm. There was not a lazy man amongst us because if there was, he would have died of cold or exposure. The severe weather was the best foreman in the world but, strange as it may seem, working in these awful conditions for ten hours a day, we stood up to eat our cheese and onion sandwiches for dinner in some awful draughty barn or cart shed. Why did we stand up? To keep warm, marching up and down the barn floor.

The amazing thing was, I never knew any of us to be ill or off work. I suppose we had the odd cold, but considering the severe conditions we were working in and the long hours we were subjected to, it did not seem to affect our health in any way. I know we were all super-fit, because the very nature of our physical work made us that way. None of us, young or old, ever put on an ounce of weight. Everything we did took effort – going to work, for a haircut, or meeting up with friends in neighbouring villages – as we had to walk or cycle.

The weekends were very important to us. After work on Saturdays, I would go ferreting for rabbits in the afternoon with my friends and Toby, the family dog, in the hedgerows and ditches of

Alpheton Hall. We would catch on average half a dozen and share these out as far as possible.

I would hang my brace on my mother's great back door, and my father and Jep and Wally would do the same. My mother, Liz, would take her pick for the week for our dinners, and the rest were sold to Mr King, poultry and game dealer in Sudbury, who delivered our Sunday News of the World. We used to get sixpence each, but since the war and meat rationing, we now got one shilling.

Why did we go out Saturdays hunting and ferreting for rabbits, you may ask, after working out all week in severe weather? Why didn't we sit around the fire in the warm and comfort of our cottage home? No, we could not. It may seem strange to you now but we were born to work and to hunt. Something from our primitive ancestors, I expect, but when we had the chance of comfort we did not appear to take it. Looking back, the whole family did the same and, indeed, the whole village.

In the long, cold winter evening, after working on those cold, bleak sugarbeet fields all day, Harry and I would go and meet up with Ernie Bugg, William and Dusty Frost and our other friends for a chat on the old bridge at Bridge Street. This was our meeting place and vantage point to watch the air war going on, which it did most nights over our part of Essex and Suffolk.

It was a great scene to stand and watch this great spectacular being fought out night after night. The whole sky, in all directions, was ablaze with lights, hundreds of searchlights sweeping the skies for enemy aircraft in this winter of 1940. When they did pick up, they shone like diamonds in the night sky. When out of reach of one light, they were handed on to the next and so on across the sky.

On occasion, the pilot or crew member must have got fed up when he could not shake off the searchlights and he would fire tracer bullets down the beam. As if by magic, out went the light, but it would return almost instant. Then more tracers, then another aircraft would join in, then they were gone from our view for perhaps other boys to watch in another village or town. We would continue to watch and listen out for the rumble and flashes of gunfire out towards the east coast. At ten o'clock, our little gang dispersed, Harry and myself to Rose Cottage and our feather beds.

Our Sunday breakfast was egg and bacon at eight o'clock, with hot cups of tea although not too sweet, as they used to be. There was not much sweetness in wartime Britain, but there never is in a country at war. I would take a walk out of the back door, across Serpenpan Meadow. The grass was crisp and white after frost down my beloved Dark Lane and Lower Meadows beside the Chad. It was stark and bare against the pale winter sun, sparkling hoar frost hung everywhere, from the reeds and grasses of the wetland meadows to the top of the tallest trees. It was silent, only the Chad made any noise as its winter waters splashed and crashed over fallen trees lying in its path.

Walking back, a few isolated snowflakes were falling and a bitter north-east wind began to freshen and howl around the high frosted hedges of Dark Lane. I went past Ford Hall stackyard where hundreds of wild birds and farm chickens were feeding off old kayvin heaps left behind by the thrashers. As my mother's cottage lattice windows came into view, it looked lovely, nestled down on the edge of the white, crisp meadow, with its three strands of barb-wire to stop cattle from rubbing on its low, clay lump walls.

I walked in by the great back door, and my mother was cooking dinner. "We're sinking into the darkest days of the year, now," said Liz. "A few more weeks and we'll be past the shortest day. 'The days will lengthen, but the cold will strengthen.' Did you enjoy your walk down to the meadows, Jim?"

"It's stark, white and lovely."

"Yes, it's lovely in all four seasons, but I only get to see it in spring and high summer when I go down there with Mrs Frost to get my wild fruits to make jam and wine."

Jep and Wally came in, from sawing and splitting logs. "Here come our woodmen, in for their dinner," said Liz. "We must have plenty of fuel at hand, weather like this." We needed a big pile of logs for cooking, fires to keep us warm and for the copper to do the washing. Even Liz and Dusty Frost's mother would go gathering wood together during the year. If any of the men from the village was ill, Mr Wallace would send round a load of wood from Ford Hall as this was a vital necessity to keep body and soul together.

After eating, my mother and sisters washed up the dishes. It was nearly always dark in our cottage because of its tiny windows and overhanging thatch, and the flames from the fire danced shadows on the walls and ceiling. Wally and Jep barrowed the logs into the log house near the cottage door for easy access and to keep them dry.

My older sisters Constance and Margie and their boyfriends would arrive home about four o'clock. The old single-burner oil lamp would be lit, throwing its weak, yellow light around the room. The wooden shutters would be put up over the windows because of the blackout. We all had tea, mostly hard-boiled egg sandwiches because of food rationing. We had a good supply of eggs and it was eat it or leave it. Some Sundays, the old gramophone was played, and by ten o'clock, my sisters and their boyfriends had departed into the cold, white, frosty night.

Then it was Monday again. Up at half past five, and up Cold Hill with a thousand stars shining above us, just Harry and myself on this lonely road, heading for the frozen sugarbeet fields of Lavenham Lodge once more. It was still dark when we arrived at the Lodge cart shed. There was already several men standing in there. These were the beet pullers who had finished their taken pieces, mostly twenty-four rows. They had been piece-working since late September and were now back on day work, waiting for George to give them orders for the day.

Harry and I made our way to the stable to help Vic harness up the horses.

"We will work the same as always," said Vic, "but we won't need a trace horse. The ground is frozen solid, and that will release a horse for other work, but you mustn't load too heavy. Just use your common sense and Jimmy – be very careful you don't get your foot caught in a narrow rut or something when you're driving to and fro. It's very dangerous out there with the ground rough and hard. Keep well out of the wheel alignment. Keep an eye on him, Bert. George won't be with him for a while. His got to set up a gang for carting and spreading shoddy around the blackcurrant bushes – good weather for that job, wheels will run clean." Shoddy was waste from the cotton mills, made up of soot and waste cotton, and was used as fertiliser.

Vic went on, "George is sending a labourer down to remove the beet tops covering your heaps. You'll have to watch him, don't let him get too far ahead of you – they don't want to be left uncovered too long in this cold, and he can always fall back and help you fill. And he's sending me down a load of straw to cover up at the clamp, so George is a busy man this morning."

So, the great door of December 1940 closed in on us. It got darker and darker and the cold intensified. Bitter winds blew in from the north, freezing our hands and feet, our faces almost numb. There was no shelter on this great, open plateau for man nor beast, but we struggled on until the last loads of beet were offloaded.

The ploughmen were following close behind us with their great crawler tractors, turning over the deep racked-up soil before it froze solid, their drivers wrapped up in great army overcoats and pulp bags around their legs to keep warm, for there were no cabs or heaters in those days. Very skilled people indeed, these ploughmen. Although they had powerful machines for their day, they had to know when to apply it and reduce it, for these big Ransome ploughs had a great weakness. Their cast-iron parts were very susceptible to frost and had to be handled very gently. But turning the land over – the best one could, under these awful conditions – was essential to get the winter frost into the newly turned soil to make a good seedbed for the spring barley that would follow.

With the completion of the sugarbeet season, George said, "You gotta go back to Alpheton Hall tomarra, Jimmy. And you, Bert. You have got to meet the boss on Church Field at seven o'clock tomarra morning."

Bert said, "That will be better for us, Jim boy, not so far to go to work. I'll meet you at the field gateway just before seven, so we're there before the boss man. Don't forget to bring your spade. We can't dig with our hands." We had to supply all the hand tools at our own expense in those days.

Blackthorn Winter

I left home around half past six to cycle my old familiar route along Aveley Lane and up the long track to Alpheton Hall. It was as dark as black hogs, and a bitter, icy rain was hitting the side of my face. I arrived at Church Field gateway, adjacent to the church. Not a soul in sight, not a sound to be heard. I waited in silence and suddenly heard footsteps approaching.

To my relief it was Bert. He was with Dick Talbot, who I'd worked with at Alpheton Hall before. They were both wrapped up in pulp bags against the foul weather. Dick greeted me, "Morning, Jim. At last we've all met up again. This is our old home, really, a bit like old times. Well, here comes the boss – that's the lights of his car."

We watched it twisting and turning on the long, narrow road to Alpheton Hall, then it stopped opposite the gateway to Church Field.

"Morning, everyone."

"Morning, sir."

"We'll walk along this ditch and I'll show you where I would like you to start."

We walked along together for a hundred yards or more, when he suddenly stopped. "Right, Dick, this is our starting point. This will be the main drain running in a straight line right to where the ditch ends. Its length will be about five hundred yards, depth will be three spits deep. First spit – topsoil to right side. Second spit – clay to left. Bottom spit dug with proper drainage spade to take a six-inch pipe. That will make it three foot cover to top of pipe."

That was going to be some work.

The boss continued, "You've got a natural fall, though it be slight, so you must hold your depth. At every one hundred yards, take an eye-drain off to the ditch and connect your main drain. I think that's about all. Any questions?"

"No," said Dick, "that's plain and simple enough, but what about a drainage spade?"

"There's a new drainage spade in the car boot, three new digging spades and a pipe boss, so you can take your own spades home. I'll leave them on the edge of the field and the lad will go up and get them for you."

Then he turned to me, "Now, sonny, your job is to help and assist Bert and Dick in any way you can for the next day or two. As work progresses, your main job will be this. First, help offload the pipes as they arrive at the farm. You must see they're stacked so they don't fall and break, and check the number of pipes delivered so they tally with tickets before you sign for them. Then, get a horse and tumbrel and take them over to the men who'll be laying them. Lay them out alongside the trench, ready.

"Now, there are workmen clearing out those huge clumps of blackthorn from Back Meadow. They'll lay them ready for you to load your tumbrel. Take them onto Church Field and just tip them in heaps. Then I want you to get a slasher and trim the blackthorn so they fit in the trench. Lay all the ends the same way to keep them neat and tidy.

"The last part of the job is this. When you've got the blackthorn laid over the pipes in the trench, cover them with clay. That will gradually push the bushes down. When you've got plenty of clay on top, get your horse and walk up and down the trench, that'll aid compaction.

"Dick and Bert will keep an eye on you, so do whatever they tell you. There's plenty to do, so there will be no need to stand around. The first thing you can do is go up to the wood and cut out eight or ten straight hazel sticks, then go back to Dick and help him set out the line of the drain with them."

I went off to the cart shed to collect a slasher and cut some string from a ball of binder twine. Then up Wood Drift and onto Wood Field – a very high point at Alpheton Hall – where I could look down into the valley below. Drizzly, cold rain was still falling, not a soul or a bird in sight.

The wind howled around my right ear-hole and water drips were falling from my flat cap and running down my face, mixed up with matter from my nose. It was the type of day when the cold went through the flesh into the bones and one gets shivers up and down the spine.

I entered the wood by the main glade next to Park Ley. It was dark and creepy in here. Just off the main glade, I found a good hazel stub loaded with just the sticks I required. I cut down about ten, trimmed them up and tied them together. Now for the mile-long walk back to Church Field.

When I got to Wood Drift, I had to stop and put down my

hazel sticks – my face and hands were frozen. I clapped my arms across my chest, banging my hands under my armpits to get some life back into them. As the feeling came back, as always they ached like hell. I managed to get my nose rag from my pocket and wipe my frozen face. Then, feeling a bit more comfortable, apart from my aching hands, I picked up my sticks and slung them over my shoulder for the last leg of the journey. When at last I reached Church Field, Dick and Bert were digging away.

"Good lad," said Dick. "Put them down there and pour yourself a cup of tea from your flask. Get both hands round the hot cup, and when you can feel the warm, get up and flack your hands across your chest."

"You need to get some hot tea and a sandwich in your belly. You'll soon be all right," said Bert.

"He should have known better than to send a boy all that way for hazels, it's a bloody long way to carry them. It's over a mile up there."

"It's a good thing he didn't send me, because I wouldn't have had the wind to plough all that way."

After we'd had our nineses, Dick said, "You can set the line out, Jimmy boy. Take it from where we've started digging, one hundred yards out from the ditch. Here, I'll help you get a start."

He put one stick five yards from where he was working. "Now, walk up the line and drop another one in at about a hundred yards, then come back fifty yards, and I'll eye you." That done, he said, "There you are, you can manage on your own from now, if you back-sight." That job complete, Dick said, "Go and get old Sharper from the stable and put her in a tumbrel and bring me up a load of pipes. Don't load too heavy – it's hard going now with all this rain."

I pulled up beside the trench with the first load. "Lay them out in a straight line, one yard off-set from the pipeline to leave room for trench arisings." Dick gave me a hand to offload. Then it was time for me to take Sharper to the stable and give her some dinner. Afterwards, Dick sent me down to Back Meadow to fetch up the blackthorn with the horse and cart.

"Before you go," he said, "put the front ladder on the tumbrel, that'll stop the bushes pricking her arss. Take a slasher with you in case some need to be trimmed. There's enough men down there to help you load and show you how to go on. Mind your hands – blackthorn bushes are sharper than needles. Once they get into the flesh, they'll go right through to the bone. Need proper leather gloves, really, but because of the war we won't get them. You'll just have to be careful. Perhaps we can find an old bit of leather in the stable somewhere. We can soon make an old glove with a bit or two of binder string and a sack needle. After all, you only want a left-handed one. You got your slasher in the right hand."

Off I went down Back Meadow with the old mare, Sharper. She was no show horse but she had a heart of gold and a lovely character. She was also rat-tailed and had brittle hooves so she had special shoes. She was small for a farm horse but willing and hard-working.

My brother Harry was with the workmen cutting the blackthorn. They came over and gave Sharper a pat on the nose. They showed me how to select the best pieces for the drain – long pieces with plenty of brushwood on the ends.

"Lay them all the same way on the cart. Don't, it will get into one great mess." They loaded the tumbrel for me, and trimmed bits and pieces off here and there.

"Get your rope ready, Jimmy." They roped it from one corner to another. "There you are, off you go. No, hold it a moment. You'll need a glove, boy. Oh my God, you can't handle them without a glove for your left hand."

They produced a piece of old binder canvas, cut two flat pieces with their shut knives, and with a sack needle they stitched the two bits together with old leather strips from an old horse collar.

"There you are, friend, now off you go."

Off I went with Sharper, feeling quite proud of my load of blackthorn, through the farmyard, onto the public lane, past the stackyard and Hall Farm's great timber barn, entering Church Field adjacent to the churchyard gateway. We turned right and I led Sharper along the headland, then left towards the site of the main drain.

Dick guided me. I removed the rope and the safety pin, pulled the tipping iron forward and up it went. "Forward a bit," shouted

Dick, then there it laid, a lovely neat bundle of bushes.

All winter long, week in, week out, in all weathers, Dick, Bert and myself laid these drains on Church Field. The pipes went in and the blackthorn was laid over the pipes, right to the top of the trench. The hard part for me was lifting the wet clay as back-fill on top of the bushes. It was really hard work, but much better when Dick told me to use a fork instead of a spade. Then I walked my old mare Sharper up and down the trench to compress the bushes, finally putting the topsoil on top of the clay – complete!

I feel I must tell you a bit about my two companions, Bert and Dick, both probably in their sixties. Great mates these two fellows.

First Dick, a lovely, happy, carefree man who had the most heartiest laugh. Nothing put Dick under the weather, he was as tough as old nails. He had a haircut about twice a year, a shave about every two months and a rat-tail moustache consisting of no more than twenty hairs in all. He had a permanent drip on his nose and when that let go, another formed instantly. He had no teeth whatsoever. His feet were always wet because of holes in his boots and he couldn't get new ones because of the war. He was nearly six feet tall and very thin with massive hands.

Now Bert was a more grizzly character, but I think this was because of his health. He seemed to have attacks of asthma but was quite a cheerful old soul when his breath was easier. He was quite a tough man. He did not let his disability stop him from working. He was very disciplined, probably coming from his army days, never late for work or early leaving off. Like Dick, he was tall and thin.

They made a great pair. They got on well together. Dick seemed to be the boss, and Bert happily let him lead. Dick did most of the digging. Bert shovelled the crumbs. On and on they went, day in, day out, in all weathers, never sheltering from wind or rain. The clocks were so that the morning start would be pitch dark as the three of us walked across the field to our drain to commence our day's work. They would start immediately and tell me to go back-filling.

"You must keep working, Jimmy boy, to keep yourself warm on these raw winter mornings."

One day, the boss turned up and queried the fall of Dick's

pipes. No slope on the trench, the water wouldn't drain out of the pipes meaning time and money wasted on the drainage scheme. They argued for a bit, then the boss man said, "How do you know?"

"Well now," said Dick. "If you're asking me to prove myself, I shall have to tell you I p*ss in it every twenty yards – nothing truer than water."

The boss said nothing but walked away.

"He must think we're bloody daft, digging here all bloody day on the wrong fall," said Dick.

After that, the boss must have been satisfied because we were left to get on with the job.

One wet December afternoon, Dick and Bert were working peacefully laying their pipes. Sharper and myself were some way off, working, when all of a sudden, this cold, dark day was split wide open with a terrific noise and voices shouting. My old mare took off like a bolt out of the blue. With my reflexes on full alert, I looked up and what I saw amazed me.

A German bomber was flying well below the low cloud bank. I could see the propellers swishing the rain and mist around and around. I could see the crew members looking out of the windows, and above all, I could see the black crosses under each wing.

I fell flat to the ground in the mud and slime and then, like a fleeing moment, it was gone. I jumped to my feet and saw my old workmates raise their heads above the trench, laughing like hell.

"You did the right thing, Jimmy boy," said Dick. "This is wartime. Now go and get your old mare. I can see her near the hedge a hundred yards down. Talk to her nicely and pat her neck to get the fear out of her."

Then, Sharper and I were sent to fetch old heaps of straw left lying about the stackyard, to lay along the trench-line ahead.

"Lay it on the ground a foot thick," said Dick. "The winter's in front of us and the earth will be frozen solid. We'll never be able to dig if we don't cover it to keep out the frost."

Soon enough, the days got colder and colder, everywhere was white with hoar frost. Dick had some advice for me in the early morning.

"Put a scarf around your ear-hole, Jimmy. Don't, they'll get frostbite and you'll know all about it. You haven't been out enough winters yet to get hardened off. And get a chaff bag for your old mare's back, and put it under the saddle and britchons, not on top. Poor old bugger will get frozen to death standing about here. Always remember to look after your hoss, Jimmy boy. Now go and light a big bronze. There's tons of sare [lumps of deadwood] in that hedge. Pull it out and break it up into small pieces. Use a handful of kisk [weed stalks] first, then the small bits of wood on top and put a match to it. When the flames are shooting out the top, then you can pile the big old sare chump on. And you can pull some big bits out of the hedge for us to sit on, as well."

I soon had a lovely bronze going, the flames shooting up looked good on this bitter morning. On the dot of nine o'clock, the three of us sat around toasting cheese on a crutch stick from the hedge – this, of course, was a farm worker's early morning picnic.

"Mustn't stay here too long," said Dick when our time was up. "If the boss man comes, he'll think we've been sitting round all day. But keep the fire going, Jimmy. We'll need it lunchtime – and by the way, if the boss asks you anything about the fire, you tell him to come and see me. Bosses don't like the working man to have any comfort. Their idea is we should work like hell to keep warm, but I haven't wintered and summered this man up yet, so I shan't condemn him until I have."

Just before midday, I rounded up the fire, and Dick and Bert sat on their old wood seat pieces. From their frail baskets, they opened up their little hessian grub bags, and pulled out a bottle of cold, black tea wrapped in an old grey army wool sock, and sat it as near to the fire as they dare, as too much heat would burst the bottle. "Just to take the chill off," said Bert. As they ate their half-loaf with a hole cut in for a lump of butter and peeled an onion, they chatted away about the war.

"They stuck the fear of hell into the captain of the Graf Spee – he blew the bugger up. He knew better than coming out of the river into the open sea."

Both men were First World War veterans and were following this war very closely and with great suspicion. They did not really trust our High Command, having lost faith in them some years ago.

After eating, Bert removed a fag from its packet, tapped both ends hard on the outside case and returned the case to his pocket. He lit up and the smoke curled up into the cold December air. Dick was enjoying his pipe of tobacco and they sat in silence together. Both men seemed very content and interested in their work.

Bert broke the silence. "Can you hear that, Dick?"

"What's that?"

"The wind in that tree."

"I can, mett [mate]."

"That's moving round to north-north-east."

"Seems all the signs of snow on the way."

"Yes and it's three minutes to one, so we'd better stroll back."

They kept their time to the minute and were very conscientious workers. It was so warm and cosy, sitting around the blazing bronze, I felt reluctant to move. However, back to work it was. I went and got Sharper away from her treacled chaff and crushed oats and we got down to Back Meadow again. The labourers were making progress in clearing huge areas of blackthorn. They always helped me load the tumbrel.

A crawler tractor and disc plough was working in cleared areas, attempting to cut the roots of the blackthorn to stop its re-growth. Men with picks and mattocks were cutting off the roots which the ploughs couldn't manage. Huge fires were burning up the trash and roots. It was a very intensive working area. I watched the tractor and plough for a bit and was very impressed by what the plough was doing to the roots.

We kept working until half past four, then Dick said it was time to take Sharper back to the stable. "By the time you get her harness off and feed her, it will be five o'clock. We've all had enough out here today in the cold, it takes its toll on us olduns. We need some hot grub in our guts."

The three of us met up in the cart shed, where Dick and Bert removed the hessian pulp bags from their legs and from around their waist. These were placed between the spokes of one of the parked harvest wagons, together with the string which was stretched and hung up straight, ready for the morning.

"Well, we'll make our way home, old partner," said Bert, and with our farewells said, Dick set off up Church Lane to Alpheton. These men never parted at the end of day without wishing each other a warm 'Goodnight, mett'.

Our House Did Not Always Smell Of Violets
The lights of Alpheton Hall glowed as we made our way towards Bridge Street, out of the valley basin. The Hall was now occupied by two Alston Estate workers and their families. Tom Mott, the horseman, had moved in from the Black House in Church Lane – tarred pitch black against the damp – with my second cousins Evelyn, Nancy and Beryl Mott. Sam Swallow, the foreman, occupied the other half.

The lights of the Hall were soon a memory, as we pushed our bikes into the cold and dark. The stars were shining in a clear sky and it froze like hell. On reaching the track that led down to Aveley Lane. Bert said, "I think I'll walk all the way home. It's bloody icy for me to sit on this thing."

"I'll walk with you," I said.

He looked a poor, pathetic figure, pushing his cycle with a slight stoop, in his flat black cap and long overcoat. His frail basket cord seemed tight around his neck, but he did nothing to adjust it. We would stop now and again, for the cold night air made him cough. The night was silent, the cold intense, just the sound of stones, moving under our feet.

Bert said, "It's Christmas next week. We'll get a couple of days off, at least. We can stay in the warm around our firesides and have a pint or two in the Rose and Crown. I'm looking forward to a couple of days' rest."

"Well, perhaps Father Christmas will pay us a visit, Bert."

"That's most unlikely. His bloody stags couldn't pull a sleigh full of feathers across Suffolk fields of clay, let alone loaded with toys and the old man sitting on there."

At that moment, this quiet night was split open as a lone Wellington bomber made its way across the night sky, flying very, very low just ahead of us, west to east.

"Where the hell do he think his off to? He ain't going to do no bloody good over there on a cold, dark night like this. He may just as well turn round and go back home."

Within seconds, the plane was gone and the silence returned to the night. We had, by now, reached Aveley Lane and the tar and stone road. Bert walked slowly, well into the verge as hobnail boots and the ice-covered surfaces did not mix. At last, we reached the pathway to Bert's house. "Farewell, Jim boy, thanks for walking with me."

I stepped into my mother's cottage, where the old black kettle was, as always, singing on top of the old oven hotplate.

"Come on, Jim. You're late home."

"Walked all the way home with Bert. Everywhere's covered with ice. He dared not ride his bicycle and he had to be careful when he walked."

"It's good of you to walk with him. He could slip and break his leg and no-one would last long laying out there tonight, young or old." Liz was busy with the dinner. "It's sprats, tonight."

"Yes, I can smell them."

"Here's a bit of newspaper to put the heads and backbones on. Your father eat the lot, but you don't eat those bits."

My father looked up and smiled.

"Get them into you, Jim," said Harry. "Lovely grub on a night like this."

Nice and warm, and with our bellies full, we all sat around in the kitchen afterwards in the yellow light of the old single burner oil lamp. My father stoked the fire up from the heap of logs in the hearth. We sat around with our working clothes on, and as Wally and Jep looked after pigs and cattle at the mill, when they warmed up the house did not always smell of violets.

Mother said, "Don't forget, after the pigs have finished drinking, turn those cast iron troughs upside down. Any water left in them, and they'll crack in this severe frost. Make sure everything has got a good warm bed, and don't forget the poor bloody old dog – he want looking after, too."

So my father and older brothers put their hats and winter coats on, lit their hurricane lanterns and disappeared outside to feed the pigs, rabbits, chickens and collect the eggs – some at the house and some at the allotments.

Water was our big problem in severe winters. It wasn't possible to store it in buckets, or any containers overnight, or for any length of time. It just turned to ice. All water for the animals had to be fetched from the spring on Spring Meadow, which never froze because it ran in at the bottom and was forced out at the top. All of us living in this tiny hamlet of Bridge Street were lucky to have such a great asset, and we were never short of water.

In the dark and perishing cold of another winter morning, I arrived at the cart shed the next day. My old pal, Bert, sat in there on his drainpipe, smoking his Woodbine. He had two small hessian bags tied around his boots to stop him slipping on the ice. Dick arrived.

"Morning Bert, hello Jimmy. Rum travelling this morning."

"You're telling me," said Bert. "Talk about freezing the balls off an iron monkey. I don't know that it ain't beginning to touch me up a little."

We had to keep moving.

"Come with us, Jimmy," said Dick. "You can leave the old mare in the stable until it get daylight."

We made our way across the stackyard together and back onto Church Field, walking along the headland, then up to our drain. Dick pulled the shovels out from under an old sack, and both men slipped their boot irons on then started digging.

"You'd better be putting the blackthorn over the pipes, Jimmy," said Dick, "and backfill the clay on top. Keep working to keep yourself hot."

Lights flashed in the field gateway and the boss man came walking towards us. He went over to talk to Dick and Bert first, then headed towards me, inspecting Dick's pipe-laying in the trench.

He walked past me, saying, "Good morning, sonny."

"Good morning, sir," said I.

He walked on, inspecting my work, then turning back to me, he said, "How old are you?"

"Fifteen, sir."

"Well, you're making a very good job of bushing up and backfilling, but where are your gloves?"

"We can't buy gloves, sir."

"How on earth do you manage, then?"

"Well, I don't need one for my right hand, because that's my slasher hand. For my left hand, I have an old Wellington top."

"That's ridiculous," he said. "One must have protective clothing, war or no war. I will look into it." And with that, he went back and talked to Dick.

At half past eight, Dick said, "Go and light the fire, Jimmy, ready for breakfast."

I walked down to the headland, down into the ditch, and pulled some good pieces of sare wood from the ancient hedgerow. I had a lovely bronze going in no time. I piled on the wood then went back to work until Dick shouted nineses.

We sat there warming ourselves and I pulled a lump of cheese from my lunch bag and toasted it over the fire with a crotch stick cut from the hedgerow. It tasted gorgeous. Out here on this frosty morning, after they'd finished eating, Dick and Bert sat in silence smoking their tobacco. The wood smoke from our fire climbed lazily into the bleak winter sky, the embers glowed and faded in the light, whispering breeze. My two old pals were drifting off into the world of nod. I removed Bert's lighted cigarette from between his fingers and threw it into the fire.

Hard work, hard times, hard winters had taken their toll. I would have let them dream on, but it was time to go back to work.

"Come on," I said. "We mustn't sit here any longer."

"Bugger me," said Dick. "I nearly dropped off to sleep."

"I was bloody near gone, as well," said Bert. "It's the heat from the fire. I thought I had a fag on. I must have been dreaming."

"Well, Jimmy," said Dick, "today is Friday and Tuesday is Christmas Day. You've got to get mangol-worzels for the stockman to use over the Christmas holiday, but you've got to get enough blackthorn up here as well, to bush up the trench tight. We mustn't leave any bit of trench open – if a thaw come, the trench could cave in, then we'd have a bloody job on our hands. So you've got today, Saturday morning and all day Monday. Jimmy is going to be a busy lad – and keep your north eye open because the man we work for will be round to pay our wages."

So for the rest of the day, I carted blackthorn from Back Meadow to the trench line, as well as keeping Dick supplied with drainpipes. At five o'clock, I took Sharper to the pond for a drink and on to the stable for her food. By that time, it was dark and the cold was intense. The stars glittered like diamonds in the sky, and thousands of birds were tucked up on the beams of the stable and cattle yards keeping warm from the cattle's body heat.

But I was not to make my way home just yet. Dick, Bert and myself were walking through the farmyard, when headlights shone through the darkness.

"It's a bloody lorry," said Dick.

It pulled up beside us. The driver put his head out of the window and shouted, "Drainpipes, mate."

"Right over here, beside this wall," said Dick, then turned to us. "Run and get our hand rubbers, we'll have to protect our hands."

The driver jumped up on the lorry and pitched the pipes to us, and wearing our squares of rubber cut out of old lorry tube, we caught them and placed them on the stack, with Dick building up the ends so they wouldn't roll or slip.

We finished around half past six and I walked home with Bert to keep him company, for this had been a long, cold day. I walked into Rose Cottage at half past seven.

"Come on," said Liz. "This is too much – out there in this weather with no hot food all these hours. Come on, I've got soup and twenty-minute swimmers – your brother shot a pheasant up the garden, that'll make the soup taste good."

I looked round the empty kitchen. "Where is everybody?"

"All out feeding the pigs and seeing to the animals. Water's the biggest problem, it's no sooner in than it's solid. The ice is on it in minutes. Then they've got all the logs to saw up and split for Christmas, we've got to have a stack near the house. With Christmas Day on Tuesday, there's still a few cockerels to pluck and dress. Perhaps you could give a hand tomorrow night. I'd like to get finished and labelled up. I only need another half-dozen to complete the orders."

"I'll give you a hand as long as you promise to give me a clean shirt and vest and a big kettleful of hot water so I can have a good wash down. I've had enough of chicken lice dancing on my back and in my hair."

"I'll grant you all that."

"Good, then I'll help."

Saturday was another raw morning, back at Alpheton Hall. I harnessed up my old mare, Sharper. A pale yellow light came from the small bottle of TVO, which was all that lit the stable. A string wick had been threaded through a hole in the metal screw-cap. Sharper and I made our way to the cart shed to collect our tumbrel. Men were hammering away at the pond in a desperate effort to keep it clear of ice for the farm stock. Their blows were ringing out through the farm buildings on this otherwise silent morning.

Everywhere there was ice. Sharper seemed to be aware of the danger and walked very slowly. At the mangol clamp, I had to remove tons of straw to gain access but at last there they were, beautiful, round, bright orange globes with small yellow and green leaves sprouting from their crowns. They had a glow about them, tucked up in their dark, frost-free cave. I stabbed them one by one with my two-tined fork and bounced them off into the tumbrel.

After three loads Sam Hart, the stockman, said, "That's enough. Just help me pull the tarpaulin over and it'll keep the biggest part of the frost out. I hope you sealed the clamp up well with straw again? It's time to put your old mare up – twelve o'clock finish on Saturday and it's past that now. I'm off home."

Then he'd gone. I took dear old Sharper to the pond for a drink, then to the stable. I took off her harness and gave her crushed oats and treacled chaff for her dinner.

On Monday, it was Christmas Eve. I decided to walk to work. I left home early at six o'clock and made my way to Spring Meadow, following the footpath which ran beside the Chad. It was cold, and the echoes of a barking dog could be heard miles away in the distance. There was no wind, it was wild, dark and absolutely lovely.

At the cart shed, Bert sat with his fag aglow, puffing Woodbine smoke into the air. "Hello, Jimmy. Did you walk up here this morning? You didn't come by the farm track."

"No, I came by the fields."

"How did you get over the river?"

"It's iced over."

"You must be bloody mad, clambering over bloody stiles, five-bar gates and skidding over iced-up rivers at this time of morning. It's pitch dark and freezing like hell. Did you see anyone?"

"Not a soul."

"No, you're the only soul stupid enough to be out there on a day like this."

Dick arrived. "You're early, Jimmy – p*ssed the bed or something? Because I reckon I've drained off ten times since I left my old cottage this morning. What with that and a dripping snout, these sharp frosts don't half tickle up some parts of my old frame. Never mind, it's Christmas Eve – tonight we'll have a drink in the Rose and Crown. You come in there, Jimmy? How old are you?"

"Fifteen."

"Well, the old girl will let you in, just for once. After all, it is wartime, no need to be that strict. I'll have a word with her."

"She's afraid of the police," said Bert.

"No need to be. There's only bloody granddads and specials now the young ones have been called up. Well, Bert, me old mett, we'd better get to our land drain. That'll be cold comfort today. Jimmy, you've got to spend the day with the stockman again, so you'd better get your horse and cart."

Sam was glad to have help. "Right, first we'll feed the stock, then drive them down to the pond for a drink. We'll litter up the yards, that's including the horse yard, and we should complete strawing up by lunchtime. This afternoon we must mix up enough food for Christmas Day, Boxing Day and the first feed for Thursday morning. So we'll need chaff, thrown out of the chaff house onto the barn floor, twelve bags of barley meal from the mill house and at least twelve barrowloads of mangol-worzels to put through the mincer.

"Then we have got to feed all the cattle and drive them down to the pond for a drink this afternoon. So we've got a hell of a busy day in front of us. We'll have to work in the dark because there are no lights – we haven't even got a hurricane lantern. Never mind, we'll make it somehow."

We worked on all day with hardly a break. At five o'clock, the great barn doors opened and in came Bert and Dick.

"How are you getting on, my old partners?"

"Got a bit to do, yet," said Sam. "Hell of a lot of work to getting forward like this. Jimmy and I have earned our Christmas holiday. We've done four days' work in two."

"Well, we'll stay on and give you a hand, won't we, Bert," said Dick. "What do you want us to do?"

"Mix up those four heaps of chaff, put on one sack of barley meal, four bushels of ground-up mangols and ten shovels of beet pulp to each heap. Jimmy will keep grinding up mangols and I'll keep filling the hopper."

Dick said, "Is anyone coming in to break the ice in the morning?"

"Christ, yes," said Sam. "That is a must."

It was dark, cold and eerie in this great timbered barn and I did not wander far from my old workmates.

"There," said Sam, "that's it. Thanks, everyone for your help."

"It would be much better if you had a lantern. Have you asked for one?"

"No," said Sam.

"Well, you won't get one if you don't ask. How the hell would we get on in an emergency, all these bloody cattle here and haven't got a light. I'll speak to the boss – he'll get one. Blast, he got Jimmy a new pair of gloves and Bert and me a new spade apiece. He's not that bloody tight. Anyway, let's get home. Got to celebrate tonight in the Rose and Crown, haven't we, Jimmy."

Gingcrade And Auld Lang Syne 1940

There was no bright star to guide us home that night before Christmas as I walked home with Bert, but there was someone who provided us with the right sense of direction, for we both arrived home safely.

I lifted the latch on Rose Cottage door. Liz had flames shooting up the chimney and our old, black kettle could still sing, even if she was getting her bottom burned.

"Come on, Jim boy – nearly seven o'clock and Christmas Eve.

What's the excuse tonight? Your dinner's been keeping warm in the oven. Not so nice now."

"Never mind, Mother. Don't keep worrying. There are thousands worse off than us, this year."

"How right you are. Your sisters put up a few paper chains this afternoon, make it a bit like Christmas. All the firewood is in, the cockerel's ready, and I managed to get enough stuff to make a Christmas pudding – albeit a wartime one. Now come on and give yourself a good wash down. There's no chance of you bathing in the outside wash-house this weather, so I have put a bowl of water in your bedroom with your clean clothes. Come on, smarten yourself up for Christmas – we have to stop moaning and make the best of what we've got."

Into the Rose and Crown, shining like a new penny, the old Sunlight soap had done its job. The landlady, Mrs Penborough, greeted me. "You may go into the tap room with the older men, but because of your age, you can only have gingerade."

"Thank you, lady," I said. I could hear the sound of laughter coming from the tap room, and my father's voice. In there with him sat my brother Harry, now seventeen, George Day and my old workmates Dick and Bert, Sid Bugg, Tom Bush and lots more.

An open fire blazed away in the grate and logs lay on the hearth which the customers had brought in, supplying their own fuel in wartime Britain. The room was full of tobacco smoke. Old-timers and young men were chattering away.

The landlady came in and out with orders on a tray. All of a sudden, from across the room, came a few notes of music. I looked up, and Tom Bush had taken his concertina from its box and a loud cheer went up.

He played 'To Be A Farmer's Boy' and 'Only A Beautiful Picture.' By now, the men were quite merry. My old pal, Dick, stood up and sang 'I Put Aside My Plough'. Someone else sang the sad song 'Just Break The News To Mother', with the words 'Tell her that I still love her, kiss her dear sweet lips for me, because I'm not coming home. Tell her there is no other to take the place of mother,' and so on. Then 'The Homestead', 'Pack Up Your Troubles', 'The Sailor Boy', and lots more I cannot now remember.

Then a voice screamed across the tap room, "Last orders, please."

Tom packed up his music box. All the old and young stood up and sang 'Auld Lang Syne' unaccompanied, and that was the end of our Christmas Eve party in December 1940.

They bid each other goodnight and a merry Christmas, then to their cottage homes for a Suffolk supper of bread, cheese and pickled onions. Then up the wooden hill to their feather beds and above them, the sparrows were already fast asleep, warm and deep inside the straw thatch.

As the clock struck twelve and the first minutes of Christmas Day ticked away, all was still, dark and quiet at Rose Cottage. In the kitchen and pantry, the little grey mice that lived here with us crept from their hidey holes in the old beams and floors and tiptoed across the old coconut matting. They gathered up all the crumbs, then searched the pantry for anything that was eatable and when their bellies were full or they could find no more, they retired under the trivet of the still warm kitchen range to sleep the rest of the night away, huddled up in the warm.

So you can see we catered for almost everything in those days, welcome and unwelcomed guests. Four or five mousetraps were constantly in use, trapping on average about three a week, but another three or four moved in, and our ginger cat took his share. When they thrashed the stacks across the meadow at Ford Hall, we were invaded by them and had to put down poison along the outside walls of the old cottage. It was a desperate bid to control the numbers getting into the house but we never won, they were always there.

We also had living with us huge black beetles, woodlice and ticking spiders. We also had some mysterious thing that used to do five or six laps around the loft area, three or four times a year. We called him or her 'Bullace', but it never showed its face.

On one of our bedroom staircases, footsteps could be heard coming up the stairs but they never reached the top and we never saw anything. Perhaps it did reach the top and we did not know because we had our heads under the sheets.

Now forget all the creepy crawlies that surrounded us, because today was Christmas Day, 1940. In wartime Britain the food for us was still good, as we had home-reared chickens and home-grown vegetables. But this Christmastide, things were not quite the same. The church bells of Long Melford and Lavenham were silent, their echoes no longer heard in Lineage and Spelthorne Woods.

Searchlights had replaced the Star of Bethlehem that we kids looked upwards to the heavens for. There was no glitter this Christmas, only from the frost outside. Father Christmas will not come this year, that's for sure, but Adolf Hitler might.

On Boxing morning, off I went to Alpheton Hall to meet all the workers there, for today was Rabbiting Day for those of us who lived and worked in the countryside. We all met outside the old cart shed, about fifteen of us. Some were carrying ferrets, others twelve-bore and four-ten guns, rabbiting spades, nets, probing spears and a collection of mongrel dogs that all loved the cart shed posts.

"Right, off we go," said Sid Andrews, part-time Keeper of the Lavenham Lodge Estate. He never did swear but he might as well have done, as 'drat', 'darn' and 'blow' did the job for him, and it was 'blow this' and 'blow that' all day long.

We all followed him down Back Meadow to some great 'old holds' as we called the great rabbit earths. Men moved forward with slashers and cleared the area of blackthorn, others moved on to drive the hedgerows and some made their own arrangements. Sid insisted every gang would work well out of each other's shotgun range. I stayed with the first gang, who netted some holes and left some open. I was given my job.

"You, Jimmy, go well out on the meadow and search in the rough grass for bolt holes. If you find some, don't touch them – just put a stick up, so the men with guns can keep them covered."

When everything was set up we were told to move away for fifteen minutes, so the area went quiet as we crept away. Two polecat ferrets were lifted from their box and they swiftly disappeared down the holes. We stood, watched, and waited. The net men stood at the back of the holes, so the rabbits wouldn't see them. It was so quiet, my heart was pounding. Then all hell was let loose. Nets jumped up high in the air and men were scrambling to catch the struggling rabbits caught up in the nets. Guns blazed away as rabbits streaked out of the holes left un-netted. Dogs were screaming to be let off their leashes to join in the fun.

Amongst the noise and confusion, some men were shouting, "Jimmy! Jimmy! Near your feet!" Two rabbits were struggling in the nets, hitting against my legs and feet in an effort to escape. I bent down and tightened one drawstring, putting my foot on it to hold it. Then I bent and grabbed the other net and rabbit. Within seconds, two men ran up and took over, leaving me to set the nets again.

And then it was all over. The last shot rang out as the last rabbit made its break for freedom. All that was left to do was to clear up and catch the ferrets. The nets were pulled up. The dead rabbits were all hocked – one rear leg twisted through the other – with all the shot ones threaded onto one pole and all the clean-killed on another.

The ferrets were still down the rabbit hole somewhere, but the men knew what to do. They took one rabbit, gutted it and lay its innards just outside the hole. The ferrets soon got a whiff of this and after a few minutes they came out for the bait. They didn't see the man lying flat on his belly at the back of the hole, or the big hand that grabbed them and returned them to their box.

By three in the afternoon we all had a brace of rabbits, one clean-killed and one shot. The rest was sold, and the money divided. I made my way home down the private track from Alpheton Hall to Bridge Street. It was icy and I was pleased to have reached my old thatched homestead as I was bitterly cold. I lifted the latch and walked in. The family all looked nice and comfy, sitting around the kitchen range and the old cooker looked red hot.

"Come in, Jim. You must want a job, being out there rabbiting on a bleak old day like this. Hang that brace on the back door, then come and sit by the fire and get yourself warmed up," said Liz.

I wasn't going to get too comfy yet, though. Mother's rules meant a strip-wash and change.

"Give us a knock when you're ready, and I'll wash ya back. You're not sitting around smelling of rabbits and ferrets on Boxing night – and not no other night! So come on, get yourself moving."

Then I joined the family, all sat around the wood-burning fires in the kitchen and front room reading magazines like 'John Bull', 'The Red Letter', and old copies of 'Farmer's Weekly', and comics. We had quite a good wartime tea. Liz had managed a little bit extra: cold pork, cold chicken, beetroot, homemade pickles, home-baked seedy cake, shortcake, with jam puffs for the young ones.

We counted our blessings, as we had learned a new word – Blitz. In London, German bombers had been pounding away night after night since September. As we sat cosy and warm in Rose Cottage, at the back of our minds we knew there were many poor souls who had lost their homes this Christmas.

Then it was Thursday, Christmas holiday over, and back to work on the drainage field at the tail end of 1940. Out here at Alpheton Hall, it was another bitter cold morning. I met Dick and Bert in the cart shed.

"Come on, Jimmy, we had better get out on that field. The Governor is sure to be around this morning." We walked across the field to our drainage trench.

"Not a lot of cheer out here today, Bert," said Dick.

"No," replied Bert. "Nothing else is so bloody silly as us, even the birds are still in bed."

"Well," said Dick, "they'll find out there is not a lot to sing about when they do get up. Hello, here he comes. I can see the lights of his car coming down the hill."

Within ten minutes, he was beside us.

"Morning, Dick."

"Morning, sir."

"I would like the lad to go with the stockman this morning to help him catch up after the holiday."

"Well," said Dick. "It's like this. You want Jimmy today, you want Jimmy tomorrow to help catch up for the weekend, you'll want Jimmy again on Monday to catch up again….. Well, you're the boss, you find our wages, you do what you like as long as you know how many hours Jimmy is helping with the stock and how many hours he is with me. I only had him about two half-days last week, but don't blame me if progress here goes behind."

Manpower was low, farms were mostly kept going with old men and boys helping the skilled workers not drafted into the army and we knew that as soon as we turned eighteen, we had to expect our call-up papers. The boss considered the problem.

"I see your point, Dick. If you can spare Jimmy, just for today, I'll make other arrangements for the rest."

"All right," Dick agreed, "but I'd like to keep Jimmy with me."

I went with the stockman. The stock at Alpheton Hall were all beef cattle. I think they were bought in from Ireland. They were mostly about one-year-olds, perhaps about one hundred total. They were yarded up from October to the end of March. They were useful because they stamped up the straw from these great grain fields which littered the cattle yards, to make muck which was later transported to manure the fields.

The cattle also ate up vast amounts of sugarbeet tops, which would have been wasted otherwise; sugarbeet pulp – a by-product of the Bury St Edmunds sugarbeet factory; barley straw chaff produced on the farm by a chaff-cutter machine; and a small amount of barleymeal ground up on the farm mill.

At the beginning of April they would be turned out onto the meadows where they grazed all summer at their leisure, and then back they came to the yards for their final year on the farm. Their food intake was increased and of better quality as their purpose now was to put on weight ready for the spring beef market and for the farmer to get a return on his capital.

They would never really make good beef because of the diet they had been fed on but nevertheless, they had done the job they were purchased for. Good beef cattle, top-grade, never go out to grass but spend their entire life in sheds or yards on a very rich diet.

The days and weeks of the bleak, cold dark winter gradually died away. The hard frozen earth gave way to mud and water. Our land drain was nearing completion but it was hard and heavy going. The three of us were now equipped with mud scrapers for our boots, made with wood from the hedgerow. To walk or to work was almost impossible. Bert said, "It would help if we could get our feet out of the sticky stuff but you can't bloody well do it."

"Aar, it's a bloody hard job," said Dick. "Next thing will be the March winds tickling round our arss. That'll be enough to turn heavy clay like this to dust and if we don't treat that with respect and wrap up well against it, it will turn us into dust as well. It's a cruel and bitter wind for people like us who have to face its wrath, but it's more friend than enemy to the East Anglian farmer. It turns his fields into gold dust but 'Farmer Fred' won't agree to that. He's never made gold in his life, poor old thing."

The great East Anglian landscape was now waking up from its long winter sleep. Buds of the hazel shrubs, catkins, first peep at the world and in the hedgerows, wild plums are showered in their white blossom. As Dick had predicted, the bitter cold east wind arrived. It howled around the houses and farm buildings bringing with it crazy winter showers of sleet and snow. Dick had been taken from us to go harrowing behind the old Smythe drill. Bert was left behind to carry out the last remaining jobs to our land drain.

I was sent off to the blacksmith's to collect fifteen handmade dock irons – tall hand tools, made to weed out the deep tap-rooted docks from compacted land. I had to make three journeys, tying five to the crossbar of my bicycle on each visit. As you will have guessed, I was paid no mileage money for the use of my bike.

Huge March dust clouds appeared on the bare land and fields as the ducksfoot harrows lashed deep into the friable March tilth, pulled by the great crawler tractors of Alpheton Hall, their drivers working from sun-up to sundown to create the perfect seedbed, and speed was essential. All the skilled men on the farm were out seed drilling, harrowing and top-dressing.

Two Boys Are Nothing

Winter work such as hedging, ditching and draining were now stood down. All the labourers and boys were sent to Church Field. Fifteen of us, equipped with dock irons and an assortment of old buckets, marched onto Church Field on this lovely April morning. The sun was rising bright over Felixstowe way and the morning was clear as crystal as we viewed the barrage balloons on the east coast.

The bitter east wind had lost its ferocity and a gentle, sweet-smelling breeze was blowing east to west, making the growing wheat on this forty-acre field dance, bend and bow to its command. It was a perfect spring morning as we stretched ourselves out in line, each searching a five-yard area, digging out the long-rooted docks and putting them in our buckets. Harry was there, and Jack Long – the great talented cricketer of my schooldays. Barney Andrews was with me, and Dusty Frost was alongside his older brother Harold who had now come to work at Alpheton Hall. As the sun rose higher into the sky, the skylarks rose with it on their vertical singing flights. The more they sang, the higher they rose into the light morning air. On reaching the top of their upward flight, they would stop singing and drop to earth like a stone. Here, near their landing point, us young ones in the docking pack would find their nests in a little hole in the field, full of nestlings with mouths wide open. We would dig into the soil with our dock irons and find little worms and break them into small pieces and drop them into their open mouths. They appeared to love it, but our behaviour did not suit the older men. They soon brought us back into line.

"Come on and get those bloody docks out and behave yourselves and do the job you're supposed to do. Birds are quite capable of feeding their young without your help. Now stand your dock irons in the ground, lads, or you won't know where to start back – it's nineses time."

We sat on the brew of the field with our legs dangling down towards the ditch. We all had a pulp bag under our rears as protection from ant nests and damp grass. Here and there were huge clumps of primroses tucked well down in the thick grass, on the opposite bank, well out of the way of Suffolk's bitter east wind should it decide to blow. Young leaves were bursting out in all the hedgerows and the blackthorn blossom hung white and heavy. On the ground, in every ditch and brew, the peggles were out in bloom or their buds about to burst. Blackthorn and peggles in bloom together were a sure sign of cold weather, sometimes accompanied by powerful hail, sleet or snowstorms, commonly known as a 'blackthorn winter'. But today was one of those lovely April days, what the old men called a weather breeder.

"You don't want to take your jackets off, you silly young buggers. You'll want your overcoat on tomorrow." The old stagers had wintered and summered the Suffolk scene for many a year and it would take a lot more than a couple of days of April sunshine for them to remove any garment.

We continued with our docking, working in the same direction as the corn was drilled. Two older men followed the drill wheelings on the outsides of the line and us young ones (or as they said, 'silly little buggers') were herded into the middle of the row and they kept a north eye on us. Even a simple job, like docking, had to be done and done correctly. As the foreman said, "One boy is half a man, two boys are nothing."

But as farmers' boys, we had our laughs.

One old man would say to the other, "My old leg don't half take on this morning."

"Why's that?" said the other.

"Screws, I reckon, right in the thick part of my leg."

"Put some hoss oils on it. That will bloody soon put that right. There's plenty in the stable but don't forget to wash your hands after. Get that in the wrong place and that'll make yer eyes water – strong stuff that!"

So it seems hoss oils cured their few ailments and what hoss oils didn't cure, Greene King did. Chewing tobacco pickled their teeth so they did not need a dentist. They never swallowed a tablet in their lives and most lived into their late seventies or eighties. Remarkable, isn't it? Simplicity. The answer is diet and work.

We stayed on docking Church Field for five to six weeks and enjoyed every day we were there. Some days in April it was warm and some were bitterly cold, but it was pure joy after the winter we had been through.

Now it was May and we moved onto the beet fields. The foreman sent me to lead the horse on the horse hoe, with Tom Mott. The rest of the docking team were sent chopping out sugarbeet, leaving one little plant around ten to eleven inches from the next, to grow on to a big sugarbeet.

Our horse hoe worked two rows at one pass. It was equipped with discs to cut down close to the seedling beet, and 'L'-shaped hoes followed the discs. We worked twelve-hour days, and until four in the afternoon some Saturdays, to keep in front of the beet hoers, who were working fast on piecework.

Progress was slow as we could not work continuous. The horses had to be rested for five or ten minutes at the end of each bout, depending on the terrain, as they were pulling heavy implements.

On Sundays, the horses had a day off from their heavy labours and had a well-earned rest in lovely green and wildflower meadows. It was also the worker's day of rest and I and my friends from the hamlet would stroll down to the wetlands at the rear of Ford Hall, following the line of the Chad – the same place we walked and played as schoolboys. On Sunday afternoons, we played football on Spring Meadow and lazed on the sweet-smelling grass. The older boys were nearly eighteen, when our army call-up papers would arrive, but we did not hardly talk about it. We just took it as a matter of course, I suppose.

In those great sugarbeet fields at Alpheton Hall row after row, acre after acre stretched out before us. It looked impossible for that vast acreage to be chopped out by hand-hoeing. Men and sugarbeet wilted under the midday sun. Most of us were tanned to a hazelnut brown, sitting together under the shade of a big-top elm or overhanging hedge to eat our lunch. After the first hoeing of beet was completed, some of the men moved on to hoeing weeds from around the currant bushes at the Lavenham Lodge farms.

In the evenings, most of us enjoyed a pint in the Alpheton 'Lion' or Bridge Street 'Rose'. It was a great and simple way of life, but of course, it was our way of life. We did not know anything else. It was how our fathers and grandfathers had lived and we never imagined it could change.

The Alston farms covered land in neighbouring villages, as well as Alpheton. Dusty Frost, Barney Andrews, my brother Harry and myself were sent to work all over the place from time to time. Sometimes I did not see Harry all day, until our evening meal around the kitchen table.

Late spring was haysel time. The head horseman, Tom, cut the fresh green grass with his pair of horses and grass mower, while I sharpened the knives. About every two rounds he would shout and wave his hand and I would take the newly-sharpened knife and bring the blunt one back. The knife was clamped to a table while I sharpened it with a file.

It was wonderful being out here in the newly-cut grass-scented air, content and fifteen. I was standing there thinking what a wonderful place the world really was, when Sam Swallow, the Alpheton foreman turned up.

"Hello, Jimmy boy. Got any gaspers?"

I had to disappoint him. "No, can't get none. Sold out until Monday."

"Bloody war, I can't do without a gasper. Well don't forget to get me a packet or two on Monday then. Come on, let's have a word with Tom."

We stood beside the standing grass and when at last Tom arrived, Sam said, "Hello, bloody Tommy Tucker, where the hell have you been? Been waiting here an hour."

Tom laughed. "Fair pull up that far side, you know. Hard work for a pair of horses, grass mowing. You ain't on Lavenham Lodge plain now – this is Alpheton Hall. You're beginning to find that out. Now you know why George Colson had fine big horses. Could really do with three horses, especially up the hill. Have to rest quite a while to get their wind back."

" Well, we musn't kill 'em or break their hearts. How long will it take you to cut this lot?"

"Four or five days."

"That long? In that case, I'll send Dick in this afternoon with the swath turner and he'll get going on what you cut first."

In the weeks that followed, the hay was cut, turned and put into haycocks. At half past eight on a perfect June morning, the hay wagons rolled into this sweet-smelling hayfield. The pitchers and loaders, equipped with their frail baskets, pitchforks and wagon ropes were ready for work, and within an hour the first load was ready and roped.

"There you are, Jimmy boy. Off you go and plumb those bloody furrows."

"Come on, Captain." I felt the horse lay hard into his collar, the chains tighten, and gradually the great wooden iron-bound wheels turned and I led him forward, the old wagon timbers creaking under the weight of the heavy load.

As I drove along, everywhere was a picture to behold: the haymakers with their pitchforks, the hay wagons, the haycocks, the hedgerows hanging with garlands of wild roses. Up ahead of me, as I dodged in and out of the haycocks with my horse and great ancient wagon loaded with hay, stood the humble little church of St Peter and St Paul – the only place where the rich and poor ever met as a symbol of togetherness but alas, once outside that great oak door, it was back to Class.

That summer, we all worked solidly through the heat of the day, for as long as the dry spell held, throwing ourselves down thankfully for our short breaks before scrambling up to make the most of the day. For two weeks we worked twelve-hour days including all day Saturdays. By then, everyone was glad it was time for a pint and a rest. Two big crawler tractors moved in and ploughed it up to make a barsted fallow, while I worked with Tom on the final horse-hoeing of the sugarbeet, followed by the hand-hoers who were still on second hoeing piecework.

Then, we were into the lull before harvest. Most of the labourers were sent up to Lavenham Lodge land, hoeing around the currant bushes. Bert, Dick, Tom Mott and myself remained down at Alpheton Hall – pulling wild oats out of badly infected areas of wheat fields.

I would watch the horses enjoying a life of luxury out on Back Meadow, getting themselves steamed up for the great harvest pull. Some days I would be in the great thatched barn with Sam the foreman, checking over and renewing parts on the McCormack binder. The binder canvasses and great stack cloth were hanging in space above us, slung over one of the great oak beams, secured by a rope out of harm's way from rats and mice.

Sam pointed up towards the roof and said, "Climb up there for me, Jim, and cut the rope."

I climbed up with a hedging slasher. Straddling the beam, I used the slasher with a sawing action, until after a few minutes, the canvas and stack cloth came crashing to the ground. Then Sam secured a wagon rope to the tractor wheel and threw the loose end up to me so I could descend by sliding down the rope to the barn floor. I thought it was great fun.

When the binder was ready for a test, we took it out to the field, and slowly but surely, the flyers began to turn gently. Sam called, "That's it, Jimmy boy, running like Granny's sewing machine. Switch off. Release the canvasses and sheet it up."

Then we were off again. Sam indicated the old International 10-20 tractor. "Come on, Jimmy. Jump up and sit on the mudguard, we're off up to the wood to see how the others are getting on."

We bumped all the way up Wood Drift and along the cart track bordering Wood Field. We left the tractor at the main glade and continued on foot, quiet except for the odd call of the pheasant and the soothing cooing of wood pigeons high up in the canopy of the green leaves. We stopped after a while to pick up the sound of slashers and billhooks working away. Soon, Ron, Bert and Dick were in sight, with their bundles of split hazel sticks, cut into straight lengths called 'brorches'. Ron would be using them to thatch the haycocks, waiting in the stackyard.

"Have you got enough yet?" Sam asked.

"Enough for the stack, but what about the wheat stacks after harvest? They'll all need thatching."

"Blast, yes. Forgot about them. You'd better carry on cutting, tomorrow. It's five o'clock, time to go." He looked at us all and calculated Dick and Ron were near their footpath home. Come on, Bert, you can have a ride back down on the tractor with me."

"What's Jimmy going to do? Walk?"

"No, he'll hang on any bloody where. Don't worry about that little bugger."

He was right. I was determined to have a ride, so I stood on the drawbar and held the back of the tractor seat as we bumped and swayed our way back down the hill. As we jogged along on our spade-lugged chariot, vast sugarbeet and wheat fields stretched out before us, with the network of dusty old cart tracks twisting and turning in all directions. Bert always said that early men who walked them always travelled with the wind blowing on their rears, hence all the twists and turns.

Bert and I cycled home together down the old stone track leading onto Aveley Lane. It was a peaceful July evening, the air lightly scented with elder blossom and wild roses. A few bullocks lazed in the evening sunshine, lying in little groups half-covered in the tall grass.

We passed over the little radius bridge that spanned the Chad, just wide enough for a horse and cart, where ivy had long ago climbed its ancient brickwork. Then Bert and I dismounted and walked up Tippets Hill. Bert said he hadn't got the wind to cycle up and another thing, he was in no hurry. At last we reached his ancient cottage and off I cycled to tea. Home, where rambler roses did really bloom around the door and where the neglected flower garden, left almost to its own wild ways, suddenly looked like an artist's palette: Liz's patch, and she was proud of it.

Rose Cottage was quiet. My mother was getting used to feeding one less of us around the kitchen table. Harry had turned eighteen during haysel and by the time we started the harvest he'd got his call-up. I was getting used to having a bedroom to myself for the first time, or at least I was only sharing it with Bullace and the creaking footsteps on the stairs. I don't suppose anyone missed the early morning fights too much between the two of us, and for the first few months, Harry was stationed in Bury St Edmunds, and we still saw him quite regular. We swapped bikes, and he cycled back the eleven miles to Rose Cottage some weekends in his soldier's uniform.

At Alpheton Hall, as the fields turned into swaying gold, we geared up ready for the harvest weeks of long working days. Sam Swallow said, "Jimmy, take three horses to the blacksmith's. Get the bridles on Captain, Blonky and Sharper."

Tom Mott was in the stable and helped me lash the three together, and put the lead onto Captain. "Now, walk on the outside, Jimmy and if anything comes along, push them hard into the verge. These horses are quiet enough, but with so many army track vehicles about, they could get frightened."

I got to the blacksmiths without too much trouble, and Mr Goldsmith was his usual friendly self. "Hello, Jimmy, how many shoes do you want today?"

"Twelve, please." I handed the horses over to him.

"Right, Jim. It'll be about an hour so you can go off home for a cup of tea. These old timers won't be no trouble."

I walked along to the Rose and Crown, then up the long path to Rose Cottage. Liz took no time in getting the fire up. There was a box of dry kettle wedges under the stairs and once she'd shoved a handful of these under the old black kettle, the old girl was soon singing away as flames shot up around it. We sat together talking while we drank our tea, then she sent me back to see if the horses were ready.

Beads of sweat were rolling off the blacksmith's forehead, hitting the cobbled floor of the travis as he leaned forward, horse's leg held between his own.

"Won't be long, now, Jimmy. Just got to finish this one off."

I watched as he lowered the horse's foot to the floor. He took hold of an iron tripod with a ball on top, picked up the horse's foot and trimmed back the hoof to suit the iron shoe. Then he stood up straight and smiled.

"There you are, Jimmy boy, all ready to go."

He lashed the horses up for me and gave me the rein. At that moment a huge convoy of army vehicles started to roll through the village. Army outriders stood at the junctions of Lavenham Lane and Aveley Lane, both junctions I had got to use, with the convoy going the opposite way to me.

Mr Goldsmith said, "I'll take them up the main road for you. You run ahead and tell the outrider we need to cross."

When the horses reached the access to Aveley Lane, the outrider had stopped the convoy and we crossed in safety. The blacksmith handed the horses over to me.

"There you are, my little friend. I'll walk back to the travis by way of the allotments."

"Thank you, Mr Goldsmith," said little me.

This giant of a man looked down on me with his friendly, loving smile. "All good things are not always in big parcels." And then he was gone. Left alone with my three old carthorses, we strolled along Aveley Lane peacefully in the early August sunshine. Not a care in the world had I, and not a penny in my pocket, but even that did not disturb me one little bit. Someone at Rose Cottage could and would cough up if needs be. That was, of course, family. They were always there as security.

We turned up the half-mile track back to Alpheton Hall, through the farmyard to the horse pond, then on to the stable. I fed the horses and went back to the farmyard. Not a soul in sight – so quiet everywhere you could have heard a penny drop in straw. They had all gone to lunch, so I got my bike from the cart shed and thought to myself, "Liz is bound to have something in the pot, I may as well go back home."

I took in the view from the top of the old dusty track leading back to Aveley Lane. The great golden cornfields stretched out before me, but everywhere was hushed. The only sound was the faint rustle of the wheat, moving slightly off vertical as the light, warm breeze just touched its golden ears. Deep blue field scabious stood erect in their full beauty on both verges of the ancient track, their movement slow on this lazy summer day. There was no whispering wind, no clouds in the sky, just the sun moving slowly on towards night. I decided not to go home after all, but took a cheese sandwich from my pocket and ate it lying down in the long grass beside the worn and dusty track and enjoyed the peace and quiet for a while.

Then back to work. Sam Swallow pointed to the next job, which was greasing up the four harvest wagons. "You go and get your old mare and we'll pull them outside where there's more room."

With the aid of the wagon jack and the grease bucket, we got started. We lifted up one wheel at a time, slipping the wheel to the edge of the steel stub axle. Sam held the wheel while I smothered the yellow cart grease onto the exposed axle, then Sam slipped the wheel fully back onto its axle with a bang. We worked on the wheels and this afternoon completed two wagons, then we put Sharper in the shafts and backed the two greased wagons into the horse pond, as Sam said, "to tighten up the iron work".

Then I was sent off up the wood with the tumbrel, to collect a load of brorches for stacking in the end bay of the cart shed. Sharper and I set off, with me sitting up high on Sharper's back with the britchin's buckle leaving its imprint on my bum. Here we were, a boy and a horse, just jogging along in perfect peace, with the beautiful summer landscape rolled out before us.

We stopped at the entrance to the wood and I jumped down and took hold of my old friend's rein. I gave her a rub on her lovely soft, pink nose and she rubbed her head on my belly, just a sign of friendship between us.

We followed the deep shaded glade far into the wood. It was cool, mysterious and lovely, for this silent, green place belonged to the wildlife. Rabbits crossed our path, squirrels peeked at us from behind trees, pigeons flapped and took off in alarm. No sound of men at work. At last we came across a stack of newly cut brorches tied into neat bundles. Nearby, smoke curled from pipes and roll-ups and there were my three old pals, bundles of brorches under their behinds, taking a break. Each one had a smile on their face, a signal that today, at least, they were in quite a good mood. Some days they could be a grumpy old lot, especially with the farm boys.

They didn't need to stir to give advice. "Right then, Jim boy, you go and turn the cart a bit further up at the cross-glades. Always turn empty. Then pull in close to the heap of brorches and we'll get you loaded."

By the time I got back, they were all on their feet. One man jumped into the tumbrel and the other two threw the bundles up to him gently. Within half an hour all the bundles were stacked neatly on the cart, but they took no chances.

"We'll just rope them to make sure they don't fall. Take it steady through the wood, Jim. It's a rough track and you've got low branches overhanging."

All three men walked behind the cart until we left the wood behind and broke out into the summer sunshine. I stopped the cart, and they climbed up onto the tumbrel by standing on Sharper's rear, then they sat down on the load of brorches, making themselves quite comfortable. I jumped up on Sharper's back and did a slow trundle down the long dusty track to the cart shed.

"Right, Jimmy," said one of the old hands. " We're off home. It's past five o'clock. You make sure your horse is well fed and watered before you go, and it looks as if a good curry comb and brush wouldn't be amiss on her coat."

It wouldn't be amiss on yours either, I thought, but of course I dare not tell him that. When I got home, I was ready for my dinner – rabbit, potatoes, cabbage and runner beans with rhubarb pie and custard. Quite good for a country at war, and the season was soon coming up when pretty things would be roosting in the trees and hedgerows and my brothers would remove a few for the family pot.

Bert Gets A Surprise
I made my way to work the next morning and the sun was well up in the sky over Felixstowe way although it was only six-thirty. It was hot, with a lovely breeze blowing a hint of scented straw from the east on the dew-washed air.

Fields of black horse beans broke up the acres of golden wheat, barley and oats that stretched before me. The once-green verges had now turned to a seedy-pod brown, and swelling hips – fruit of the wild, wild rose – were showing flashes of orange to add another hue to the field hedgerows. By ten to seven when I arrived at the cart shed, most of the men were already there.

"Morning, Jimmy boy," said Dick. "Christ, I wish I was as young as you. You haven't got a care in the world, have you! As it should be at your age."

Sam Swallow arrived and I was set to finish greasing the wagons with Bert.

"Swear at him, Bert, if he don't do things the way you want him to. And when you've finished greasing, back them into the pond – and make sure you move them every day till all the wheels have been well soaked."

The big, grey, Talbot car swished into the yard – the boss had arrived. He spoke to the foreman and both got into the car and headed up Wood Drift.

When Sam got back, we knew harvest was upon us and everything was set for action. Ron was sent to get the 10-20 tractor ready and up to Eighteen Acres where the binder was standing ready. "Start cutting as soon as the heavy dew has dried off, Ron, and take Tom to ride the binder. Everybody, bring your fourses with you this afternoon. We'll work late. And I want to keep setting up close to the binder just in case the weather breaks."

Bert and I worked steadily greasing the wagons, and I was just going to get a horse from the stable ready to reverse them into the pond when Sam Swallow arrived on the scene. He was in a rush and spoke sharply to me.

"Jimmy, get your bike. Cycle home and tell your mother you're having dinner at one o'clock not twelve today. Tell her to pack you up some fourses. You're working late. And don't be gone half a bloody day, it's harvest time. You and I will keep the binder going at lunchtime, so be in that cutting field at twelve o'clock sharp. Now off you go. I could do that journey in fifteen minutes, so at your age, you should be back in ten. Bert, you can complete the work on the wagons and when Jimmy gets back you and him can join the men standing up the sheaves."

When I got back, Bert had finished the wagons and put the horse back in the stable. On this hot and humid morning, we walked up Wood Drift to the harvest field to join our friends. The smell of new-cut straw was lovely to the nose and a few rows of golden corn shocks had appeared as if by magic. The old 10-20 International tractor was trundling round the field, towing the binder with its flyers high in the air, flashing against the mid-morning sun. Swallows in their hundreds wheeled and twisted around the binder as it progressed round the field.

Bert and I dropped in to our uniform piece, taking six rows, three each. We met at the half-way stage to start our row of shocks. "Take the outside three, Jim boy. That will save my steps a bit. It's a long day from seven in the morning until half seven at night when you're getting upwards, and your legs are younger than mine."

We soon had a lovely row of golden shocks across the field.

"If I were you, Jimmy, I'd be making tracks to the field gateway. It's five to twelve – you mustn't be late taking over from Ron."

Off I went, jumping over sheaves and running along beside the standing corn. Sam was already waiting. We watched as Ron approached us. What a wonderful picture: wide blue Suffolk skies, the machine working in a ghostly haze of heat and dust, the whole scene was ablaze with light and colour for this was August in lovely England in 1941. But there was also the downside to the above picture, and things did happen to remind us, as just then a squadron of Hurricane fighter planes flew low over us on their way to do battle with the enemy.

Ron reached us with his tractor and binder, and Sam said, "I thought they were going to shoot you up, Ron."

"Christ, they were low," said Ron.

"Right, Jimmy Mott," said Sam. "On that tractor seat, full cut, full throttle and no garping about."

After an hour, Ron and his binder man, Tom, returned to take over the machine from us, and Sam said to them, "I want to keep going while the weather's good, so have your fourses at five o'clock, and Jimmy and Bert will keep the binder going for half an hour." Sam and I walked across the golden stubble and down Wood Drift towards the farm. "Look up there, Jimmy, there's a battle going on."

Miles up in the sky, planes like little black dots were diving and climbing, twisting and turning. We could just hear the sound of machine-gun fire. A parachute was drifting along, high up in the clear blue. We watched for no more than two minutes, then they were gone from our view.

"Peaceful enough down here, Jimmy, but a different world up there. Well, go and have your dinner and don't be late back. You can team up with your old mate Bert and continue shocking. Then you can take over the binder at five o'clock with Bert, while Ron and his mate have a bite to eat."

I joined Bert after lunch. "Thank God you're back. Bloody lot of shacking backwards and forwards on your own."

"Just tell me when it's five o'clock, Bert. The two of us have got to keep the binder going while Ron and Tom have their tea."

"What? I've got to come with you?"

"That's what Sam said."

"I don't know nothing about binders."

"Perhaps not, Bert, but you can sit on the seat and just hold on tight and shout if it fails to tie the sheaves. I shall be looking round as well, so don't worry."

"No, and I'm not bloody going to."

At five o'clock, Bert climbed up onto the high binder seat.

"What's all these levers for?"

"You don't have to do anything with them. Just sit where you are and watch. If you think there is anything wrong, just shout."

I climbed onto the tractor, trying to ignore the look on Bert's face, dropped into power drive, spun the canvasses to clear them of straw, then off we went. The sun was still quite high and hot, though making its descent into the western sky. Bert was doing an excellent job on the binder and seemed to enjoy it.

We did several rounds before Ron and Tom came over to claim back their machine. Bert and I retrieved our fourses bags from the hedgerow, then settled down on the shady side of a completed stook and enjoyed our tea: Bert, his bread and cheese and onion, myself, bread, beef dripping, pepper and salt. We worked on stocking sheaves until seven-thirty, then made our way home to Bridge Street via the old familiar stony track.

The older men of the village made their way to the Rose and Crown for their pints – if they had any. If they'd sold out of beer, oh dear, it broke their hearts. The younger men and boys would sometimes bathe in the Chad. Dusty, dirty work, harvest work, and we never had good facilities in our cottage homes. You were either spotlessly clean, clean, dirty or bloody filthy. So you see, the old Chad stopped us from being the latter. For all the drawbacks of our humble cottage homes, we were happy and contented people. We never went to the doctor very often, if at all. He lived at Long Melford, five miles away. Bugger that – ten miles there and back for a bottle of fizz.

As the harvest went on, Bert and I continued putting sheaves into shocks, following the binder from field to field. I had my turns on the tractor, with Bert behind me on the binder, relieving the regulars for meals. It was a joy out here in these great open fields, stubble, sheaves and shocks ablaze with sunshine.

"So dry and lovely," said Bert. "You can sit down anywhere without feeling the damp."

At that moment, the big grey Talbot car made a slow and careful approach into the field and drove between two rows of shocked corn. "It's the boss," said Bert, "heading right for us."

The car stopped and the boss spoke to Bert through the open window.

"You're keeping the machine going while the men have their meals?"

"Yes, sir, that is the arrangement."

"Will you finish it tonight?"

"Job to say," said Bert. "What do you think, Jimmy?"

"If no breakdowns, easily."

"Well done," said the boss man, and then he was gone.

"Well, he's happy enough," said Bert. "Come on, we'd better do our bit. Not one minute must we lose, Jimmy boy."

Ron removed himself from the old tractor, rubbing his legs. "Stiff as a bloody stake, sitting there all those hours."

I climbed aboard this huge, all iron machine for my half hour, opened the throttle wide, and looked round to see if my old pal was comfortable and safe. There he sat, surrounded by levers and controls he knew nothing about, but he always laughed and said, "I only come for the ride." He acknowledged my glance with a wide smile. I let in the clutch and we were off, surrounded by a cloud of paraffin smoke from its side exhaust.

The swallows were around us in their hundreds as the flyers put thousands of insects on the wing. Summer sun played its heat beams down hard upon us. The so gentle westerly breeze was just whispering into the ears of the golden swaying corn and lifting the light white thistledown high into the early evening air, like angels on their way to heaven powered by the hand of God. As we worked on, the scent of wild summer stubble flowers filled the air.

I looked around for my old mate, Bert. I could only see him through the heat haze, chaff, thistledown and dust as we rocked and bumped along on our springless iron seats, driving to the very edge of the binder's capability.

Our short shift finished, Bert brushed the thistledown from his clothes and chose a lovely place for us to sit, under an old Todd Oak in the shade, and here we ate our fourses in peace. Then Bert lit up a Woodbine. He just sat there, looking out across the harvest fields of his native Suffolk, the rows of standing shocks and the acres of uncut corn. I sat silent beside him, not prepared to disturb his silent thoughts until the Woodbine had burned to its bitter end. He stubbed it out on the side of his boot. His hand moved to his watch pocket, and we were off again.

I could guess where my old friend's thoughts had turned. Bert's family was big like ours, and our friends William and Dusty

Frost were about the same age as Harry and me. Labouring in the fields, we were not classed as essential workers in wartime.

We continued shocking, walking back and forward carrying sheaves under each arm, until our legs ached and our arms were sore. At last Bert looked at his watch again. "Thank God, it's time to go home. Now for a pint."

We made our way off the field to the old stone track, known as 'The Private Road'. Why it was called that I do not know, for at its access with Aveley Lane it had a white painted five-bar gate with 'Private' on it, but at the other end of the lane to the east was a stile, also painted in white, properly constructed with hand-hold and footplate. It was, of course, a footpath to the church for the people of Bridge Street living on the west side of the village in the parish of Alpheton. A path for them to worship in their local parish church and attend to their loved-ones' graves. So who blocked it up?

I parted company with Bert at his cottage home in Aveley Lane and made my way home to tea at Rose Cottage. At harvest time, dinner was in the middle of the day and we all came home to eat and collect our harvest field fourses. In the evening, Liz would make us wait for my father and brothers to get in so we could sit and eat together. Afterwards, however late it was, there were pigs and chickens to feed and dogs to let off the chain for a good run.

I had my share of work as well. From an early age, my mother had made us look after some of the rabbits, and there were jobs like carting water to do. Liz always told us, "You'll have to bring up a family one day, you two boys, so you've got to work." Beryl and Iris never seemed to get the same treatment as Harry and me, but if we said anything our mother said, "Don't you worry about your sisters, someone else will look after them."

At Alpheton Hall the next morning, Sam Swallow said, "We'll start carting wheat from Eighteen Acres, but first let's get stack bottoms made in the stackyard – they're all marked out with sticks. I should think that's a job for the field gang. And get the tarpaulin near the stack – it's in the barn – just in case of a thunderstorm." We would also use it to cover up the stack every night, until the roof was complete. Sam continued, "The thatching ladder and half-thatching ladder are under the eaves of the cart shed. Get all the gear ready, then have your breakfast. By then the dew should be off the corn and we'll make a start."

I was given the job of driving the wagons. Sam reminded me to check the wagons had their ropes, which were slung on a hook at the rear.

So around nine o'clock on this lovely golden harvest morning, with stack bottoms ready, the men and the boy sat on a heap of surplus wheat straw, the smell of the mayweed strong in our noses where we had disturbed it by working on it. Here we all sat enjoying our early morning cup of tea in these picturesque surroundings, with the harvest wagons in their faded blue and orange paintwork, the early morning dew disappearing into vapour by the heat of the rising sun.

Tommy Mott, the head horseman, was Lord of the Harvest, organising the harvest workers. "Right, time to get those wagons moving."

I jumped up onto the shaft and onto the horse's back. Men of the field gang climbed up the great rear wheel of the wagon with pitch forks and frail baskets. Then we were off out of the stackyard and onto the road, left up Wood Drift and then up to Eighteen Acres, followed by the second wagon.

"Up to the top, Jimmy boy. We'll load downhill, take the first two rows near the hedge. They're in full sun, so no fear of dew hanging on in there."

With two men on the wagon and two wielding pitchforks, loading proceeded with me leading the horse forward until the wagon was fully loaded. Then a shout, "Hold hard, my beauties! Ready to rope up," and soon we were heading back to the stackyard.

The harvest dragged on into late September 1941, and the wheat stacks gradually rose high above the yard. Now we were into the barley harvest and Bert Death's thrashing machine from Lavenham was here at Alpheton Hall to thrash out the barley straight from the field. With the grain separated from the stalk, the barley straw was built into more stacks alongside the unthrashed wheat stacks already in the yard. Straw was used everywhere around the farm as litter, and ended up on the muck hills that were spread back on the land.

As the late September dew was falling early and lifting late, this shortened our thrashing day considerably and so, to overcome this, every evening around half past six the thrashing machine would stop and all the farm wagons and three-laddered tumbrels were loaded and sheeted up.

At seven o'clock sharp the next morning, the old engine with a full head of steam started to turn the pulleys on drum and pitcher. Men climbed the ladder up onto the straw stack, horses drew up the first wagonloads beside the drum, the old engine increased its revs and the first barley sheaves of the day fell into the drum with a bang and so we were off for another hard, hot, long dusty day.

Now, as the power of the summer sun began to fade, the last wagonloads of harvest barley rolled off the great wide fields of Alpheton Hall in the dusk of this late September evening, making their way home to the stackyard. Then the wagons were lined up and sheeted, the horses to the pond and the stable, the harvest men to their cottage homes, walking under the light of the harvest moon.

The next day, with the last of the thrashing done, Bert Death's crew packed up their gear, coupled the machine behind the engine and drove out of the stackyard, done for another year. I stood looking around at the stackyard, now graced by five or six beautiful straw and corn stacks, and where the harvest wagons were just left here and there.

With the rush of harvest gone, and the tarpaulin stretched out on the remains of the mayweed floor, the thatcher and his mate were left to complete work to the stack roofs in the peace and stillness of a mellow late September. As the month faded into October and October into November, the great white feathered owls who lived here at Alpheton Hall would patrol this old, misty, haunted stackyard for the pickings of mice and rats its stacks had to offer.

Defence Of The Realm
It had been quite a year. It was the end of my first twelve months working for the Alston family and I had enjoyed it. George Eady, the foreman, was kind and considerate. The cold, wet sugarbeet and drainage fields, at age fifteen, had been a challenge to me, but it was

a challenge I was determined to win. For those of us sowing the fields and bringing in the harvests in the lovely rolling fields and meadows of Alpheton Hall, and the flatlands of Lavenham Lodge, life was quite good.

But the news all through 1941 had been very grim indeed. The German bombers had come night after night, knocking the heart out of the dockland area of London and the City of London itself. I did wonder, after listening to our old crackling radio, if we would ever make it. It looked impossible.

Through the crackle and hiss, we gathered round and heard… London in ruins and on fire…. Germany invades Yugoslavia…. The great battleship Hood sent to the bottom, sunk by shellfire. Germany invades Russia…. (switch the bloody thing off and hope things get better).

We did have one incident in May that gave us just a little ray of hope. I was in the cart shed at Alpheton Hall with Bert and Dick when it came up in conversation.

"Heard the news, Dick?" Bert asked.

"No, haven't got a wireless. Why, what's up?" said Dick.

"Bloody old Hess flew over here last night."

"He did? Flew over, you say? I shouldn't of thought he could drive a bloody airplane."

"Well, he did. Jumped out of the bugger when he got to Scotland."

"He never did! What the hell has he come here for, I wonder?"

"Not to have his bloody hair cut. I reckon old Hitler was going to shoot him fer suffin, so he buggered off when he saw his chance."

"You're probably right, Bert old mate."

Some time around my sixteenth birthday that October, the officer in charge of the Bridge Street & Alpheton Platoon, a Mr Rackham of Bridge Street Farm, approached my mother asking her permission for me to join the Home Guard as a despatch rider, which she gave without hesitation.

After some weeks, I was given a uniform and with other boys from the two villages, we were taught small-arms drill on Sunday mornings on Ford Hall meadow, beside the Rose and Crown. On

Wednesday evenings, we had lectures in the Mission Room. Some Sundays we all had to cycle to Chadacre, where we met up with the Lawshall and Shimpling Platoons. We practised small-arms drill and officers and NCO took turns to shout (Wait for it!) Orders!

One cold Saturday December night of 1941, at around 19:00 hours, there was a loud knocking on our cottage door. My mother opened the door. "Do come in," my mother said. "Surprised to see you on a night like this," and on our doormat stood Mr Wallace, the farmer of Ford Hall.

"You're the little chap I want," he said, pointing at me, for he was Sgt. Wallace, Home Guard. "Jimmy, we've got a call-out from Headquarters. Get your uniform on, travel without lights, fast as you can to Lineage Cottage – and get the Home Guard out."

First, on with my uniform, to the shed for my bicycle and I was away – out onto the main road, sharp right at the travis and on to Lavenham Lane. Now the hard pedalling, up the steep winding hill out of the valley, taking in deep breaths of the cold night air. A thousand searchlights roamed the skies, with flashes and rumbles of gunfire towards the east coast.

The night seemed exceptionally quiet, apart from the distant gunfire. I pedalled on, half-way to Lavenham past Duncan's Farm, and at last Lineage Cottage came into view. It stood there stark black against the starlit night. There wasn't a crack of light from the cottage, nowhere. It almost seemed deserted. I rested my bike against the hedge. I couldn't find the latch on the little wicker gate, but painfully cocked my legs over the top, then down the path into a very dark porch. A very ghostly place, this, with high hedges and the great dark forestry wood to the rear.

I found myself hammering on the door. Nothing, not a sound. I just stood there in the darkness, wondering whether to run away or try again. I hammered like hell again on the cottage door and every cock pheasant in Lineage Wood called out. It was probably the gunfire, not my knocking that set them off. Ah, in luck. Someone was unlocking the door.

It opened about two inches wide. A grey-haired lady peeped through the crack and quickly shut the door with a bang. I heard her say, "It's a soldier." A few seconds later the door opened again and the lady said, "Can I help you?"

"Oh, yes!" I said. "Please don't be alarmed. I've got a message for your sons, Fred and Charlie."

"What do you want them for?"

"Well, is it possible to speak to them, please?"

"Fred! Charlie!" And after a bit of a wait, they appeared at the door.

"Hello, Jimmy."

I was brief. "Charlie, there's a call-out. Report to Ford Hall as quickly as possible."

"Oh my God!" exclaimed the grey-haired lady. "Are they here?"

"Oh no, I think it's just an exercise," I tried to sound reassuring.

"There must be something wrong," she insisted. "But he's only a boy. Charlie, he must be scared, poor boy."

I thought, "Yes, Mam! How right you are."

Now, off we flew back home, down the hill all the way. No ghost or German will catch me. Head down and bottom up, I rode like the wind. All went well until I reached the blacksmith's travis and from the stillness of the night a voice called out, "Halt, halt."

Oh no! Bloody Germans! No good running, I'll get shot!

A rifle was laid across my chest. "Where are you going?" said a voice.

Thank God! He's English! I knew the voice.

"Hello, Arthur," I said.

"Oh, it's you, Jimmy. Where have you been?"

"To get Fred and Charlie out. They'll be coming this way in a moment."

"OK, Jimmy, thanks for telling us."

Then I was off again, chasing Home Guard members who lived in isolated farm cottages up long, lonely farm tracks. At about 21:00 hours we were all paraded outside the Rose and Crown and a roll call was taken.

2nd Lieutenant Rackham stepped forward, saying, "Good evening everyone. I would like to thank you all for turning out at short notice and I feel very proud of the efficient way our forward plans have worked out. We have taken over the old stables at the Rose and Crown for our sleeping quarters. If this gets full up there is the Dutch barn that Mr Ruffle says we may use at the mill.

"Our mess will be the Brewer's at the blacksmith's shop, which, unfortunately will only serve tea. Whether there is an invasion going on, or whether it's just an exercise, I do not know but if we are overrun by the enemy, we shall make our way over to Ashton Grove Wood. So any of you who may be cut off from the main party should make their way to Ashton Grove. And don't forget to use your pass code at all times. Now! Any questions?"

"Yes, sir. Only one," said a lone voice. "If we get cut off we won't want to worry about going to the wood because we shall die of fright, sir. And the Germans will die laughing at us."

At 11:00 hours on the Sunday morning, we were all paraded on Ford Hall Meadow and stood down. The exercise was over.

PART FOUR

The Invasion Of Alpheton

Destruction
In December 1941, we heard about Pearl Harbour. The Americans had entered the war. I'm not sure what we thought about it, that Christmas. At first, we were probably thinking more about Harry being away from home. But the next year, things started to change.

First, we heard that the government had taken over most of the land in Alpheton belonging to the Alston family. Only much reduced acreages were left to cultivate at Lodge Farm, Manse's Farm and Elms Farm but these were farmed very efficiently.

In time of war, the farmer did not choose what to grow on his land. The Ministry gave the orders, and the farmer did his best to obey, or else face a fine or worse. Local farms which were not run well were taken over, as part of the war effort to feed people in the towns and cities with their food rations.

We worked hard, and we were paid fair. I was 'sonny' for a long time, but Mr Alston eventually learned my name, and I learned he was a gentleman. He never lost his temper, and even if the weather turned on us so we couldn't get on with harvesting, he just said, "Oh, well, we'll just have to wait another day."

Perhaps the biggest surprise came after the war, when we found the boss had paid for us all to have an outing to the seaside at the end of harvest. It turned out it wasn't a dreary place to work at all. David Alston let us have fun, and there'll never be no more like him.

In September 1942, John Laing Construction, who were the main contractors, arrived with heavy earth-moving equipment and hundreds of Irish labourers, to start work on the land that had been taken over by the government. It took a year of chaos and upheaval around us, but by the following September a large United States Air Force base had appeared on the flatlands at the top of Alpheton village.

Destruction of the countryside was on a large scale. Trees,

ditches, hedgerows, telegraph poles, even the old and lovely Turnpike Road and sleepy Dead Lane disappeared. Manse's Farm, that lovely old medieval farmhouse, was left to decay, and out of those acres of farmland Lavenham Airfield gradually appeared.

Nothing was sacred, nothing was spared. It all went to hell and nothing came back. No, and nothing did come back, not ever.

The old sowers and reapers of Alpheton and Bridge Street stood in amazement one evening, to find that their seats, which they thought of as their own and had been theirs for twenty or thirty years in the Rose and Crown and the Red Lion, had been invaded by Irish labourers. They were no longer the masters of their own pub who turned the local young men out of their seats should they happen to be in one of them. Their happy days, sitting around the old Tap Room open fire drinking their pints, had come to an end.

On the land, the sweet and mellow days of autumn were rolling in fast. Before us stood one hundred acres or more of sugarbeet, and perhaps forty to fifty acres of potatoes all to be harvested by hand.

Besides beet and potatoes to harvest, there was also the ploughing, the seedbed and the drilling of the winter wheat – a task that looked almost impossible, especially as the farm's skilled labour was being lost to the army, and the management were anxious to press on hard before the November rains and mists turned the heavy clay soil to mud and slurry.

To cope with the heavy rootcrop harvest and loss of skilled labour, Land Army girls were brought in. Their hostel was at the Old Rectory, up near the boundary of the airfield by Buxtons and Clapstile Farm. We did scratch our heads and have a laugh over that one, putting the Land Army right next to the US Air Force.

We set out for the beet fields, Tommy Mott to clamp and myself to drive the tumbrels. We were joined by four land girls to fill the tumbrels, whose names were Joan the forewoman, Betty, Janet and Alice. Joan was from London and the rest were from Stoke-on-Trent. Lovely girls, who didn't know the first thing about farming but what they didn't know they made up for by hard work in their strange surroundings. There were some embarrassing moments.

One girl approached me on their first day.

"Umm, excuse me, but where's the toilet?"

"Oh, we don't have one."

"So where do you go?"

I almost said against the cartwheel, but corrected myself in time. "In the ditch."

She whispered something to the other girls and they all laughed, but they soon got used to our Suffolk ways and the farm's toilet facilities.

The land girls settled in, and eventually the Irish labourers began to depart. A few of the village elders came back to their old Tap Room to drink their beloved nectar and sit again on their favourite bench – things seemed to be getting back to normal.

A few US personnel arrived before all the Irish workers had left. We stood amazed one day, watching Americans lifting out telegraph poles with a machine that gripped the pole and out it came. I think by then they were in a bit of a hurry.

The first bomber arrived before the runway was finished. We went to have a look at that. We saw it come in to land one afternoon. 'Lucky Strike' it was called, after the brand. It had a pack of cigarettes painted on it, with one cigarette sticking out of the top. I remember seeing holes that had been shot clean through it, and before it left they had just patched it up with some sort of silver tape. It had just enough runway to land and take off and it must have been running out of juice, because as soon as it had refuelled it went.

That was the first of the Flying Fortresses, that swept over our Suffolk skies.

Before we knew it, the greatest air armada ever seen touched down on East Anglia's newly built airfields and brought with it thousands of fun-loving American airmen, smartly dressed and polite and oh-so-different, travelling round on khaki military bicycles.

They invaded our pubs, our dance halls, our towns and our cities. They were everywhere. Our girls loved them and they brought something new into the East of England from which we never recovered.

As daylight broke over the Suffolk countryside and I was cycling to work I probably saw one, or part of one, of the greatest air armadas ever seen anywhere in the world. Morning after morning, I watched with great interest as these huge aircraft formed up in their correct slots. Fairy lights of all colours shot up by these aircraft added to the spectacular. Hundreds of aircraft seemed to fight for position on their slow climb to the heavens.

After what seemed ages, the last of these great aircraft had gone, and silence returned again to our little piece of Suffolk, but not for long. By midday to one o'clock, the great return home began, some still in their orderly formations, but alas, some alone and in distress as we boys stood with bated breath to watch these loners struggling to reach their Lavenham home.

Some made it, some didn't. Many a wreck of a Flying Fortress lay deep down in the Suffolk clay in some lonely field. Wreckage from these aircraft is still being churned up by the plough as it passes over a Fortress's grave.

We first met the airmen one Saturday night when the Tap Room door opened and in walked a dozen or so smartly dressed American servicemen, each with one trouser leg rolled up to the knee to protect them from cycle chain grease, showing the white of their legs.

"Hiya, pops. We're from America. Glad to meet ya. Have a drink with us." Then they came over and sat beside us young men and boys, saying, "Hiya, guys. Got 'ny sisters?"

After buying us all a drink and telling us where they came from and a lot of things about their own country, they left us to explore the next village down the road.

And that, of course, was the last straw and the end of our peaceful way of village life. It just disappeared. Gone forever our lazy Sundays lying in flower meadows beside the Chad or going to our little village church. All had gone – even the parson had gone off to war.

In its place, a new way of life. For the rest of the war, us farm boys spent most of our evenings in Alpheton's Red Lion in the company of the land girls and American servicemen.

One evening, I was outside with a crowd of people when I

heard someone calling my name, and pushing their way through to reach me. I didn't trouble much with girls as a rule. My brother Harry had a sweetheart, but I usually preferred my own company. Amy wasn't even working on our farm, but somehow she'd heard I came from Bridge Street and was determined I was going to show her my village.

There was no way I was going down Cold Hill with Amy that evening, with so many heavy vehicles around. But Amy was as keen as me to wander the countryside and for the next few months she followed me around as game as anything, clambering over stiles in her wellington boots.

On Saturday nights, we would all go to the pictures in Sudbury on the local bus from Stanstead and we had many a good wartime sing-song on Honeywood's old crates on our way home. But one by one, as we reached the age of eighteen, we were called into the army – Jack Long, William, Dusty and Harold Frost, and Barney and Dick Andrews, as well as Harry and me.

The summer before I turned eighteen, in 1943, we got the harvest in with the help of the land girls and young farm boys. We seemed to get very violent thunderstorms in those days. On a hot and humid day, a dark cloud started to appear.

"Keep your eye on that cloud," the foreman said. "There's going to be a hell of a storm, so keep the stack cloth handy. And keep the middle of the stack full, so the water will run off and not pond on the cloth. Jimmy, see the field gang get home to the farm in time to cover the wagon, and get all the horses to the stable."

Out in the field, one man said, "We'll keep going for a little while longer. It's slow moving and every load helps."

An old timer in the field gang said, "It's going to be a bloody sharp one. It's following the Chad and coming against the wind, so it's got its own power. First we get the calm, then there will be no birds in the sky and nothing, not even a twig will move. Then we'll get the wind that's powering it and, my Christ, we'll have to watch out then. So I say we go on the calm – and that means now."

So across the fields came the field gang with their loaded wagons and the land girls sitting up high on the load of corn. The thunder cloud was over them and the lowered daylight was turning to darkness when the wagons rolled into the stackyard.

The stack gang had got the stack cloth secured tightly to a ladder, and ran to help the field gang, then we all ran for shelter in the great barn of Alpheton Hall. Their timing was perfect. The rest of the afternoon we lay on the sugarbeet pulp stack, listening to the rain and thunder.

It was essential to keep moisture out of the stacks – particularly the hay, stacked for animal feed. When the stack was opened, if there was any sign of mould, the men would keep the farm boys away from the area. They would cover their mouths with cloth to prevent breathing in mould spores which could cause farmer's lung. Then the mouldy hay would be taken off and burnt. I never saw a mouldy stack at Alpheton Hall.

In October 1943, I turned eighteen and eventually got my call-up and headed for training in Bury St Edmunds, but I got home regular.

The road through our village of Bridge Street was in constant use by military vehicles supplying the airfield. There were convoys of American vehicles loaded with bombs in open trucks. Huge American tankers, loaded with fuel, passed slowly through, dragging chains along the road surface. Military police seemed to patrol the road all day in their jeeps.

Accidents were frequent, as the road wound its way around the houses with a turn at the bridge. On my way home one day, bombs lay all over the road from Aveley Lane to the Rose and Crown. I was stopped by a huge, coloured American soldier, dressed in an all leather and wool uniform with a matching hat. Stamped on his back were the words BIG DICK in bold white letters.

He looked at me and said, "Just ride between them. They won't go off, and if they do, you won't know, boss." A big white smile followed. His truck lay on its side beside a broken telegraph pole and a mass of wire tangled up with bombs.

But the old road stood up well to its wartime traffic, even if its verges were covered in debris. Long gone were the days us children searched its banks from High Cross to the top of Cold Hill for cow-mumble to feed our tame rabbits, and for flowers to add a spice of colour to our homes. Then and now was a sad contrast.

I was away from home, back in the army, in April 1944 when Liz got the telegram to say Harry had been killed in Burma. The day the news came, my brothers arrived home for their dinner but there was nothing cooked for them that day.

This was a hard year for my mother. She lost four of us over a few months – my father, my big brother Wally, my big sister Nora, and Harry.

I got home eventually, released Class B to go back to work on the farm. The war was over. Barney Andrews came back to work for D Alston Farms with me. Our friend William Frost was killed in the D-Day landings in June 1944. His brother Dusty was wounded.

Home Sweet Home

The war ended in April 1945. After my time in the army, it was good to be back home with the people I loved, the fields and bridleways, and above all, the great blue Suffolk skies.

After a few days' holiday, on a Monday morning in August, I cycled up to Alpheton Hall with my old pal Dusty Frost to start work. We pedalled into the cart shed and here we met all our old friends – including Dick and Bert and the land girls – and there were lots of handshakes and kisses.

Then it was work, chopping out sugarbeet on the great field. We each took twenty-five rows on piece-work. The sun was high and hot on this lovely morning, and we were home, sweet home.

At nine o'clock, we all sat on the shady side of the fence to eat our nineses. Just a gentle August breeze was blowing through the leaves and it was peace, perfect peace.

I looked down towards the valley and there it was, just as beautiful as when I left it. The heat haze was dancing on the beet rows and everywhere was fair and lovely.

"Come on, Jim, time to go back to work," said Dusty.

Later, we cycled home to dinner. The bees were busy on the flower banks of the old private track. The tar surface of Aveley Lane was bubbling in the heat, looking tired and lazy, but all I could think was how peaceful everything was.

I completed a week on the sugarbeet field, and on my first Sunday off, I walked down to the lower wetlands, across Serpenpan

Meadow, down to Dark Lane where the old broken-down farm carts and machinery still lay here and there, covered in bushes. The crab apple trees were still here, unchanged, the sun still shining through the many holes in the leafy roof above me. Ahead, the old five-bar gate still lay wrecked beside its gatepost.

I walked on, towards the banks of my lovely river Chad, water flowing over its clean pebble bed, tiddler fish swimming in their thousands, watercress flourishing in mid-stream.

I sat under the shade of an old ash tree and memories of the children of Bridge Street came flooding back, playing and paddling in the clear river water.

Where have they all gone?

I sat here in a dream, but then got a rude awakening. It was the church bells, the holy bells of Long Melford and Lavenham, their great peals crashing through the woodlands and bouncing off the waters of the Chad, rolling out across hundreds of acres of our beloved Suffolk fields.

And here I sat, listening, and I remembered how as children we used to mimic the church bells, all those years ago. About ten of us would line up and sing, to the tune of the 'bob major' peal, "Who killed the fox in Lineage Wood, who killed the fox in Lineage Wood? The huntsmen did from Bury-ary, the huntsmen did from Bury."

I carried on working with Dusty at Alpheton Hall through the summer, and we have stayed close friends throughout my life, as have many of the friends of my young days. Farm work continued through the seasons, and as time went on, I was given the job of driving the sugarbeet to the big sugar factory in Bury St Edmunds, which was a challenge at times.

At the beginning of the beet harvest, we were allowed to take in as many loads as we could manage, to fill up the silos so the factory could start up. After that, all loads were controlled by permits. It was a busy job with long, difficult hours as the management didn't like wasting permits.

When the weather held good through September and October, we could load straight from the field, with land girls and labourers pitching the beet straight onto the lorries. By November, the rain would mean there was no more driving onto the field and we would load from the clamps. We would drive back from the factory with our quota of beet pulp, a by-product used for cattle feed.

By December, we had to cope with freezing fog and snowed-up roads. We had no heaters in our trucks, our windscreens froze and I had to drive all day with my head out of the side window. I was lucky that I was driving a US Army truck with left-hand drive, so I could follow the verge and, also, see any cyclists who were making their way to work in Bury St Edmunds. There was no salt in those days, only sanded here and there, with hundreds of beet lorry drivers on the road, but somehow we always got there.

One Saturday in December, I took two loads to the factory. Travelling had been dangerous and slow, roads packed with hard snow. I was home for dinner around two o'clock, then decided to go for a walk with the dogs to take a good look at the snow scene around Alpheton Hall.

My walk took me along the banks of the ice-covered Chad, towards the stile that led onto the footpath, overhanging bushes weighted down with snow bending gracefully over its top rail.

Then across the meadow, down the earth ramp, sliding across the ice and up the other side. Next, over a five-bar gate to a field called Bushlons. Now the climb through deep virgin snow, up the hilly field towards the private track to Alpheton Hall. On reaching the summit of the Hall drive, I crossed it to enter Church Field.

Drifts were beginning to form as the north-east wind was blowing clouds of frozen snow, all of it settling in the low areas. My dogs did not like the cold, although they enjoyed rolling in the snow. I kept them both on the lead because if a hare should surface from its pug-hole, they would chase it and some of the areas blown clear of snow could be frozen sharp enough to cut their paws.

The dogs and I were very exposed now as we crossed this high and open field. I looked across to the church of St Peter and St Paul, which means so much to me.

I came here as a child to learn to pray and sing the hymns, and I came here as a choir boy. As my mother once said, "Off you go, Jim boy. It will help you grow up to be a decent citizen and you can go to worse places than that."

Inside that little village church, the name of our friend, William Frost – Dusty's brother – is written on the wall and read out every Remembrance Service along with Arthur Matthews and Owen Reynolds.

You will not find my brother's name there, William and Harry were friends in life but their names are separated. Bridge Street – just a few houses, not much more, really, than a crossroads in a valley – is divided by the road that runs through, with Alpheton on one side and Long Melford on the other. My brother Harry's name, Cyril Douglas Mott, is listed with many others in that great church of Holy Trinity, Long Melford.

> Both from the hamlet of Bridge Street
> Both gave their all, so all of you who live
> In this little Chad valley, now and in the future,
> May walk in the fields, footpaths, bridleways
> In peace and freedom.
> They do not see the flowers of spring
> Or hear the thrush or blackbird sing.
> They do not see men in summer fields
> Harvesting their heavy yields,
> They no longer see the autumn leaves
> Turn from green to red, and then to gold.
> They will not feel the cold of a winter's day.
> They lie in silent fields, so far away.

The dogs and I left the church behind us and continued on our way through the blowing snow, out of Church Field onto Shimpling Hatch, crossing it to Shimpling Dodser and along the edge of Alpheton Wood. We took a right turn into the main glade, then right again after three hundred yards, heading south through the deep, dark wood.

I came across what I was looking for – a huge, still smouldering ash and charcoal fire adjacent to Wood Field. This was the beet pullers' eating and rest place, where that morning they had eaten and dried the hessian bags they had worn around their middles and legs to keep their clothes from a soaking.

I stirred up the fire with a wooden poker and there they were, glowing red embers. A wonderful sight on a day like this. I sat here on a beet puller's seat, the dogs lying snug and happy beside me.

I looked out across Wood Field at the pale winter sky, leafless trees here and there appearing dark against the lonely landscape. This is why I came here, to sit beside the glowing fire and look out at a wonder of the world – mysterious, cold, icy.

The dogs seemed restless and they sat, looking into the wood, ears standing up high, listening. Then they stood up. Someone, or something, was coming our way. I could hear breaking sticks, then someone stepped out of the darkness, laughing and pointing a finger at me. It was Margaret and then Barbara, land girls I worked with, approaching out of the shadows.

"I hope you don't mind us disturbing you, Jim."

"No, not at all. Sit down."

"We got fed up being in the hostel, so we thought we'd go for a walk. I know you follow the beet pullers around on your Saturday afternoon walks, so we thought we'd come and find you."

"We can't stay long, our tea is at five o'clock, so just half an hour then we must be off," said Margaret. We sat by the fire.

"Why do you come to such lonely wild places?" said Barbara.

"Well, I like wild and lonely places and I love the landscape."

"I think you're a loner, Jimmy."

"No, I'm not. Only on a Saturday afternoon."

"Are you coming to The Bush in Shimpling this evening?" I shook my head. I would be at home by the fire, keeping Liz company tonight. "Will you be there tomorrow night?"

"Yes, I suppose so. So I'll see you there, then."

Off they went into the darkness, and I got the dogs together and walked towards home down Wood Drift. By now, the moon and a thousand stars with their silver light made the snow and ice sparkle ahead of me all the way to Aveley Lane.

The thatched roof of Rose Cottage was loaded with untouched snow, and woodsmoke rose into the night air as I walked up the long path.

I reached the cobblestone apron of the cottage, lifted the latch on the old oak door and stepped in. Inside, it was quiet. There sat

Liz in her horsehair chair, with flames leaping up the chimney.

"Come in the warm, Jim, do, out of the cold." I quickly shut the door behind me. "I can't understand why you have to go out walking those fields in weather like this. Why don't you stay here in the warm?"

"If you were able to come with me, Ma, you would find out why. The landscape, the lonely fields, the very silence – you have nothing, only the wind. It's a poet's dream."

"Well, I don't suppose I will alter you."

Then my mother went off to get my tea, reminding me to look after my dogs with plenty of straw to make a warm bed for the night.

Stars, Stripes And Union Jack

I carried on driving the sugarbeet lorries up to Bury St Edmunds, then homeward past the Lavenham road, taking a left turn at the entrance onto the airfield. I drove back towards Lavenham Lodge farm across a great expanse of nothing on a wet or misty night and one could soon get lost without Bill and Irene Eady's light guiding me to Elms farmhouse.

The Americans had gone home. The Lavenham airbase lay deserted, its Nissen huts, huge kitchens and hangars abandoned, their doors unlocked and left to swing and bang in the wind. Only thieves and ghosts travelled the narrow concrete tracks now. The runways lay drab, cold and deserted, the last Fortress gone with its crews and ground staff.

None of us was here to wave them a goodbye or to say thank you. They had all gone home to America, just as we had come home to England. Now there were no Stars and Stripes fluttering in the wind over this desolate airfield. Everything was left to the elements, to rot and decay.

The light of Elms farmhouse faded in my rear-view mirror as I travelled on to Lodge farm for fuel, then took the road through Alpheton, heading down towards Alpheton Hall.

As I passed the Red Lion, memories flowed back of all the great times I had there, all of us together, land girls, Americans, farm boys and soldiers on leave, singing war-time songs like their favourites – 'Someone In The Kitchen With Dinah' and 'Ghost Riders In The Sky'.

Of the thousands of men who came and went during 1944 and 1945, over two hundred young airmen, mostly volunteers about my own age, had been killed while flying from Lavenham Airfield. I may have met some of those men in the Lion, drank with them and sang with them. I shall never know, but we shall be forever grateful for their sacrifice and the support of the American people.

In the early years of the war, my family had crowded around our kitchen table, my father, mother, brothers and sisters, listening to the bleak news. Nothing had seemed to stop the enemy's march towards us.

Later, I had raced my bicycle up Lavenham Lane as a member of the Home Guard, past tank traps and land defences in fear and trembling to defend my country. At that time, we could not see anything that would stop Hitler invading our English fields.

Then came the Mighty Eighth.

Proudly we stood in our villages and on our farms, watching the skies. Men ploughing in the fields stopped their horses and looked up to the heavens. They took off their hats to shield their eyes from the morning sun to watch these silver, shining Fortresses climbing slowly to the edge of space in a never-ending line, all in a great and orderly formation, not one seeming out of line.

They called themselves the 'Gentlemen From Hell' and they faced their own fear and dread to bring terrible death and destruction to the enemy.

At the end, by some miracle, the Union Jack was still flying over our island home. In our Suffolk villages, we shall never forget their sacrifice. In Lavenham Church is an American memorial – "I remember you, my brothers, as we were, as it was. This is the resting place of our memory, as it always will be."

I left the lorry at Alpheton Hall, and went to look for my bicycle. It was now well past seven o'clock on this dark, misty night. I cycled along the familiar private track to Aveley Lane, then on to Bridge Street.

At last, I pushed my bicycle up the long path to Rose Cottage and lifted the latch. Inside, my sisters sat around the blazing kitchen fire. With Jep married, there were only four of us at home now – my mother, Beryl, Iris and myself.

"Come on, Jim – late again," said Liz.

"Yes, I know. The sugar factory works all hours."

"Get yourself cleaned up a bit, while I get your dinner. It's rabbit pie, swede and potatoes, then apple pie and custard."

It was my favourite dinner, with lovely gravy. Afterwards, I would have nodded off by the fire, but my mother said, "Get yourself up those stairs and get some rest. What time in the morning?"

"Five o'clock." I made my way slowly up the stairs one more time, towards my lovely warm feather bed under the thatch.

"Goodnight, everyone."

The End

Postscript From The Editors
We moved to Alpheton in 1999 and got to know Jim and Daphne Mott at the fortnightly 'Coffee Pot' mornings at the village hall – coffee, tea and home-made cakes made tirelessly by community-spirited residents. It makes for a noisy get-together, some compensation for the absence of a pub, shop or post office in Alpheton these days.

We soon realised we had chosen a fortunate place to live, where the landowners had farmed for generations and played a full part in village life. Small family farms help Alpheton retain its old-fashioned air of self-sufficiency, providing anything from straw, logs and eggs to building and maintenance work.

Alpheton is a place of deep roots and long memories. We live in Vic Simpson's old house. Vic, horseman at Lavenham Lodge, lived to the age of 104 with sharp recall to the end of his life. In 2004 David Eady was presented with a long-service medal for his work at Lavenham Lodge, as was his father Bill Eady, as was his grandfather George Eady, between them putting in 150 years' service on the farm... and counting. And over those generations, life changed.

Jim Mott's account struck us as a unique glimpse into the daily life of those at the sharp end of a revolution in farming. Looking across the picture-perfect fields that surround us, we know we ourselves have little real understanding of the way the fortunes of the countryside have risen and fallen with the times.

Agricultural depressions in the late nineteenth century, and then in the 1920s and 1930s, saw great hardship for both farmers and farm workers, with farms abandoned and land values at rock bottom. Ashley Cooper in his book "The Long Furrow" writes of twenty thousand acres of land lying derelict between Colchester and Haverhill. The heavy clay wheat fields of our area suffered badly.

War brought revolution. The dairy herd, flocks of poultry, colts and heavy horses that processed out and away from Alpheton Hall in 1940 seem to symbolise the loss of a mixed arable heritage and the dominance of the prairie cultivation of today – what Jim has called the coming of the 'ghost farms'.

We can only imagine the pressure on landowners, suddenly

responsible for the efficient production of food for a wartime population. Local landowner David Alston found himself with five thousand acres under his direct control – his own and those of a relative serving in the armed forces.

In addition, the County War Agriculture Committee on which he served had to take charge of under-performing farms. The reclamation of land was a priority, despite minimal mechanisation and equipment shortages. The controlling hand of government has not relaxed its grip since those times, but the farmer still has some choices to make.

In our time here we have watched David Alston's grandson, John Pawsey, convert the many surrounding acres to organic production, establishing beetle banks and small plantations of trees, sheep grazing on fields of clover. John believes his grandfather would approve, as he had a keen regard for wildlife.

The lovely medieval farmhouse, Alpheton Hall, is a family home for a branch of the Alston family and their huge and ancient barn is now a busy wedding venue, in close proximity to the village church. There is that kind of silence in the valley which is only achieved through the absence of traffic noise. It is easy to appreciate why the landscape meant so much to young Jimmy Mott.

Time has passed. A dwindling number of American airmen who served at Lavenham Airfield are now able to return to show sons, daughters, grandchildren, where they served in the war. The footpaths retain their memories, the broken concrete still having names – Hospital Road, Burma Road – passed on by word of mouth. These days, the paths are frequented only by dog-walkers, horse-riders, and the occasional speeding Royal Mail van, their verges resplendent with wild flowers and butterflies.

'All went to hell', but at last, something did come back.

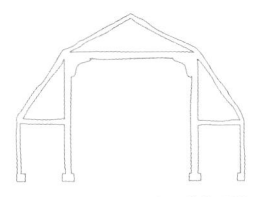

www.Alpheton-Hall-Barns.co.uk
@10ᶜ Historic Wedding Venue

Recently renovated to provide a bespoke wedding venue, Alpheton Hall Barns sit comfortably alongside the Hall and Parish Church to provide an all in one wedding venue. With the parish church only a few steps away, the West Barn dedicated to Civil Weddings and the Large South Barn with its cathedral like open space providing room to seat 200 with space remaining for the evening's entertainment without the need to move tables and chairs around.

We provide a "Quality Frame & Canvas"
You Provide the "Picture"!

The Barns have been restored with great sympathy and attention to detail, from home felled oak to sheep's wool insulation and Venetian Plaster panels. We seek to apply the same attention to detail in attending to our Guests, whether it be last minute alterations and improvements to a bagpipes send off.

Located at the end of a single track road in a gentle fold in the countryside, the barns are easy to find being just off the A134 between Sudbury and Bury St Edmunds.

Don't take our word for it do contact us and arrange a visit: Contact:
Nicholas or Carol Willcocks: barns@alphetonhall.co.uk
Tel: Home: 01284 830 200 Office: 01787 248 188
Alpheton Hall, Church Lane, Alpheton, Sudbury, Suffolk, CO10 9BL

St Nicholas Hospice Care

we care because you do

We are a local charity which helps people live with life-shortening and terminal illnesses. We support them and their families in a variety of ways.

Since 1984, St Nicholas Hospice Care has been providing care and support to people in West Suffolk and Thetford. This care is offered not only to its patients in the Hospice building itself, but also in the community via the Community Hospice Team, giving help to people in their own homes or wherever they may be.

The organisation supports people with life-shortening and terminal illnesses. Many people think of this as cancer – but it also includes Multiple Sclerosis, Motor Neurone Disease or AIDS. The Hospice cannot cure these illnesses, but it can improve quality of life for those affected by them. This is not just for patients, but for their family and friends too.

St Nicholas Hospice Care provides absolutely all of its services free of charge – but many people do not realise that the Hospice itself is a charity.

At full capacity, St Nicholas Hospice has annual running costs of £4.6 million, with only 27% of these costs received through statutory funding. The organisation therefore has to fundraise £10,000 per day to keep running, and relies on the generosity of the local community for this – without their help, the Hospice wouldn't be here.

At any one time there are over 300 people, plus their family and friends in the Hospice's care. The care we give:

The Community Hospice Team: Our specialist service cares and supports people at home or wherever they may be.

Orchard Day Therapy: Providing activities, peer support and rehabilitation therapies.

Orchard Clinics: One to one appointments with doctors, nurses, complementary therapists, occupational and physiotherapists and other health professionals.

Sylvan Ward: Offering round the clock specialist medical nursing care, tailored to each person's needs.

Family Support: Confidential counselling and psychological support for adults known to patients. We also offer an independent social work service giving help with money matters including benefits claims. Spiritual and pastoral support and a befriending service are also some of the support services offered.

Nicky's Way: Bereavement and grief support programme for children and young people.

Education: Offering a programme of specialist learning opportunities, room hire and DVD loan service.

Chaplaincy: Providing multi-faith spiritual and emotional support to patients and families.

Information: Guidance on illness, treatment and support.

serving the local community

St Nicholas Hospice Care

A Registered Charity No. 287773

THE LAVENHAM PRESS LIMITED
HIGH QUALITY COMMERCIAL COLOUR PRINTERS

◆ Design ◆ Typesetting ◆ Publishing
◆ Pre-press ◆ Printing ◆ Binding ◆ Mailing

High quality production of books, magazines, journals, catalogues and promotional material for customers locally and nationally

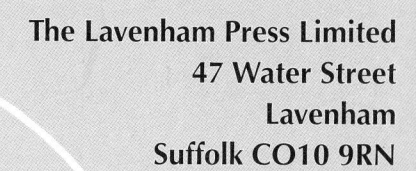

The Lavenham Press Limited
47 Water Street
Lavenham
Suffolk CO10 9RN

Please contact Bill Byford
Email: bill@lavenhamgroup.co.uk
Telephone: 01787 247436
Web: www.lavenhampress.co.uk

Your print partner for the 21st century